Robert Williams Buchanan

A Look Round Literature

Robert Williams Buchanan

A Look Round Literature

ISBN/EAN: 9783337205096

Printed in Europe, USA, Canada, Australia, Japan

Cover: Foto ©Thomas Meinert / pixelio.de

More available books at **www.hansebooks.com**

A LOOK ROUND LITERATURE.

A LOOK ROUND LITERATURE.

BY
ROBERT BUCHANAN.

I never bowed but to superior worth,
Nor ever failed in my allegiance there!—YOUNG.

LONDON:
WARD AND DOWNEY,
12, YORK STREET, COVENT GARDEN, W.C.
1887.

CHARLES DICKENS AND EVANS,
CRYSTAL PALACE PRESS.

PREFATORY NOTE.

MOST of the articles in this volume are reprinted from the critical and other periodical papers of the day. They have no arbitrary connection with each other, but they sufficiently indicate the point of view of a writer whose opinions are somewhat independent of current criticism.

Some of these opinions will doubtless awaken animadversion in quarters self-considered authoritative; but the literary Inquisition, like its religious prototype, will soon be a thing of the past, and, in the meanwhile, I am fortunately not alone in refusing to accept all literary religions merely because they are based on good historical evidence, and possess quasi-miraculous pretensions. At the same time, I have quite as great a distrust of my own discernment, as of that of any of my contemporaries. I simply put down my impressions for what they are worth, and leave the rest to the common-sense of the reading public in general.

R. B.

LONDON, *October*, 1886.

Dedication.

To THE QUARTERLY REVIEWER.

"*Ave Cæsar, te saluto moriturum.*"

SIR,—Permit me to inscribe these Essays to you, as a slight expression of the estimation in which I hold you. If you survive long enough to read them (for the booksellers report that you are fast sinking, with a circulation so languid as to be hardly perceptible in the pulsation) they may perhaps do you a little good; at any rate, they will so far gratify and serve you as to remind the world of your existence; and when you are dead and buried, they may perhaps help to preserve your name from unmerited oblivion.

I know that you have many enemies, who rejoice at your decadence and downfall. I shall do nothing of the kind, for I hold you have done good public service by bringing pedantic criticism into discredit. When you were young and strong and clever, you had the courage of your opinions, and cordially hating every form of literary revolt, you served the cause of retrogression with no little success. Later on, even, your very audacity in evil-doing made you amusing. But that is all over now. Your time has come, and in your last sickness you have this one consolation—that you have been evenly and triumphantly malicious, thoroughly and roundly unintelligent, from the first to the last of your career. You have never said a generous word to help a rising reputation; you have never failed to crawl obsequiously on the ground before every form of mediocrity. You have seen a poetaster in Mr. Tennyson, and a brilliant poet in the writer of the "Lays of Ancient Rome." You have hated progress, derided originality, insulted every honest spirit of your period. It may comfort you a little on your deathbed, to know that even your opponents admit your consistency.

It is sad to reflect that the doom of dotage has fallen upon a spirit that once seemed so playful. The day appears to have passed when public interest could be awakened by the appearance of some half-dozen ill-natured pamphlets in a paper cover, or by the phenomenon of an antiquated literary watchman rushing out into publicity, months after the henroost is robbed or the house burnt down, with cries of "fox!" and "fire!" The spitefulness you once expanded into a long article, is now concentrated by your successors into half a newspaper column. You affected to be scholarly; they pretend only to be plain-spoken. Other times, other manners. When I read the journals which have superseded you, I almost regret your extinction. Be comforted, however, by the assurance that no critic of the future will ever surpass you in the sincerity of his endeavours to promote the science of misconstruction and the art of nepotism, or exhibit a more splendid record of literary mistakes.

I am, Sir,
Your obedient Servant,
ROBERT BUCHANAN.

LONDON, *January*, 1887.

CONTENTS.

		PAGE
FROM ÆSCHYLUS TO VICTOR HUGO:		
I. Prometheus	. . . .	1
II. Gilliatt	. . . .	10
III. Æschylus	. . . .	20
IV. The One God	. . . . . .	29
V. Victor Hugo	. . . . . .	32
VI. The Promethean Myth	. . . .	40
VII. Summary	. . . .	48
THE CHARACTER OF GOETHE:		
I. The Amours	. . . . . .	54
II. Goethe's Toryism	. . . . .	69
III. Sources of Agitation	. . . .	83
A NOTE ON LUCRETIUS		96
FREE THOUGHT IN AMERICA:		
I. Robert Ingersoll	. . . . .	135
II. Octavius Frothingham	. . . .	140
III. The Hope of the Human Race	. .	148

CONTENTS.

	PAGE
A NOTE ON DANTE ROSSETTI	152
THOMAS LOVE PEACOCK; A PERSONAL REMINISCENCE	162
SYDNEY DOBELL, AND THE "SPASMODIC SCHOOL"; A SOUVENIR	185
THE IRISH "NATIONAL" POET	204
HEINE IN A COURT SUIT	210
A TALK WITH GEORGE ELIOT	218
THE LITERATURE OF SPIRITUALISM; "POST MORTEM" FICTION	227

THE MODERN STAGE:
   I. NOTES IN 1876 239
   II. A NOTE IN 1886 281
   III. THE DRAMA AND THE CENSOR . . . 297

FLOTSAM AND JETSAM:
   I. A NOTE ON ÉMILE ZOLA 303
   II. CHARLES READE; A SOUVENIR . . . 308
   III. GEORGE ELIOT'S LIFE 314
   IV. EPICTETUS 322
   V. THE GOSPEL ACCORDING TO THE PRINTER'S DEVIL 330
   VI. "L'EXILÉE" IN ENGLISH 333
   VII. THE CHURCH AND THE STAGE . . . 338
   VIII. THE AMERICAN SOCRATES 341

FROM POPE TO TENNYSON 347

A LAST LOOK ROUND:
   I. CIRCUMSPICE 359
   II. FIRST, HEAR THE CARDINAL . 361
   III. THE ATTITUDE OF SCIENCE 365
   IV. MINOR RESULTS AND INFLUENCES . . 370
   V. THE NEW GIRONDE 374
   VI. THE OUTCOME IN SOCIETY 377
   VII. CONCLUSION 382

A LOOK ROUND LITERATURE.

From ÆSCHYLUS to VICTOR HUGO.

"*Look on this picture, and on this.*"

I.

PROMETHEUS.

THE scene is Mount Caucasus, a craggy desert, silent, inaccessible; the clouds come and go silently above, the Euxine glimmers faintly far away. All the eye beholds is sombre, terrible, colossal, shadowed with the mystery of some awful event. Three gigantic Shapes rise, leading a fourth in chains. The first is the god Hephœstos, accompanied by two formless and awful figures, Kratos and Bia.* He whom they lead is Prometheus, called the Fire-bringer, because he has brought fire to men, and thus incurred the wrath and avenging hate of Zeus, the "new tyrant" of Olympus. He is silent, while Kratos speaks. "Bind this crafty one to these rocks, and so fulfil the behests of the Father." Reluctantly, tenderly,

---

* Generally, with an unpleasant allegorical flavour, translated "Strength" and "Force;" but they are entities, not abstractions, and it would be as reasonable to introduce Prometheus simply as "Foresight," or "Forethought."

as beseems a god, Hephœstos performs his duty, uttering at the same time a prophecy of almost inconceivable suffering.

> And thou shalt here behold
> Nor face nor form of any living man,
> But scorching in the fiery breath o' the sun,
> Shalt lose thy skin's fair bloom ; and thou shalt joy
> To see the spangled night devour the day,
> And yet again to see the sun return
> Scattering the dews of dawn ; and evermore
> The ever-present ill shall crush thee down.

The crucifixion is complete; arms, legs, ribs, every joint and thew, are fast bound, and to complete all, the sharp tooth of the adamantine wedge is driven right through the Titan's chest. At last the servants of Zeus withdraw, leaving the sufferer alone with Nature ; and now, but not till now, the pent-up agony of his heart bursts forth in one great wail, one passionate appeal of immortal pain : " O holy ether, and swift-winged winds, O springs of rivers and innumerable laughter of the ocean waves, O earth, mother of all—you I invoke, and the all-beholding circle of the sun." This, in the most wonderful of untranslatable iambics, followed by a scream of indignant anapæsts equally untranslatable : "O see by what pitiful bonds worn away, I shall wrestle through æons of pain !" His call is quickly answered. A music and odour are blown to him from the far-off sea, and soon the air trembles with the stir of wonderful wings. The Chorus rises—beautiful ocean spirits hovering over him with soft and soothing song. As they float above him, fixing their gentle eyes on the lineaments of his sorrowful countenance, he tells them who and what he is, his story, and the story of his offence against Zeus.

When confusion and anarchy arose among the

gods, some wanting to depose Kronos that Zeus might reign, others striving that Zeus might never reign, Prometheus was the only Titan who stood on Zeus's side; and by his help Zeus conquered.

> But this disease exists in sovereignty,
> Never to trust one's friends.

No sooner was Zeus seated on the ancestral throne, than he began to persecute the race of men, with a view to their utter annihilation and the creation of a new order of creatures. But Prometheus interposed on behalf of humanity; firstly, by teaching men to be less fearful of the supernatural, to cease, in other words, from "dwelling on their doom;" and secondly, by teaching them the use of fire, parent of innumerable arts. The Titan has arrived at this point of his narration, when the Chorus alight on the ground, surrounding him, and simultaneously Okeanos their father arrives, riding on a gryphon. The ancient sea-god comes to proffer counsel, which is gloomily received, for he recommends a certain amount of submission to the powers that be. He will himself, he suggests, intercede with Zeus. For reply, Prometheus reminds him of the fate of the other Titans—Atlas and Typhon:

> And by the fortunes of my brother Atlas
> My soul is troubled;—he who stands i' the west
> Upbearing on his shoulders silently
> A burden borne not easily by arms,
> The pillar of the heaven and of the earth.
> And troubled was my soul when I beheld
> The earth-born dweller in Sicilian caves,
> The hundred-headed Typhon, fierce as fire,
> Crushed down; for he, the foe of all the gods,
> Rose hissing horror with terrific jaws,
> And from his eyes a gorgon fury glared,
> Threat'ning red havoc on the rule of Zeus.
> But on his head flashed Zeus's fiery levin,

> The burning and unsleeping thunderbolt,
> Which clave him even as he threatenëd.
> Smit to the vitals, to a cinder burned,
> His force devoured by lightning, prone he fell;
> And now a corse effete, outstretch'd he lies
> Close to that ocean strait prest down between
> The leaden weights of Aetna; and Hephœstos
> Forgeth the liquid mass of glowing flame,
> Seated above him on the mountain heights,
> Whence in the time hereafter shall outspring
> Rivers of flame with fiery mouths devouring
> The furrow'd fields of fruitful Sicily.*

Finding his task hopeless, Okeanos withdraws. The Chorus surround the Titan, uttering music of infinite tenderness. His voice trembles as he tells them of his gentle deeds, his love for humanity. It was not enough to give men fire; he gave them living souls. Before his beneficence, they had been as "phantoms seen in dreams" (ὀνειράτων ἀλίγκιοι μορφαῖσι). They dragged their weary lives along. Houses they had none whether of wood or stone, but they dwelt, numerous as gnats, in the sunless hearts of caverns; and they knew not how to distinguish the seasons, until Prometheus instructed them in the risings and the settings of the stars. He then taught them Number (ἀριθμὸν), and the arrangement of letters (γραμμάτων συνθέσεις), and Memory, handmaid and Mother of the Muses. Nor was this all. He instructed them in horse-taming and horsemanship, and in navigation of the ocean; what medicines to use in sickness, where to find, and how to combine them; how to divine auguries and omens, both ordinary and extraordinary; and how, delving in the deep earth, to discover the precious metals. He concludes—

> Summed in one little sentence hear the truth,
> All arts to mortals from Prometheus came!

---

* This and the other renderings in the text are original.—R. B.

The dialogue now touches on divine Mysteries. Prometheus prophesies. After thousands upon thousands of years, he is to find a deliverer. The thing is fated, and even Zeus is the creature of fate. "What, then, shall be the fate of Zeus?" ask the Okeanides; but Prometheus refuses to answer, the time being not yet ripe. An unconscious answer comes, however, through a sudden apparition. Io, in the shape of a white heifer, enters, rolling her wild eyes round and wailing loudly. In a frantic song, she bewails her miserable fate, and calls upon Zeus to pity her. She is still moaning, when Prometheus utters her name—"Io, daughter of Inachos, who filled the heart of Zeus with love, and who is now, through the hate of Heré, driven from land to land." Presently, while her soul is soothed for a time by the sympathy of Prometheus and the Maidens, she tells the whole story of the divine love and persecution.

> But now in clear narration you shall know
> All of these things ye crave ; but ah, I grieve
> Ev'n while of that same heaven-sent storm I tell,
> And of the cruel changing of my form,
> The way it came upon me miserable !
> For ever thronging in my virgin bowers
> Came nightly dreams with smooth and honeyed words
> Beguiling me : " O maiden, triply blest,
> Why linger on in cold virginity
> When most exalted wedlock waits for thee !
> For shafts of love outshooting from thine eyes
> Are burning in the breast of highest Zeus,
> Who now would mingle with thee amorously.
> Wherefore, O child, disdain not Zeus's bed,
> But hie thee forth to Lerna's deep green mead,
> Where feed thy father's oxen, flocks and herds,
> That so the Eye Divine from its desire
> At last may cease." At voices such as these
> I wretched trembled nightly, t'll at last
> I dared to whisper in my father's ears
> My visions. Then did he send messengers
> To Pytho and Dodona frequently,

> Seeking to know how best to please the gods
> In words or deeds ; and ever they returned
> With numberless ambiguous oracles,
> Most dim of meaning and most dark to read.
> At last there came a clearer oracle
> Charging upon my father Inachos
> To thrust me from his threshold and his land
> That I might wander homeless, desolate,
> On the remotest limits of the earth ;
> And threatening if he failed in this dark deed,
> That fiery lightnings should be sent from Zeus
> To sweep away the remnant of his race.
> So, overawed by Loxias' oracle
> Unwilling he drave me unwilling too
> Out of his house, since Zeus's cruel curb
> Constrained him to this deed in love's despite.
> Then suddenly my senses and my shape
> Became transformed, and even as ye behold,
> Hornëd as any beast and driven on
> By the fierce pricks of the sharp stinging fly,
> With maniac leaps I rushed until I came
> To the soft stream Kerchneian and the fount
> Of Lerna. And the Herdsman born of earth,
> The fierce and headstrong Argus, followed me,
> Watching my track with eyes innumerable.
> Him sudden accident surprised and slew,
> But I abide, by maddening pangs impelled
> From region into region of the earth.

The Okeanides utter their pity in loud wails. Then Prometheus describes to Io the whole of her future fortune; and to prove the truth of his prophetic powers, he follows with a recital of her wanderings past, describing point by point, and picture by picture, the whole extent of her toilsome journey. Midway in his recital, he comes to a more explicit prophesy concerning the fall of Zeus. A day shall come when a child of Zeus, mightier than himself, as Zeus was mightier than Kronos, shall hurl him down from heaven ; before or about the occurrence of this event, a child of Io, the third generation after her, shall release Prometheus from his bonds. Not to be misunderstood by too dark an augury, the Titan

concludes by recurring to the end of Io's wanderings
and the birth of the Deliverer :—

> Remotest of the land, a City stands,
> Canopus, at the very mouth of Nile ;
> There verily shall Zeus restore thy soul
> Smoothing thee only with his outstretched hand,
> Touching, not terrifying thee ; and lo !
> Of that same touch thou shalt conceive and bear
> The dark-skinned Epaphos, "Touch-born ; " and he
> Shall gather in the fruit of every land
> Whose fields are watered by broad-bosom'd Nile.
> There in the generation fifth from him
> Shall fifty children come of female seed,
> And these against their will shall journey back
> To Argos, flying nuptials with their kin,
> These kin their cousins ; and these last, as kites
> Not lingering long behind the doves they seek,
> Shall come pursuing evil marriages,
> But God shall grudge to yield unto their arms
> The bodies of the virgins. And at last
> In bloody woman-watches of the night,
> Those men shall perish, stab'd and smit to death,
> Darkly, within the land Pelasgian ;
> For by his bride shall every husband die,
> Staining with his red blood the two-edged sword.
> But love shall soften one of those fierce maids,
> And trembling, hesitating, choosing rather
> To be deemed weak than to turn murderess,
> This one shall spare the sharer of her bed ;
> And from her seed shall spring the royal race
> At Argos. Long and tedious 'twere to tell
> These things at length and clearly ; but i' the end,
> Of this same seed a hero shall be born
> Mighty to bend the bow and hurl the dart,
> And he it is who from my sufferings
> At last shall set me free ! This oracle
> The Titan Themis, my ancestral mother,
> Rehearsed unto me darkly long ago.;
> But how and when the thing shall come to pass
> Tedious it were to tell, tedious to hear,
> Nor could ye gain at all by hearkening.

As he ceases, Io bursts into renewed lamentations, and stung* again by her grief, rushes onward down

---

* It is rather puerile to render the οἶστρος of v. 567 and 880 literally, as most of our translators do, as if this οἶστρος were the mountain side. In a low monotonous song, the Okeanides sing, while Prometheus falls into a gloomy trance; awakening from which, with a bitter smile, he repeats his awful threats against the King of Heaven. His words are wrapt in mystic darkness, trenchant and terrible though they be. One point is certain—Zeus is to fall. The Okeanides, again surrounding him, look on him sadly, for the frightful power of the Deity has terrified them, and they regard the Titan, still with the old pity, but with a new despair. Their terror and submission irritates him anew, and he exclaims:

> Worship then, flatter him, the King of the Hour!
> For me, I care for Zeus, yea less than nought.
> Let him abide this little while, and rule
> Even as he pleases,—long he shall not rule
> O'er the immortal gods!

As he speaks, he beholds, brightly approaching, the god Hermes. The terrible threat has been heard in Olympus, and the messenger of Zeus has been sent to demand, in no measured language, the full explanation of when and by whom Zeus is to be overthrown. In the angry scene that follows, Prometheus still preserves his dignity, coldly refusing to gratify his persecutor with one syllable of the awful truth, but still defying him to do his worst. That worst is soon to come. Horror is to be heaped on horror, torture on torture. Even as Hermes speaks, the earth begins to tremble, the heavens to flash fire.

---

the ὀξύστομος μυώψ of v. 674. Still more ridiculous does it seem to conceive that the Spectre of Argus of which Io raves in v. 568 was actually present on the stage. Professor Plumptree, in his excellent translation, falls into this error of stage direction—" Enter Io," etc., followed by *the Spectre of Argus*— as if he were glaring in the background, like Banquo's ghost, and rolling his hundred eyes to affright the groundlings.

While the Okeanides cower and moan, Hermes withdraws, and on the Titan's head falls the full thunderbolt of Zeus. To the very last the mighty voice is heard intoning:

> Yea, now, in very deed,
> No longer only in word,
> The earth is shaken and stirr'd,
> The fiery levin is freed.
> The thunder rolleth by,
> Storms whirl the dust on high.
> Downward with madden'd motion
> The mighty whirlwinds leap,
> The sky is blent with the ocean,
> And deep is mingled with deep.
> Such is the horror hurl'd
> From Zeus's terrible hand,
> In dark confusion whirl'd
> I tremble and shake, yet stand.
> O holy Mother, see;
> O all-encircling air,
> Light of all things that be,
> Behold what wrongs I bear!

With the immortal appeal, the voice ceases; all is silence and darkness.

Such is a brief sketch of the "Prometheus Bound" of Æschylus, a work so familiar to students that a detailed description of it would be superfluous, were such a description not absolutely necessary for the purpose of the comparisons to be instituted in the present article. This immortal piece bears the same relation to tragedy that the "Laocoon" does to sculpture; it is absolutely solitary and supremely great.* In the depth and infinity of its suggestions,

---

* Thirty pages of close print would contain this masterpiece. It is about as long as a single book of "Paradise Lost," and not very much longer than Mr. Tennyson's "Enoch Arden." The whole trilogy, of which it was a part, could have been included in the space of one of the volumes of an ordinary three volume novel!

it is even more pregnant now than it was to the contemporaries of its author; every century adds to its significance, every literary remove heightens its grandeur. It has no equal because it has no rival. It deals with shapes so colossal, with ideas so sublime, that we still tremble before them in wonder akin to superstition. If the Bible overshadows us like a cloud, the Prometheus overawes us like a mountain. Its peaks touch the stars, its base is rooted deep in human soil; wind, rain, and snow abide upon it, and mystery dwells upon it; it stirs with the blind motion of supernatural powers—Zeus slipping like an avalanche to his doom, the Titan towering far above in the beauty of unimaginable power. A Voice comes from it, with such music as shall be never heard again, for "that large utterance of the early gods" is dead for ever.

II.

GILLIATT.

I HAVE given one picture. Let me turn now to the other.

The scene is scarcely less wild and desolate than was the Scythian Caucasus. It is a lonely reef of rocks in the midst of the ocean; nothing is seen but the cloud, rock, and the water, no sound is heard save the sound of sea-birds, the plash of the silent sea. Suddenly the eye becomes conscious of two things that it had not seen before—of a large vessel, wrecked and sucked up between two mighty masses of rock, where it hangs suspended, and of a solitary figure which stands behind it, looking upward—the figure of a man. This man, too, is Titanic; so at least he seems in the dim low light that surrounds him. This form too is in revolt, not against a cruel and malignant Deity, but against those powers of Nature which are even more cruel and malignant; and he too will endeavour to conquer, but by active resistance, not sublime endurance. His work lies before him. If, in defiance of the elements, he can detach that suspended wreck from its niche, piece it again into a goodly vessel, set it again afloat upon the sea, and all this by the unaided craft of his own brain, and the strength of his own arm, why then, the Tyrant is conquered, and the human Spirit rises irresistible and supreme. The man, however, has a lower end in view—he hopes, by his miracle of salvage, to win to himself the love of a woman, the daughter of the man whose wealth has been lost in that missing vessel. For this being in mid-ocean is no Titan, no colossal comrade of gods and demigods, but only a poor Toiler of the Sea, dwelling in a poor home in the island of Guernsey, and earning his subsistence by the work of his own hands. "Tel était Gilliatt. Les filles le trouvaient laid. Il n'était pas laid. Il était beau peut-être. Il avait dans le profil quelque chose d'un barbare antique. Au repos, il ressemblait à une Dace de la colonne trajane." He was thirty years old, but he appeared five-and-forty; for he "wore the dark mask of the wind and the sea." Gilliatt, then, is here on the Douvres, a desolate reef of rocks out in mid-channel, resolved upon a work which, to all intents and purposes, is impossible—the rescue of a steam-ship, which, instead of sinking to the bottom as is the usual fate of wrecks, has been suspended miraculously in mid-air.

> La coque était perdue, la machine était intacte. Ces hasards sont fréquents dans les naufrages comme dans les incendies. La logique du désastre nous échappe.
> Les mâts cassés étaient tombés, la cheminée n'était pas même ployée ; la grande plaque de fer qui supportait la mécanique l'avait maintenue ensemble et tout d'une pièce. Les revêtements en planches des tambours étaient disjoints à peu près comme les lames d'une persienne ; mais à travers leurs claires-voies on distinguait les deux roues en bon état. Quelque pales manquaient.
> Outre la machine, le grand cabestan de l'arrière avait résisté. Il avait sa chaîne, et, grâce à son robuste emboîtement dans un cadre de madriers, il pouvait rendre encore des services, pourvu toutefois que l'effort du tournevire ne fît pas fendre le plancher. Le tablier du pont fléchissait presque sur tous les points. Tout ce diaphragme était branlant.
> En revanche le tronçon de la coque engagé entre les Douvres tenait ferme, nous l'avons dit, et semblait solide. Cette conservation de la machine avait on ne sait quoi de dérisoire et ajoutait l'ironie à la catastrophe. La sombre malice de l'inconnu éclate quelquefois dans ces espèces de moqueries amères. La machine etait sauvée, ce qui ne l'empêchait point d'être perdue. L'Océan la gardait pour la démolir à loisir. Jeu de chat.

His first care is to find a place of shelter for himself while he remains on the reef, and this he at last finds in a sort of hole in the rock. As he prepares his lodging, multitudes of sea-birds hover above him. " C'étaient des mouettes, des goëlands, des frégates,* des cormorans, des mauves, une nuée des oiseaux de mer, étonnés." A week passes away. This first week

---

* It is as consistent to introduce the "frigate-bird" here as to write of the sea-serpent. The mistake is trifling, but it points to a general want of veracity, which would be repelling in a writer of less genius. Further on, he describes a purely impossible flight of cormorants. Here as elsewhere, he writes like a man who has got his notion of the sea from books, and had never seen a sea-bird. Who doubts the genius? but it is genius reckless of all consequences and indifferent to all verification.

is employed in gathering together all the flotsam and jetsam of the wreck—ropes, chains, pieces of wood, "broken yards," blocks and pulleys. Then—

> A la fin de la semaine, Gilliatt avait dans ce hangar de granit tout l'informe bric-à-brac de la tempête mis en ordre. Il y avait, le coin des écouets et le coin des écoutes ; les boulines n'étaient point mêlées avec les dresses ; les bigots étaient rangés selon la quantité de trous qu'ils avaient ; les emboudinures, soigneusement détachées des organeaux des ancres brisées, étaient roulées en écheveaux ; les moques, qui n'ont point de rouet, étaient séparées des moufles ; les cabellots, les margouillets, les pataras, les gabarons, les joutereaux, les calebas, les galoches, les pantoires, les oreilles d'âne, les racages, les bosses, les boute-hors, occupaient, pourvu qu'ils ne fussent pas complètement défigurés par l'avarie, des compartiments différents ; toute la charpente, traversins, piliers, épontilles, chouquets, mantelets, jumelles, hiloires, etait entassée à part ; chaque fois que cela avait été possible, les planches des fragments de franc-bord embouffeté avaient été rentrées les unes dans les autres ; il n'y avait nulle confusion des garcettes de ris avec les garcettas de tournevire, ni de araignées avec les touées, ni des poulies, ni des morceaux de virure avec les morceaux de vibord, un recoin avait été réservé à une partie du trelingage de la Durande, qui appuyait les haubans de hune et les gambes de hune. Chaque débris avait sa place. Tout le naufrage était là, classé et étiqueté. C'était quelque chose comme le chaos en magasin.

These *disjecta membra* were arranged in one great hollow of the crag which he used as a storehouse. Another hollow close by he determines to use as a forge. The preparation of the forge need not be described in detail, but it is successfully accomplished. With forge and magazine all prepared, Gilliatt sets to work in earnest, with a "fierté de cyclope, maitre de l'air, de l'eau, et de feu." It is necessary, however, to nourish himself while so doing, and he therefore spends a certain portion of the day in searching for crabs and other shell-fish. While so doing, he penetrates, through a narrow fissure, into a mighty water-cavern situated in the very heart of the rocks. The water therein is of "molten emerald" (*de l'émeraude en fusion*), a cloud of delicate beryl covers the shadowy walls and overhanging arches, pearls drop momently from the long water-mosses that cluster overhead, and through all the dimness the sea shudders like a palpitating heart. Beautiful as this cavern appears, it is fatal. Empty of all life as it seems, it is nevertheless a habitation. An evil spirit dwells within it, a monstrous and horrible Ocean-form. Of this master of the mansion, Gilliatt, during his first visit, got only a glimpse.

> Tout à coup, à quelques pieds au-dessous de lui, dans la transparence charmante de cette eau qui était comme de la pierrerie dissoute, il aperçut quelque chose d'inexprimable. Une espèce de long haillon se mouvait dans l'oscillation des lames. Ce haillon ne flottait pas, il voguait, il avait un but, il allait quelque part, il était rapide. Cette guenille avait la forme d'une marotte de bouffon avec des pointes ; ces pointes, flasques, ondoyaient ; elle semblait couverte d'une poussière impossible à mouiller. C'était plus qu'horrible, c'était sale. Il y avait de la chimère dans cette chose ; c'était un être, à moins que ce ne fût une apparence. Elle semblait se diriger vers le côté obscur de la cave, et s'y enfonçait. Les épaisseurs d'eau devinrent sombres sur elle. Cette silhouette glissa et disparut, sinistre.

This is Gilliatt's first glimpse of the "Pieuvre," or Poulp, a creature to which gorgons and chimeras were trifles, and which, scientifically speaking, is simply a ridiculous exaggeration of the octopus. For the time being, Gilliatt withdraws, attaching little importance to the apparition. By a series of manœuvres, in themselves impossible from first to last, he releases the vessel from its perilous position, pieces it together, fixes the engine again in its proper place, and softly deposits the whole in the sea beneath. It would be tedious indeed to linger over the details of this miracle; enough to say, the deed is done, and all by the unaided might of one man. The weather is calm, and little more remains to do but to depart to

Guernsey. The elements, however, have determined not to let Gilliatt depart without a struggle. "L'Abime se décidait à livrer bataille." It is the period of the equinox, and Nature is gathering her powers. Gilliatt has not long to wait. The wind is arising—"le vent, c'est tous les vents; toute cette horde arrivait; d'un côté, cette légion—de l'autre, Gilliatt!" The tempest comes, the battle between Man and Nature. Fortunately, Gilliatt, at the first warning of danger, has fashioned a rude sort of breakwater, by which the full force of the sea is broken, and the vessel preserved from destruction. Now roars and shrieks a tempest as awful as that other which Zeus hurled upon the head of Prometheus. It is superfluous to repeat in detail how the fight proceeds, till finally Man conquers. For twenty hours lasts the Titanic strife. Then suddenly the heavens turn blue, and Gilliatt, overcome by his efforts, drops like a stone and sleeps. When he awakens, all is calm, but he is famishing for food. Stripping himself to his "pantalon," and taking with him a large knife to detach stray shell-fish, he creeps down to the nether-caves seeking cray-fish (*langoustes*) and crabs. While in pursuit of a large crab, he enters that very cave which he discovered weeks before. Thrusting his hand into a fissure, he suddenly feels his arm seized. An indescribable horror seizes him. "Quelque chose qui était mince, âpre, plat, glâce, gluant et vivant venait de se tordre dans l'ombre autour de son bras nu. Cela lui montait vers la poitrine." As he stands stripped, tentacle after tentacle (*lanière*) slips round him, till he is embraced on every side, in every limb. He shrieks in horror. "Brusquement une large viscosité ronde et plate sortit de dessous la crevasse. C'était le centre; les cinq lanières s'y rattachaient comme des rayons à un moyen ; en milieu de cette viscosité il y avait deux yeux qui regardaient. Ces yeux voyaient Gilliatt. Gilliatt reconnut la Pieuvre." *

Now begins the second combat, between Man and the Execrable. It is quickly decided in Man's favour, and the "viscosity," with its head hacked off, tumbles into the water, dead. Directly after his victory, Gilliatt explores the lair of his enemy, and finds, among other horrible evidences of its predatory habits, an entire human skeleton, having around it a brazen belt containing a large sum of money lost by the owner of the wrecked vessel. Fortune has indeed been favourable to the mighty Toiler. The vessel saved, a lost fortune discovered, miracles of achievement done, and mountains of difficulty overcome, he points the steamer's bow for Guernsey—" homeward ho!" The rest of the tragedy—for a tragedy it is though told in modern prose—may be given in a few words. The prize for which he has wrought throughout is not to be his. Déruchette, the dream of his desire, loves incarnate weakness in the shape of a Protestant priest. For Gilliatt, when he appears before her in all the glory of his triumph,—" tel qu'il était sorti, ce matin même, de l'écueil Douvres, en haillons, les andes percés, la barbe longue, les cheveux haussés, les yeux brûlés et rouges, la face écorchée, les poings sanglants, les pieds nus,"—Gilliatt, thus

---

* " Pour croire à la Pieuvre," the author here naïvely remarks, " il faut l'avoir vue!" Everybody has now seen the Octopus, which distinct anti-social creature may be taken as the " Pieuvre's" representative. In some Japanese pictures of gigantic cuttle-fish, lately published in the *Field*, there is a parallel to Victor Hugo's exaggeration. One monster is depicted embracing and overthrowing a large sailing-vessel ; its tentacles are as long as the mast.

returning, is simply an object of horror. The father may exclaim "c'est mon vrai gendre," but the woman looks on with sickening despair. The end of all is very sad; for here one misses that Titanic will which overcame the tempest, tore a fortune out of the very teeth of the winds, and slew the Poulp, or "Chimæra." Nobly indeed does Gilliatt resign Déruchette to him she loves, nobly does he join their hands, concealing his own ill-fated passion. But his heart is broken. As the pair sail away from Guernsey, Déruchette accompanying her husband to the far-off scene of his gentle pastoral labours, as they sit on the deck of a sailing vessel hand in hand, they pass close by the sea-cliffs, and standing out from these a detached rock in which is a stone seat, called Gild-Holm-'Ur. Now, at high water this seat is entirely covered by the tide, and in this seat Gilliatt sits,—and the tide is rising. With his eyes fixed on the vessel as it glides away, he sits awaiting his doom. The tide rises to his waist. An hour passes, and it rises to his neck. Slowly the vessel fades away on the far horizon line. At the moment it entirely disappears from view, the head of Gilliatt is submerged. "Il n'y eut plus rien que la mer." The Titan, then, is no Titan after all. All the glory of his victory, all the beauty of his victory, has ended in the basest of all self-abnegation —suicide. To the "anarchy" of Nature he was equal, but he is far too weak for the "anarchy of the human heart." He is utterly fallen.

Such, then, is the "Travailleurs de la Mer" of Victor Hugo, a work in many respects the writer's masterpiece, and well known to many who have not read it by its exaggerations about the "pieuvre," or poulp. To convert this work into a masterpiece worthy to rank with "Prometheus" would be im-

c

possible, for its form and music alike belong to a lower art; but if its imperfections were obliterated by the simple process of reducing its bulk to one-third or one-fourth, its literary worth would be far higher than it is. It contains ideas and creations of unequalled grandeur—forms worthy of Greek sculpture—a sublime certainty of power which leaves all other contemporary fiction far behind indeed—a colossal imagery which has perhaps not been surpassed since Æschylus lived and died, and which has certainly not been rivalled by any poet but the one who painted the wondrous picture of Nimrod in the "Inferno." Though written in splendid prose, it is intrinsically a poem; and because it is a poem in essence, one wishes it had been a poem in fact. I am not so blind to the wonderful advantages of its prose form as to wish that it had been written in *verse;* that is quite another matter; I merely regret those portions which owe their inspiration to Alexander Dumas, just as I regret those portions in "Les Misérables" which catch the inspiration and follow the style of Eugène Sue. These deductions made, the "Travailleurs de la Mer" remains a marvellous work; to be read not merely once but many times; yet once read, never to be forgotten. Despite its faults, it approaches nearer to the Æschylan ideal than any other modern work not written by its author.

The preface to "Les Travailleurs de la Mer" is as follows:

> La religion, la société, la nature; telles sont les trois luttes de l'homme. Ces trois luttes sont en même temps ses trois besoins; il faut qu'il croie, de là le temple; il faut qu'il crie, de là la cité; il faut qu'il vive, de là la charrue et le navire. Mais ces trois solutions contiennent trois guerres. La mystérieuse difficulté de la vie sort de toutes les trois. L'homme a affaire à l'obstacle sous la forme superstition, sous la forme préjugé, et

sous la forme élément. Un triple anantre pèse sur nous, l'anantre des dogmes, l'anantre des lois, l'anantre des choses. Dans Notre Dame de Paris l'auteur a dénoncé le premier ; dans les Misérables, il a signalé le second ; dans ce livre, il indique le troisième.

A ces trois fatalités qui enveloppent l'homme, se mêle la fatalite intérieure, l'anantre suprême, le cœur humain.

Whether or not this idea is, as some expect, an afterthought of the author, frequently over anxious to fashion his works into imaginary unity, it is not for me to decide; but if the idea be admitted and found penetrating the three works in question, it simply renders conclusive the measureless despair of the author's moral teaching. Centuries upon centuries have passed since Æschylus wrote his Promethean trilogy, and only the gloomiest part of that trilogy remains; since that masterpiece was lost and found, Christianity has been, with its lights and its awful shadows; not a god of the old mythology remains, not a shadow of the lost superstition abides; empires have risen or fallen upon this truth, that Zeus is not, but that Christ, whether in the flesh or the spirit, is and shall be—a truth which, nowadays, is as much the spirit of Mr. Spencer's teaching as of that of the late Mr. Maurice ; and yet, for all this, for all the lapse of centuries and the roll of opinion, that sculptured "Prometheus" remains a more enlightened and enlightening thing than the figure of this other Toiler, working in all the illumination of the modern "idea." If the greatest poet of our generation has read upon the page of modern history only this one word "ἀνάγκε," or fatality, and if this miserable word is the centre of his creed and ours, then well may we wish that we, like Æschylus, had been Pagans, "suckled in a creed outworn." I shall endeavour to show, further on, that the defects of Victor Hugo are not necessarily those of his generation, and that, for those who read between the lines, even his most hopeless utterances are far removed from sceptical despair; but his fault is, that while his reason is illuminative and propagandist to a degree, his imagination, for reasons partly national and partly literary, is to a deplorable extent retrospective and overshadowed with gloom. Feuerbach in his darkest mood is as cheerful as this poet in his brightest. He preaches a breezy doctrine of democracy, as if he were opening one of the seals of an Apocalypse. His ideas are often divine, his creations are more frequently devilish. At his highest he is a dark angel, moving in the shadow of his own wings; at his lowest, he is a nightmare. From a literary point of view even he is alarming. Two-thirds of his words are about as valuable as the contents of the daily journals. The remaining third is more precious than any other imaginative utterance now heard in Europe, and yet, though its power of putting great and vague ideas into colossal forms is unexampled, it contains a philosophy of mere misery, a morality to be surpassed even among the sweepings of those sophists Mr. Grote loved "not wisely but too well."

III.

ÆSCHYLUS.

LET us turn back to Æschylus, and examine a little closer into his altitude as a poet and his claims as a teacher. Every one knows that he remained throughout his life what Victor Hugo began by being

—an aristocrat, a worshipper of the ancient order. He was a Eupatrid, a member of the proud old nobility; and he preserved to the end the dignity, the hauteur, and the prejudice of his class. More noteworthy still is the fact that he was born at Eleusis. It is no part of my purpose to enter into the controversy as to whether or not he was actually "initiated" into the Mysteries; certain it is he preserved for them a holy and deep-seated awe, and that they had a mystic influence upon his intellect and on his style; so that even Aristophanes, in the "Frogs," makes him invoke Demeter:

Δήμητερ ἡ θρέψασα τὴν ἐμὴν Φρένα,
εἶναί με τῶν σῶν ἄξιον μυστηρίων! *

It would be more to the point to examine what these Mysteries eventually were, had I leisure and erudition for such an inquiry; the truth, however, is involved in hopeless darkness, and scholars are hopelessly disagreed, some seeing in the Mysteries a solemn and sublime preservation of primitive theology, while others find in them only Phallic symbols and debasing orgies. With the last-named opinions, however, only pedants could agree. The grandeur of the very temple itself, the style of its architecture, the solemnity of its surroundings, were alone enough to dispel merely debasing associations; and when we add to the testimony of Æschylus himself that of such men as Sophocles and Pindar, we cannot but believe that the Mysteries, whatever some of their external forms may have been, had a deep and beautiful meaning, and a purifying influence. This much being conceded, we have little or no difficulty in comprehending the right

---

* v. 886, 887.

character of Æschylus himself. He is a veritable Priest of Eleusis, uttering his oracles in mighty verse. He accepts the ancient myths without doubt and without hesitation. The overthrow of Kronos by Zeus is as truly a fact to him as the creation of the world in six days is a fact to an orthodox English bishop. He believes in the old theogony, and he knows every one of its members as a Roman Catholic knows his saints. His faith is mighty within him. To regard these wondrous shapes as mere symbolism, as mere abstract attributes idealised into divine persons, to think of Prometheus as mere " Forethought," in the spirit of a didactic essay by a modern philologist, would be as much heresy in his eyes as to accept the Bible simply as " supreme literature " is heresy in the eyes of the editor of the *Record*. The order of things has been told him, and by that order he abides. But the very law of that order, he perceives, is constant change. The better displaces the worse, in heaven as on earth. Zeus has reigned, but Zeus must fall.

Here a difficulty interposes. It is clear that the poet uses the word " Zeus " in two ways—using it sometimes to describe the personality of the tyrant who deposed Kronos and tortured Prometheus; but at other times, and more frequently, to denote ("in a mystery," as John Bunyan would express it) the supreme and divine Idea which, through all human and superhuman interpositions, works for righteousness. Nothing could be more explicit and tremendous in its abuse of the Olympian INDIVIDUAL than the whole of the "Prometheus." Zeus is the synonym for everything that is treacherous, lecherous, incestuous, suspicious, tyrannous, loveless, hopeless, and diabolical. Milton is far kinder to the devil than Æschylus is to the Father—such a Father!—as contemptible in the Greek fragment as in the lovely English poem of Shelley. There can be no mistake about it, and the vituperation is given all round. But who can imagine for a moment that Æschylus, in the following passage of the "Agamemnon," is singing of the same Being?

> Zeus, whoe'er he be,
> Whether that name be pleasing in his ear
>   By which I call him now:
> For, weighing well all other names, I fail,
>   When seeking from my soul
>   To cast away all care,
> To fathom any but this name of Zeus.
>
>   For One who reigned of old,
>   Full of the might of war,
>   Is fallen, and is no more;
>   And one who followed him
>   Hath fallen in his turn.
> But Zeus abides, and he who woos him well
> Shall surely reap the wisdom of the wise.
>
> Yea, Zeus is he whom we must woo with prayer,
> And with ovations, would we prosper well—
> He who to wisdom leads us, making sure
>   Sad teachings wrought from pain;
>   For in the dead of night
> Come conscience-waking cares and agonies,
> And mortals then against their wills grow wise.
> Such grace, I trow, is shed by the Immortals,
> Seated above on their eternal thrones.*

No, this is not the Divine Tyrant, but the Divine Idea which has displaced him, and taken the name of which he is unworthy.

---

* Above is part of the extraordinary first chorus of the "Agamemnon," afterwards alluded to again. No attempt is made to translate it literally or rhythmically; it is quite untranslatable, and I merely attempt to convey its spirit. The confusion of Zeus himself with the δαιμόνες (here, however, translated "Immortals") is an example of the poet's perplexing way of mingling modern Athenian conceptions with the old theogony.

Again, in the "Suppliants":—

> Calm, without effort, is the work of Zeus:
> Thron'd loftily, he works, we know not how,
> His perfect will.

Again in "Eumenides":—

> All things he rules, unwearying, with no toil.

This is the one God that abides, though the many change and pass; this is the supreme Spirit, far more akin to the τὸ 'Ερώμενον of Aristotle, and the eternal "Ich" of Fichte, than to the colossal Constitutional Monarch overthrown by Demogorgon. This more resembles the "stream of tendency that works for righteousness," than the wicked Impostor who carried into divine life the indecency of a Nero and the cruelty of a Tiberius. In a word, the poet, half unconsciously, is intoning the music of that monotheism which interpenetrates all polytheistic systems, and of which he is as certain as Plato himself. Zeus, thus conceived, is not merely "mighty of the mightiest," as the same poet, indeed, calls him; he is the "secret force destroying wrong, as water weareth stone;" he is the everlasting Principle by which truth is vindicated from generation to generation, and through which suffering becomes self-compensating and divine; he is the Quiet Waters that receive the virgin corpse of Io in the end, and he is the Peace that broodeth like a dove in heart of the triumphant Titan. But, far more than this, he is Supreme Justice, Lord and Master of the Erinnyes, ever urging them on to righteous vengeance, until (as in the "Orestes"), Nature is vindicated, and they drop to sleep.

If, as is believed, Æschylus designed the masks for many of his characters, as well as assisting otherwise in the artistic and scenic decorations; and if these masks of bronze answered, as they must have done, to the tragic ideas of their creator, his heart must often have ached in their fashioning. Well might the Greek Theatre be formed on a mighty scale, with the quiet heavens overhead, figures of superhuman height moving on the stage, masks of mysterious awe glimmering far away. No human face could have borne throughout a play the fixed expression of monotonous pain of an Œdipus, an Orestes, or, above all, a Clytemnestra; no living actor could have personated these characters in what is now known as the *natural* style without emotion bordering on madness. In assisting at their show, we are passing, as it were, under the very shadow of God. The infinite sibilations of the "Inferno" are not more real than the cries we hear from those brazen throats; yet we take comfort from the very mistiness and vagueness of the forms. Lear's thin, human cry tears our heart-strings, but the wild groan of Orestes comes to us subdued into a prayer. We hide our faces from the sight of the "pretty princes smothered in the Tower," from little Arthur's pleading face held up to Hubert—

Must you with hot irons burn out both mine eyes?

This is too common—pitiful; we cannot bear it; but the slaughter of Agamemnon, and the torture of Prometheus, and the murder of Cassandra, and the death of Clytemnestra by the fruit of her own womb, all these we can bear, because they are less realities than symbols, seen in a shrine, of natural laws vindicated despite unnatural passions, and of the Divine Justice and Pity which is ever awaiting to redeem the deeds of guilt. To read the "Agamemnon" or the

"Prometheus" alone, is like ending at the murder scene in *Macbeth*, or stopping at the early books of "Paradise Lost." Each play bears the same relation to its group that each act of Shakespeare bears to a complete drama. We must read on until the end if we wish to receive the *sacrament* of a Greek Trilogy. In the Orestean group, fortunately preserved for us intact, we get the whole picture complete, with all its issues and its compensations. In the case of the "Prometheus," we have to guess the beginning and the end; and fortunately we can do so with ease and pleasure; but it is not too much to say that we could better spare three or four of the plays of Shakespeare, or, better still, one entire half of the Elizabethan dramas, than the lost "Prometheus Purophoros" and "Prometheus Luomenos" of Æschylus. The loss of the play last named, commonly known as the "Prometheus Solutus," is simply incommensurable. Not even the lovely lyric drama of Shelley, which we owe to it, can make that loss endurable. Nay, for that one lost masterpiece, one would freely exchange any existing masterpiece, with two exceptions, *King Lear*, and the "Inferno."

Only less wonderful than the "Prometheus" is the "Agamemnon." Here, as in the other, the spirit is wrathful, religious, and terrible. It is not my purpose to recapitulate its features, as I did those of the "Prometheus;" such a recapitulation is unnecessary for the purposes of this paper. In some respects, the "Agamemnon" is unequalled. The first chorus of Argive elders is, without any exception whatever, the weirdest, most wonderful, soul-overwhelming piece of *melody* to which the human ear ever listened. It is, even apart from those solemn religious suggestions in which it abounds, a sacred oratorio without any parallel; and delivered in the Greek amphitheatre, with all due pomp of accompaniment and gesture, it must have been as awe-inspiring in its rapid, mysterious imagery, as the very intonations of Eleusis itself. Unfortunately, it is untranslatable. Other Greek choruses may be rendered with a dim approach to the reality, but this chorus it is simply impossible to render at all. It has all the volume of the Psalms of David, with all the music of the ancient world. As one reads it, one cannot help believing that its melody was found in some old oracle, which caught it from the murmur of the neighbouring sea. It comes like a conjuration.

αἴλινον, αἴλινον εἰπέ, τὸ δ' εὖ νικάτω.

And no sooner has it ended, than there rises up, pale, terrible, crowned, with a mask fixed into one white gleam of murderous resolve, the shadowy figure of Clytemnestra. But God, in that deep music, has been invoked, is with us, is watching, and we do not fear. That awful woman may move on to her revenge —the bath is prepared wherein the corse of Agamemnon will soon be lying—all will be fulfilled as has been fated from the beginning (since crime breeds crime, and of Agamemnon's own sowing springs the bloody seed); but still, God is with us, with the spectators as with the actors, and we gaze on. Thus fortified, we can bear even Cassandra's piteous wail, which is soon heard rising to the very heaven of heavens. For we are not met merely beholding a play; we are partaking in a holy ceremony, by which God will be surely justified. Far different, here observe, is the art of Shakespeare. He, too, wrote his "Agamemnon," calling Clytemnestra Lady Macbeth, and Aegisthus Macbeth, and his work, far inferior as it is, parades these humanising touches which in a purely divine tragedy are incidental. Supreme pity is his last word, not supreme justice and religion. As we see the bloody Thane staggering across the stage in his last infirmity, crying,

> I have lived long enough—my way of life
> Has fallen into the sere, the yellow leaf;
> And that which should accompany old age,
> As honour, love, obedience, troops of friends,
> I must not look to have!

we almost forget his crimes, in the utterness of our pity for his poor humanity. There is pity too, but of a sublimer sense, in the "Agamemnon." When in the "Libation-pourers," Clytemnestra falls at her son's feet seeking mercy and crying,

> I reared thee—I would fain grow old with thee!

and when, after slaying her, Orestes cries,

> May the Great Sun, beholding all we do,
> Bear witness for me, that I justly wrought
> This doom upon my mother!

we are too awe-stricken for pity. Fate is speaking through the very lips of the Avenger, and Zeus is approving. Yet even as we hear we know, from vague murmurs of the Chorus and from certain sublime expressions of Orestes himself, that all is not yet well, that Orestes has violated a natural law even in avenging his own father, and that vengeance is not man's, but God's. We do not weep, as in Shakespeare; we pray. We do not turn away sadly conscious of human problems, tenderly stirred by human voices, as we do when we close a play of the great feudal poet; we come away as from a Temple, not wholly comforted, but reverent, and resolved.

IV.

THE ONE GOD.

THE great Greek masterpieces owe no small part of their inconceivable splendour as exercises of religion to the existence of the Chorus. The Chorus is, as it were, the idealised human spectator, ever prepared with comment on events too strange for comprehension. Its members, from their position round the Thymele, midway between actors and audience, are enabled, as the play proceeds, to give expression to the emotions which are disturbing the bosom of every spectator who possesses a particle of human nature. In a modern performance, we must repress our pleasure and pain, no matter how strongly they are excited. In forming actually or in imagination part of the audience at a Greek play, we are perpetually entering our fiery protest against iniquity, and calling aloud to God for His retribution. The moment our emotion masters and suffocates us, the Choragus finds voice in our name. Our human nature is vindicated. It is we ourselves, so to speak, no mere person of the drama, who conduct that fierce dialogue with the contemptuous Aegisthus at the end of the "Agamemnon." We hiss at, deride, insult, mock, and defy the obnoxious character.

> Thrive on, stuff, gorge thy fill, polluting right!

we shriek; and when he threatens us, we cry tauntingly,

> Boast on, and crow—like a cock beside his hen!

Our hootings and exclamations follow him as he retires, led off by Clytemnestra, and the curtain falls.

Again in the "Prometheus" when the Okeanides uplift their voices against the iniquities of the Olympian tyrant, *we* are the Okeanides. *We* call aloud, that the heavens and the earth may hear us,

> Of all the gods, what god is there so cruel
> That he rejoiceth in thy sufferings!

We cling around him, soothing and comforting him, and even when Hermes threatens us with the fiery levin if we remain, we do not go. Nay, *we* are even those fierce Erinnyes, hounding Orestes from land to land—for our human nature sickens at matricide, and we are not appeased until we receive full atonement, in utter contrition and devotion of sacrifice ; then, as the Eumenides, our cries are still.

Thus, as I have indicated, the spectator of a Greek play is assisting at a religious service, in which he joins when the emotion masters him—not wildly and madly, but in a solemn spirit befitting the tragedy of great human issues. He who reads his Bible and finds it holy, and yet can read his "Æschylus" and call it pagan, has much to learn as to what is and what is not edification. If Isaiah and Ezekiel are prophets, Prometheus and the rest are prophets too. The voice of one crying in the wilderness never uttered solemner warning to man than do the Argive Elders of the divine chorus. If the Lord God of the "Psalms" is terrible and overwhelming, the Lord God of the "Suppliants" is beautiful and wise :

> Our sire is He, creator of our being,
> Monarch whose right hand worketh well His will,
> Lord of our race and ruler of our line,
> In counsels deep recording ancient things,
> Planning and ordering all, the great Taskmaster!

It is something also to know that this Being, unlike

that other beloved of King David and dear to the Jews, is not to be entreated on our side when our thought is of battles and our sign is a Sword; that He will not utterly annihilate our enemies and deliver them into our hands, even when those enemies are Philistines and unbelievers; that He will avenge crime and punish sin, even after the lapse of a thousand years; and yet withal, that He is gentle and will bless us, if we only have the heart to suffer and be strong. To suffer!—This, then, is the spirit of Greek tragedy in its highest examples: the triple "anarchy" of Victor Hugo attacking Man on all sides, Man suffering at all points, yet above and beyond all, the reality and ever-abiding presence of divine compensations. More than this, the surety that suffering, though persistent and patience-slaying, is not *eternal*—that only *one* thing is Eternal, the Supreme Idea, the Infinite Pity and Justice of God. Nor does it matter much in partaking this tragic sacrament, on what God we call: whether we are addressing and thinking of the νοῦς of Anaxagoras, Plato's Idea of the Good, Aristotle's πρῶτον κινοῦν, King David's Jehovah, Comte's Grand Être, or Mr. Spencer's great Unknowable, it matters not, so long as we are agreed that this God is, as Mr. Arnold might express it, the *one* fixed Law and Intelligence which works for righteousness. Two vital principles are forced upon us—Nemesis from without, Endurance from within. The victory of the latter principle over the former, is the triumph of the human Will.

Two thousand three hundred and forty years have elapsed since the death of Æschylus, which took place two years after the representation of his masterpiece, the Orestean Trilogy. In that mighty interval many poets have arisen, but (setting aside Dante, whose genius, however, was too exclusively personal and lyrical) not one poet, so far as I know, has dared to take upon himself the Æschylan mantle; until, in our own day, a great genius has so dared, with results too extraordinary, perhaps, for a hasty contemporary estimate. The comparison may seem exaggerated, especially in the eyes of those worthies to whom no fame is first-rate that is not centuries removed in time, and who simply cannot conceive that demigods were *ever* contemporary. It is no exaggeration, however, to say that Victor Hugo is the Æschylus of this generation—the heir, doubtless, of a meaner time, and the inheritor of a lower art—but the prophet, too, in his turn, of miracles to come.

V.

VICTOR HUGO.

As headstrong as Æschylus, and as grim; as solemn in his presentation of archetypal forms and pictures, as musical sometimes in his conjuration of these forms into life; not one whit less credulous than that other, though he inherits all the knowledge of the ages, all the science of the age; sceptic, too, as to God the Constitutional Monarch, but adoring as to God the Infinite Idea; a prophet, a poet, who has never been known to smile, scarcely to weep, and therefore master neither of smiles nor tears (which were Shakespeare's birthright); physically resembling Æschylus, as any one may see by comparing the photograph of one with the traditional likeness of the other; morally and intellectually resembling him, to a degree which suggests a transmigration of souls! Such, then, is Victor Hugo, last of those sublime Frenchmen who have been, ever since the *Encyclopædia*, our intellectual spendthrifts, enriching all Europe with *ideas*, and receiving scanty gratitude in return. Even here in England, where intellectual fashions are so supremely "respectable," his genius is admitted, with the qualification that it lacks sobriety, calm, artistic finish, and that it offends too often against constitutional religion and conventional virtue. The British Matron reads him expurgated, and admits his power; "but, then," she adds, "his ideas are most alarming, and give me the shivers." Even Mr. George Lewes, in some respects an admirable critic, reviewed the "Travailleurs de la Mer," on its first appearance, without enthusiasm, and chiefly devoted himself to emphasizing its exaggerations. Again, he has the misfortune to be, politically speaking, "red." He began by singing pæans to the Bourbon; but advancing step by step, and book by book, he has ended by applauding the Commune, and by adoring one king of men who is worth a thousand kings of peoples—Garibaldi. His literary career has been peculiar. Many years have elapsed since his advent as the leader of the Théatre Romantique filled the aged Goethe with horror, and led him to predict a poetic Deluge. With De Vigny and Dumas for his lieutenants, he began a theatrical campaign in the Spanish fashion, and Romanticism was a nine days' wonder. Brilliant and clever as his dramas are, they are only dramas of purely ephemeral worth. The poet was to find his true tongue in the language of his own time, not in the language of François

Premier or Charles Quint. But in "Notre Dame de Paris," a novel which belongs to the romantic period, he began, while still attitudinising in hat and feather, to conjure in the name of Nature; and there arose, in answer to his conjuration, with the pet word "anarchy" written on his brow, Quasimodo. This shapeless Earth-geist, full of all the tenderness and passion of the earth, unbeautiful, patient, enduring, powerful, tender, was seen at war with all those evil forces which were once named Religion, and by his side there blossomed the flower of revolt, Esmeralda. The story is a lovely one, despite its pitiable gloom—almost approaching true tragedy in some of its issues; but there has passed across it the sickly breath of Balzac, and it droops into third or fourth rank as fiction.

The Spectre, the Earth-geist, once thus invoked, was not soon to be appeased. He who, in the spirit of Doctor Faustus, calls up the secret forces of the elements, and compels them into some attendant shape, has generally some difficulty in "laying" them again; and Victor Hugo, from the hour of his creation of Quasimodo, has been at the mercy of that type. Jean Valjean, Gilliatt, and the Laughing Monster in "l'Homme qui rit," are so many repetitions and amplifications of Quasimodo, engaged at the same old hopeless business—fighting Zeus, in all his horrible forms and execrable disguises. Nor is the poet less faithful to his own fragile type of woman. Cosette, Déruchette, and Dea are merely pseudonyms for Esmeralda. And here it may be remarked, in passing, that Victor Hugo, like nearly every modern, fails miserably as a painter of female character. His women, when they are not mere animals, with the passions of brewer's draymen, are so many inanities washed in water-colours. The secret of their failure is not far to seek, lying as it does in the over-strong virility of the poet's imagination. His masculine conceptions being types of exaggerated power, his feminine conceptions naturally become types of exaggerated weakness. They are pretty, they bloom, and they die. Compared with the divine female creations of Greek tragedy, they are as poor as the "beauties of Byron" engraved in an old Annual. In the ancient theatre, all the power was not reserved for man, nor all the suffering. Woman, too, was to become sublime by bearing sublime burthens; woman, too, was to rise supreme above the malignity and cruelty of Zeus, and to turn to eternal marble in the glory of her accomplished and triumphant will. A Niobe remains in stone, a thing of deathless womanhood. Electra, Antigone, and Alcestis also remain, certain of their immortality as the stars of heaven; for of their very womanhood was wrought their glory, and they were as strong to resist as Gilliatt himself, though, unlike him, they did not become hideous by aggression.

Victor Hugo, then, cannot paint women; it is almost doubtful whether he paints men; but for producing in colossal cipher the abstract forms of masculine forces, he is without a rival. He is the Frankenstein of the democratic Idea, the humaniser of the wild elements of anarchy; and the figures he uses, though of human likeness, and full of appeals to the human soul, are simply superhuman types like those of Greek tragedy, elevated like them on the *cothurnus*, and speaking like them through the mask. They move to and fro on a mighty stage, with a background of the mountains and the sea. They contend with monsters and with phantoms. The "Pieuvre" is as horrible, to all intents and purposes, as the three swan-shaped Phorkides, with only one eye and tooth between them all. The skeleton of Clubin is more appalling than the ghost of Clytemnestra. The Winds of the Douvres are as frightful as the Eumenides. The evil genius of "Les Misérables," Thénardier, is more diabolical than the "Gorgons, serpent-tressed, hating men." Again, even as to the number of performers, he never, at the utmost, exceeds the third actor. He himself is the Choragus, and a very bad Choragus; for his eternal volubility, though seeming in the name and interests of the spectator, goes far to spoil the play. For example, instead of the mighty music from around the Thymele, we get such reflections as the following:

> Essayez de vous rendre compte de ce chaos, si énorme qu'il aboutit au niveau. Il est le récipient universel, réservoir pour les fécondations, creuset pour les transformations. Il amasse, puis disperse; il accumule, puis ensemence; il dévore, puis crée. Il reçoit tous les égouts de la terre, et il les thésaurise. Il est solide dans le fangeux, liquide dans le flot, fluide dans l'effluve. Comme matière il est masse, et comme force il est abstraction. Il égalise et marie les phénomènes. Il se simplifie par l'infini dans la combinaison. C'est à force de mélange et de trouble qu'il arrive à la transparence. La diversité soluble se fond dans son unité. Il a tant d'éléments qu'il est l'identité. Une de ses gouttes. c'est tout lui. Parce qu'il est plein de tempêtes, il devient l'équilibre. Platon voyait danser les sphères; chose étrange à dire, mais réelle, dans la colossale évolution terrestre autour du soleil, l'océan, avec son flux et reflux, est le balancier du globe," etc. etc.

Protracted over innumerable pages, this sort of thing becomes distracting. It is more like Euripides than Æschylus, but it is far below even Euripides. It is worthy, in fact, of—"Monte Cristo;" still more worthy of M. Louis Figuier, who popularises science for the unscientific in illustrated volumes of rubbish. It is certainly not worthy of the master-poet of this generation. It is not merely worthless in itself, but it has a most demoralising influence on inferior artists.

A few remarks may naturally be made here on the character of the modern novel, and its relation to other works of Art. There is no absolute reason, that I perceive, why the novel should not be infinitely more perfect than our greatest novelists choose to make it, why it should not take artistic rank just under the very highest poetry; and there is this much to be said for it against all other finer products, that it appeals to all classes of the community alike, and carries broadcast seeds which our poets lock up in the ivory caskets of mystic and rhythmic speech. In our own days we have seen some half-dozen novel-poems, of the finest and most delightful workmanship — Canon Kingsley's "Hypatia" and "Westward Ho," Reade's first version of the "Cloister and the Hearth," Hawthorne's "Scarlet Letter," Thackeray's "Esmond," and Dickens' "Copperfield." None of these excellent works, however, are so distinctly and emphatically poetic as the novels of Victor Hugo. Most perfect and finished as works of Art are the novels of the late Nathaniel Hawthorne, most finished of all "The Scarlet Letter," an effusion of terrible and stupefying gloom, but wonderfully finely wrought. If Victor Hugo had been fettered by an art as rigid as that of Hawthorne, and had restricted his canvas accordingly, he would have escaped all those mad splashes of the brush which disfigure his best painting. Confined to the compass of the "Scarlet Letter," "Les Travailleurs de la Mer" would have been of double its present value. We want all its gold, but not any particle of its dross. "Les Misérables," too, might be curtailed one-half with tremendous advantage. As for "L'Homme qui

Rit," I am not so sure that it might not have been curtailed altogether, for one third of it is hideous, another third of it is nasty, and the remaining third is only a repetition of what its author has said better elsewhere. Each of these works, despite its prose form, is a poem—a work which could have been expressed as well, or better, in verse. Why then did Victor Hugo, whose command of metrical effects is so consummate, abandon them in composing his greatest works? Because, the truth must be admitted, he perceived that the Novel, with all its limitations, bears the same relation to this generation that the Tragic Drama did to the generation of Æschylus, in so far as it is the resource and study of the entire reading world. During the annual period of the dramatic performances, it was the simple duty of every Athenian citizen to attend and behold them; they were produced for the delight and edification of the Many, not for the æsthetic gratification of the Few; and although their poetic claims were privately adjudicated by delicate critics, their general appeal was to the public. It would be going too far to compare the productions of what was essentially a religious festival with modern productions created only for the pleasure of the hour; but the Novel bears at least this resemblance to Greek tragedy—it gratifies, when successfully written, an enormous assemblage of people. Its literary form may be loose, its influence ephemeral, its appeals undignified; but surely these are results which have nothing to do with the question—whether or not a prose story may not be as perfect in its way as a Greek tragedy?—or at any rate, to reduce the question to a closer issue, infinitely more perfect than any novelist, with the exception, perhaps, of Hawthorne, chooses to make it?

I know scarcely any modern fiction in three volumes, for example, which would not have been infinitely better if restricted to one volume ;—always excepting, of course, those collections of humorous sketches which constitute a story by Thackeray or Dickens, and in which an infinity of diverting characters are introduced almost at haphazard, with no very special adherence to a serious chain of interest. Examine, for example, that very elaborate work of art, George Eliot's " Romola." No contemporary work is better conceived, with more admirable characters and a more tragic plot ; yet, has any student ever read it through with anything but weariness, due to the masses of unemotional verbiage by which the ideas are wrapt, disguised, and overclouded? This, however, is an example of a novel without spontaneity, rather than of inordinate length, and it is doubtful if any mere compression could make " Romola" the tragedy it ought to have been. Turn to a work of far humbler pretensions, but of infinitely higher successes—the " Vicar of Wakefield." Here is a poem, simple, spontaneous, hearty, beautiful, and brief. This, however, is a mere *genre* picture; and for any parallel in fiction to the mighty creations of the Attic stage, we must return to Victor Hugo. Hugo has attempted, with more or less success, as we have been endeavouring to show, to use the novel, as Æschylus used the drama, as a vehicle for the highest poetry of which the age is capable. The splendour of his achievements has justified a perilous experiment, and the question is no longer one of mere Art, in which his inferiority and that of the novel is seen and admitted, but of intellectual grasp and moral teaching, concerning which there will doubtless be an infinity of diverging opinions.

VI.

THE PROMETHEAN MYTH.

ONE characteristic must strike at once the most superficial reader of Hugo's novels—their unutterable despair. This also is the characteristic of the stories of George Eliot, but while her despair is unpleasantly suggestive of the Feuerbach she translated in her literary youth, that of Hugo is the despair of a Poet. His colossal masculine types, while they triumph invariably more or less over the triple anarchy of Religion, Society, and Nature, double up like houses of cards before the anarchy of their own sentiments —or, as the writer expresses it, "of the human heart." The ocean closes over Gilliatt because he cannot with courage endure the contemplation of a rival's happiness, not because the nobler part of his life has been a failure. Jean Valjean dies broken-hearted, not because he has failed to redeem himself utterly from the shadow of crime and degraded instinct under which he was born, but because he misses the individual filial love which his own conscience assures him is not worth the winning. For Quasimodo there is justification—he is utterly and cruelly crushed down at all points—but for these others there is none whatever; they fail, despite their inexorable will, for want of a higher and solemner purpose than could ever be consecrated by the lips of a woman or the embraces of a child. They stalk on the stage like Titans—they creep off the stage like Liliputians. They win our pity in the end, but not the right sort of pity. We expect the sacrament of true tragedy, and it is not given. That one word, "Anarchy," which repelled us at the beginning, is whispered again to us at the end.

It is a solemn thing to discuss a Poet's religious belief; a solemn, and often a useless, thing. Here, however, the question being forced upon me, let me ask, in all humility before the mind of a Master, whether the gloominess of his religious faith does not leave him, so to speak, in intellectual and moral darkness? It would be difficult to state definitely what Victor Hugo believes, nor would what he believed matter—if the nature of his belief were a little brighter. In no man's pages does the name of "God" appear so often, and he uses it in the same way as Æschylus to express two ideas, one very execrable, the other very divine; but whether he regards this God as the Personal One of theologians, or the pantheistic Spirit of Spinoza, or the mysterious Unknowable of the doctrine of Evolution, one thing is certain—he approaches Him too much in a mood of despairing gloom. Nor is it Divinity alone that he approaches in this manner. Nature herself, he regards, or seems to regard, as something horrible, alien, treacherous, and forbidding. There is no love in his fear, as there was in Shelley's; for it is not her awful beauty that dazzles him, it is not her mystic voice that awes him, it is not her divine touch that thrills him. No poet of equal rank was ever so obtuse to her mere beauty. The peace of Wordsworth, the passion of Keats, the tender pang of Shelley, are far from his bosom. He folds his arms upon his bosom, and without quailing, gazes upon—the Abyss (*L'Abîme*). The Abyss fascinates him till he becomes light-headed, and raves about it till its name becomes a catchword. He sees Monsters, Portents, Shadows, Terrors, Horrors inconceivable—all entities like Gorgon, all abstractions like the Chimæra. He thinks, because he is gloomy, there shall be no more cakes and ale. He knows the names of all the Winds, but he is indifferent to all the flowers. He walks abroad only in the twilight, when bats fly and owls cry. His creations are hideous as the forces with which they fight. Quasimodo, Jean Valjean, the nameless one who Grins, are alike hideous. "Quand Dieu veut," he observes, "il excelle dans l'exécrable." Victor Hugo himself, however, and not God, is responsible for the "Pieuvre!" When Victor Hugo wills, *he* excels in the execrable, and unfortunately, he wills very often. His pictures are deficient in the all-purifying daylight. He gives us sun, moon, stars, earth, clouds, man, woman, bird, and beast—all in colossal *silhouette*.

It is hardly conceivable, then, that gloom so monotonous can co-exist with a bright and happy faith. The gloom of Æschylus is different; it is solemn more than terrifying. One does not shiver in it, in fear of cold unseen phantoms that "uplift the hair." Through it, star-like presences shine at intervals, and the presence of Zeus is ever felt. Above all, the final word is one of blessing, and the spectator is dismissed as with a divine benediction of hands. With Victor Hugo, this benediction is missed; nay, our own faith is shaken by what we have seen and heard; for if the last word of mighty natures is to be despair and suicide, what are we to hope whose natures are not mighty? This persistent dwelling in gloom has other results. It makes the poet wild, uncertain, and unsteady. It confuses his vision, so that he is apt to mistake very harmless human faces for awful portents, and to be startled by events which, to the world in general, might seem cheerful. He loses clearness of judgment, and falls into superstition. There is a character in one of Mr. Reade's novels, Jael Dence, who sees omens in everything, down to pins and needles. Victor Hugo is a literary Jael. Fortified with all the culture of the nineteenth century, deep in all its science, and strong in all its poetry, he cannot move about the earth in peace, or take his place among the creatures of gladness, even for a single moment. Very characteristic, for example, is his way of looking at the ocean. He has no joy in it, no mighty exultation such as Byron felt when he sang—

> Time writes no wrinkle on thine azure brow,
> Such as creation's dawn beheld, thou rollest now.
>
> Thou glorious mirror, where the Almighty's form
>   Glasses itself in tempests : in all time,
> Calm or convulsed—in breeze, or gale, or storm,
>   Icing the pole, or in the torrid clime
> Dark-heaving ; boundless, endless, and sublime—
>   The image of eternity, the throne
> Of the Invisible ; even from out thy slime
>   The monsters of the deep are made ; each zone
> Obeys thee; thou goest forth, dread, fathomless, alone.
>
> And I have loved thee, Ocean ! and my joy
>   Of youthful sports was on thy breast to be
> Borne, like thy bubbles, onward : from a boy
>   I wantoned with thy breakers ; they to me
> Were a delight ; and if the freshening sea
>   Made them a terror, 'twas a pleasing fear,
> For I was, as it were, a child of thee,
>   And trusted to thy billows far and near,
> And laid my hand upon thy mane, as I do here.

He knows not its loveliness, he comprehends not its serenity, as Shelley did, as all beauty-loving poets have done. He thinks of the monsters in its depths, not of the "fairily-wrought" shells upon its shore. He regards it as an enemy, not as a mighty friend. For these and for many reasons, he does not understand the sea ; indeed, it is doubtful if any Frenchman ever will. As it is with the great waters, so it is with all the rest—to him. He could have conceived Prometheus, perhaps, but not the Okeanides, with the bright sea-light shining on their wings, the love and freedom, and ἀνήριθμον γέλασμα of the waves sparkling in their eyes. He is the Rembrandt, not the Correggio, of novelists. In stature and strength he is an ancient Greek, but the Greek "joy" is an unknown gleam to *him*.

So, when I seek the last word of that divine trilogy which Æschylus wrote twenty-three hundred years ago, I have to turn, not to him who is most like Æschylus in shadowy power and colossal imagery, but to our own English poet of the dreamy eyes and the silvern-ringing voice. The missing "Prometheus Luómenos" is not wholly lost to us, so long as we can hear the wonderful voice of Shelley singing aloud his solemn and impassioned sequel. The "Prometheus Unbound" is, of course, a production far too thin and emotional in character to be classed quite in the same rank as the marble work of Æschylus; but it is a poem of surpassing modern beauties, and its choric portions form a fit pæan of triumph and victory for the Æschylan Titan. Its early passages are merely a free paraphrase of the "Prometheus Bound," and the appeal to "earth, heaven," and "all-beholding sun," is the immortal

ὦ διος αἰθήρ. . . . . .
παμμῆτόρ τε γῆ,
καὶ τὸν πανόπτην κύκλον ἡλίου καλῶ!

done into wonderful blank verse; just as the line,

δυσχείμερόν γε πέλαγος ἀτηρᾶς δύης,

is the original of Hamlet's "sea of troubles," and "ἐγγράφου σὺ μνήμοσιν δέλτοις φρενῶν," contains Hamlet's "tablets of my memory." Much that follows is too transparently propagandist to be quite pleasing, and in the scene of the Furies there is too much of Lord Byron ; but the conception of Demogorgon, and the scene in Demogorgon's cave, and the characters of Asia and Panthea, are magnificent beyond comparison. It is with the ethic flavour of the poem, however, that I have at present to deal *en passant*, and this is chiefly revealed in the noble melodies of the fourth and last act. Here, in her exultation at the freedom of Prometheus, the Earth prophesies the triumph and regeneration of man—

>   Man, one harmonious soul of many a soul,
>   Whose nature is its own divine control,
> Where all things flow to all, as rivers to the sea ;
>   Familiar acts are beautiful through love ;
>   Labour, and pain, and grief, in life's green grove,
> Sport like tame beasts, none knew how gentle they could be.
>
>   His will, with all mean passions, bad delights,
>   And selfish cares, its trembling satellites,
> A spirit ill to guide, but mighty to obey,
>   Is as a tempest-winged ship, whose helm
>   Love rules, through waves which dare not overwhelm,
> Forcing life's wildest shores to own its sovereign sway.
>
>   All things confess his strength. Through the cold mass
>   Of marble and of colour his dreams pass ;
> Bright threads whence mothers weave the robes their children wear.
>   Language is a perpetual orphic song,
>   Which rules with Dædal harmony a throng
> Of thoughts and forms, which else senseless and shapeless were.
>
>   The lightning is his slave ; heaven's utmost deep
>   Gives up her stars, and, like a flock of sheep,
> They pass before his eyes, are number'd, and roll on !
>   The tempest is his steed, he strides the air ;
>   And the abyss shouts from her depths laid bare,
> "Heaven, hast thou secrets? Man unveils me ; I have none."

Prometheus, then, has not wrought in vain ; his sufferings have not been without their reward. The creature of his sublime and never-ceasing love, Humanity, has become strong, beautiful, and free, and the "shadow of white death" has passed from the path of liberated Nature.

In this extraordinary lyric poem of Shelley there is a variegated light and sweetness, a continual flow of lovely and soul-soothing images, which redeem a certain indefiniteness and hollowness of meaning. We are comforted by sheer excess of light. Our path is rainbowed with a thousand flowers, our heavens are throbbing with innumerable stars. A pulse of happiness throbs through Nature, and we feel it. Now it is this abundant joy that we miss in Victor Hugo. He altogether lacks Shelley's divine faith—a faith born of sheer exultation in the Beautiful. While Victor Hugo is ever brooding on the shadowy side of Nature, Shelley is ever singing on the ethereal side. He has none of the strong earthly joy of Shakespeare, of the deep solemn enjoyment of Wordsworth. He soars, like his own skylark, through the heart of a shower; and such "harmonious madness" flows from his lips, that the world is constrained to listen. His "Prometheus," therefore, is, as it were, the choric portion of the last act of the Æschylan trilogy; to construct the play completely, as Æschylus would have done, is naturally beyond him. If we could conceive the faculties of Victor Hugo and Shelley blent together—Hugo creating the mighty forms and images of the drama, while Shelley supplied the music—we might imagine what the lost "Prometheus" was, or ought to have been.

I cannot dismiss the Promethean myth without briefly chronicling its influence on the mind of another English poet, the scholastic Milton. In the "Paradise Lost" of this author, we have an extraordinary version of the same story, Prometheus appearing under the character of "Satan," and Zeus under the name of the Lord God of the Hebrews. The parallel holds in minute particulars. The story of the angelic war, in which many of the archangels side with God, and many others revolt with Satan, is identical with the story of the rebellious Titans. But Satan, with all his power of diatribe, is a degraded Prometheus. His malignity is that of a petulant schoolboy, and his hatred of humanity is irrational and uninteresting.

> Farewell, remorse : all good to me is lost :
> Evil, be though my good ; by thee at least
> Divided empire with Heaven's King I hold,
> By thee, and more than half perhaps will reign ;
> As man ere long and this new world shall know.

This Devil is so morally foolish in his didactic wickedness, that we have little or no interest in him. But the idea of a titanic Human Spirit, loving humanity at large, leading them from darkness into the sun, instructing them in purifying arts, teaching them all knowledge from pharmacy up to augury, this is a sublime idea, and therefore it is imperishable. Founded also on eternal truth is the idea of a Supreme Evil with whom this Being is at war—the personification of terrible and cruel Power, administering and dominating, to damnable issues, the elemental anarchy of which he is the awful fruit. This Supreme Evil, however, is to fall ; above him and beyond him "darkening his fall with victory," is that other Supreme *Good*, the divine incomprehensible "God" of all divine poets, from Æschylus to Shelley. Nothing is more wonderful in Æschylus than his foreshadowing of problems which have been the delight of modern science. Primæval man lives again in such lines as these:

> Through all their days, like phantoms seen in dreams,
> All things they mixed at random, knowing not
> Dwellings of stone that catch the summer sun,
> Nor yet the useful work of carpentry ;
> But deep they dwelt, like swarms of gnats, within
> Dark sunless caverns, with no sign to show
> Frost-laden winter, flower-bearing spring,
> Or summer with her fruits," etc. etc.

Such a race as Æschylus pictured needed the Prometheus who surely came. For the Spirit of Man is ever far in advance of humanity at large, and might thus be justly typified in a titanic "Forethought." Moderns hungry for meanings may also discover in the figure of Io, a type of oppressed Womanhood, tortured, polluted, outcast, and utterly at the mercy of the Supreme Evil in its earliest and most hateful form of unbridled passion. The Voice that comes thronging into Io's "virgin chambers,"—

ἐς παρθενῶνας τοὺς ἐμοὺς,

was the despair and misery of Woman since the beginning; and not until Zeus has fallen, and the era of pure knowledge begins, shall the vestal creature walk abroad upon the earth in peace.

VII.

SUMMARY.

I HAVE thus endeavoured to sketch, briefly yet discursively, the connection of the great Greek tragic poet with modern writers, but especially with Victor Hugo. The poetry of the world constitutes one great and, as yet, uncompleted Poem, the last utterance of which shall not be heard until Humanity has reached the final point of divine knowledge and consummate literary expression; and the rank and worth of every poet is to be determined, earlier or later, by his relation to the cosmic music of which his song is to form a part. If these facts be admitted, as they must unquestioningly be by every student of literature, it follows that the criterion of poetry is its religious truth—its agreement or discord, in other words, with the sum of knowledge which Humanity has been diligently accumulating from time immemorial; and criticised under such conditions, many singers fall into comparative insignificance whom we have been accustomed to regard as irreproachable bards. Thus, Milton falls into second or third rank, while Æschylus rises to the very first. Dante stands firm, filling the darkest and saddest chapter of the book; while Virgil survives chiefly in the illumination of Dante's page. Goethe is sure of some consecration; but perhaps he will be deemed, when the final classification comes, less beloved and bright than our own Shelley, less colossal than this other descendant of the demigods, Victor Hugo. One can hardly conceive an epoch, however far advanced in time, when the " Prometheus " of Æschylus, the " Inferno " of Dante, the " Prometheus Bound " of Shelley, and " Les Misérables " of Victor Hugo (as divinely real a *poem* this as any of the rest), will become as tedious from all but a purely literary point of view as the " Æneid " of Virgil became with the first breath of the Renaissance, and as the " Paradise Lost " of Milton has become in the last light of modern thought. That mere style, however wonderful, will not save a poem, is proved by these examples. Style is all-important, but it will not avail *alone*. The criterion of a poem is its eternal truth to history of human nature. A work hopelessly fettered to an effete superstition, or to a weary and uninteresting tradition, cannot, however exquisitely wrought in the details, be classed with first-rate literature. To bring the question to an issue, if the gloom of Victor Hugo were less complete, if his moral teaching were less persistently suicidal, his certainty of immortality would be greater than it is. He fails to represent his generation in so far as he fails to image forth its happiness and its hope, together with those ideal aspirations which constitute in all generations what is termed "religion;" and in this respect he is far inferior, for example, to Shelley. The charge of atheism has been brought against both these poets, and with equal justice and consistency. But the atheist is he who disbelieves in light altogether, utterly repudiates that mystic Zeus of whom Æschylus sang, and believes that human nature is going headlong to ruin and despair. The atheist is he who cries with Schopenhauer that life is "a cheat, and a uselessly interrupting episode in the blissful repose of nothing." The atheist is he who grimly affirms with Feuerbach that "Der Mann ist was er isst." An atheistical *poet* is an anomaly, an impossibility; and Shelley, so far from being an atheist, is, of all modern poets, with the exception of Wordsworth, the most religious—so constantly in a white heat of divine ecstasy and worship, that his music becomes almost monotonous. Victor Hugo, on the other hand, is atheistic just in so far as he fails to perceive the triumph of human nature over all the conditions which mar it, and drag it down. He himself, in one of the finest poems of "L'Année Terrible," has expressly vindicated himself against the charge of atheism brought against him by (*mirabile dictu!*) a French Bishop! No charge is easier to bring, or harder to bear. As I write, I see it, in several journals, brought against a distinguished living poet, Mr. Algernon Swinburne. The present writer cannot certainly be accused of sympathising unduly with the school Mr. Swinburne represents, but he takes this opportunity of saying that Mr. Swinburne is an atheist in the sense that Shelley was one, and in no other. The wealth of his vocabulary of abuse should not mislead us. He utters the truth as he feels and sees it; he utters it, now and then, too madly; but the very strength of his invective is a proof that he is in earnest. He fights his adversaries with a flail, and the weapon too often rebounds, as such weapons will even in powerful hands, upon his own head. But for all that, he is one of the army of God, and we forgive him all his outrageousness when he speaks, as he so often can and will, the lovely language of Sion. There are far too many real atheists in the world—men who hate truth, and have no faith in beauty. Let us not class among them any one authentic poet, however much his non-poetical utterances may offend our prejudices, and even amaze our reason.

And finally, turning back to Victor Hugo, let us remember, what perhaps I have been rather forgetting, the utterness of his love and charity for all the created world, and especially for Humanity. There are words in his pages, syllables of divine tenderness, sweet enough to wake a soul under the very ribs of Death; inexpressibly sad perhaps, but most fond and pitiful. Read the story of "Fantine," an episode repeated a thousandfold in every city and in every street; read that narrative of miserable sin and divine maternal tenderness, and feel the blinding tears stream down your cheeks in sympathy and love. "The pity of it, the pity of it, Iago!" Turn again to the history of the good Bishop Myriel, remembering as you read that there were some diabolical enough to call even him —"atheist!" Was ever a picture more benignly soul-assuring? What "anarchy" could long resist the seraphic sweetness of the good Bishop's smile? Victor Hugo's faith is firm—in goodness, in human love, in Democracy. Dark as many of his premonitions have been, he believes in the world's regeneration. His canvas may be too full of Pieuvres, horrors, and chimæras dire; of evil monsters, and of evil men; of cruel elements incarnated in titanic forms; but over and beyond these, he paints the sunrise—dim, cold, far-off, cheerless as yet, but slowly creeping up from the eternal gates of morning. His defects are those of his country and of his race—too much faith and too little; too much faith in human strength and pride, too little faith in the Eternal Calm. Only the other day he seemed caught in the whirlwind of a national passion, mingling with those who still would conjure up the insatiable devil of Battle; this was only for a moment; and soon his voice was heard above the storm, preaching charity and peace. It would be pitiable if Victor Hugo were only a Frenchman; it would be horrible if the sentiment of nationality had eclipsed that sentiment of cosmopolitanism, which sooner or later will slay the War Monster for ever. Out of all the mist of contemporary wrath and passion, out of the very darkness of his own creed, the great poet emerges, beautiful and wise. No nobler figure is to be seen among living men. His greatness is without question, his immortality is sure. When he passes to the Immortals, his place will be close to Æschylus, if not at his side.

NOTE.—This article was written before the death of Victor Hugo. Since it was written, Mr. I. A. Symonds has published, in the *Cornhill Magazine,* an article in which he argues that the lost "Prometheus," if restored to us, would show the poet's *vindication* of Zeus himself as Divine Wisdom. Everything that comes from the powerful pen of the author of the "Renaissance," must bear literary weight, but in the present instance I fancy the arguments overstrained. It is almost impossible to regard the threats and taunts of Prometheus as merely dramatic utterances, with which the poet has little or no sympathy, and if Mr. Symonds is right, what shall we say of Prometheus' prophecy of the Divine downfall, which is assuredly to come?

R. B.

THE CHARACTER OF GOETHE.

I.

THE AMOURS.

IN selecting out of Goethe's enormous list of literary productions the one or two absolute masterpieces,* and in studying the great man's biography step by step, one is constantly doubting, in spite of oneself, whether Nature in the beginning really meant Goethe for a genius at all; and even his very masterpieces are so spoilt by barbarous foreign matter, by writing which is absolutely depressing in its intellectual vapidity, that one sometimes questions if even they could not have been produced, by enormous cultivation, on a soil naturally fruitful of merely frivolous material. Even as it was, Goethe, with a little less animation, would have made a very popular Parson. But the Amours turned the scale, decided the genius,

---

* Besides the books which are best known to English readers, "Faust," "Iphigenia," "Tasso," "Götz," "Egmont," "Werther," "Elective Affinities," "Wilhelm Meister," etc., Goethe is the author of *forty-four* dramas, melodramas, and farces, and any amount of travel and criticism; and even his poetical writings constitute a sort of enormous dumpling, with very few currants indeed in proportion to the dough.

and the world became the richer for "Clärchen," "Ottilie," "Gretchen," and, above all, "Mignon."

Certainly Goethe was not a man of genius in the same sense that Novalis, or Jean Paul Richter, or John Keats, were men of genius. His insight was a slowly-acquired thing, not a veritable flash from the spirit, such as gleams out of the dying eyes of poets "whom the gods love," or as lightens the strangely divine face of the author of " Titan." He was a man of high mettle, lively, animated, yet without any signs of purely poetic temperament. He had little or no humour of either sort—Shakespeare's and Richter's divine humour, or Fielding's and Molière's earthly humour. As a child, when he "reared an altar to the Lord," on a music-stand of his father's, and burnt thereon a pastil, as a sort of patriarchal sacrifice, he was not only, as Mr. Hutton suggests, without "awe," he was instinctively theatrical, carried away by the prettiness of the effect, but quite incapable of true religious emotion. His oracular *manners* in childhood, which his mother has described to us, were no signs of genius or of power; such manners, on the contrary, are very usually found in artificial children, who are pampered at home, and who shoot up into most commonplace men and women. Providence, however, had by no means arranged that Goethe should grow up into a parson or a burgomaster, and so, when her pet was about twelve years of age, she sent a company of French players to perform at Frankfort, and so arranged matters that the little fellow had constant access behind the scenes. Here, Mr. Hutton thinks,* the natural delicacy of his mind was first rubbed off. "Certainly he was not too

---

* Essays, vol. i.

young for that morbid curiosity about evil, which is often more tainting than evil itself." But I am by no means sure that mere curiosity of any kind is contaminating, and am inclined to believe that Goethe got more moral harm in the front of the house than in the green-room, and confirmed there the artificial personal and moral manner, both of thought and expression, which was his characteristic through life. Fit nutriment for "egoism" was to be found in the theatre. The rest was decided by Gretchen, his first boyish sweetheart. Then came the love affair at Leipzig, then the tremendous business with Frederika ; then this passion, then that; affinity following close upon affinity, until Goethe was seventy years of age. And only these affinities, as I have suggested, finally manufactured Goethe into a fine literary genius. The mystery of sex was at the bottom of it all.

Yes; but I have scarcely spoken of that one quality of Goethe's mind, which was so closely allied to spiritual perception as scarcely to be separable from it in his works—I mean its marvellous steadfastness in retaining, and clearness in receiving, impressions of all sorts from the world without. Surely this was genius; genius which, left to itself, would almost under any circumstances have produced great work? Great, good, or useful work, probably might have issued from Goethe's mind independent of the disturbing element ; but without the very weakness which disfigured the man, that mind would never have planned high literature. Bad, wretched, and contemptible as was Goethe's superficial habit of falling in love, it was the *light*, a real spiritual light, temporarily illumining a mirror—a mirror of wonderful clearness and power, but lying so deep in the nature that neither the white ray of faith, nor the bright gleam of moral rapture, nor the soft coruscating radiance of human pity, nor the moonlight of religious awe, could reach it at all. For nature, Goethe had never the kindling enthusiasm and fervid love of unsuccessful poets—Shelley for example. Of that deepest of all pathos, the pathos of human ties, he never had any inspiration. He had a calm and perfect perception of great literature, but masterly work never mastered him. He believed in God, *chiefly* as a useful and interesting "sentiment." But of Nature, Humanity, Literature, and God, as seen in the illumination of a new affinity, what man's soul ever offered a better reflection? His lyrics, his "Werther," his "Wilhelm Meister," his "Faust," all are autobiographical; in each we have the lover's apotheosis into a bold literary form—always a feminine form; and just, perhaps, for the reason that women like to be preached to, especially by a favourite of the other sex, and love to carry solemnity into matters by no means solemn in themselves, did Goethe gradually expand into the TITANIC TUTOR of modern literature, strongly resembling the insufferable person in "Sandford and Merton," who is for ever "turning the occasion to advantage" in the way of disquisitions on Providence, morality, life, death, and the musical glasses. For the spell which holds all criticism yet, and which makes us all, in spite of ourselves, criticise as if we were born in professorial wigs and had academic gowns for swathing-clothes, we are thus indirectly indebted to Goethe's sweethearts—to Frederika, to Annchen, to Lili, and even to little Bettina. Modern criticism thus arose, and has naturally been so extremely merciful to its parent. If Goethe had been discouraged a little oftener by his favourites, we might not have got more, but we certainly should have been spared much. As it is, he is ever resembling, even in his finest passages, the "Bourgeois Gentilhomme" of Molière, and talking "prose" (for the world's edification) without knowing it.

The affair with Frederika may be described as the decisive point in his career. Had he hesitated then, and married the poor girl, his aphrodital impulses might have exhausted themselves at the outset, and we should never have had "Wilhelm Meister" and the other cerebellic autobiographies. Frederika, as every one is supposed to know, was the daughter of Pastor Briou, who lived at Drusenheim, near Strasbourg, and in whose little circle Goethe detected a strong resemblance to the family of Dr. Primrose in the "Vicar of Wakefield," a book which, at Herder's instigation, he had just then been reading. His theatrical instincts were clearly displayed in his connection with this family. He first appeared in the character of a poor student in theology; then he "dressed up" as the "innkeeper's boy;" and finally he appeared as Dr. Goethe himself. Be that as it may, the pastor's youngest daughter, in whom he thought he saw a resemblance to Goldsmith's Sophia, fell passionately in love with him. Then ensued the same result as in the case of Annchen, in Leipzig, with the exception that in the first case his treatment had quite alienated the lady. Directly he had won this poor girl's heart Goethe began to repent, and the more her passion deepened the more he drew back and trembled. It was clear that he did not love her; but it was also clear that he had wilfully won her heart. He determined to say "good-bye," and he gives us quite a pretty artistic picture of the "situation," which he, with his everlasting double identity, seemed to enjoy as spectator as well as actor. It was quite an effective stage-parting, quiet, but powerful. "I reached her my hand from my horse; the tears stood in her eyes, and I felt *very uneasy.*" Much as he fretted over the injury he had done (for Goethe could never bear to be troubled even with his own conscience, and *it* reproached him often enough), he rejoices in his triumph over his first inclination for the maiden, and calculates with delight that, by stifling it thus early, he prevented himself from losing "two years of his time."

The first decided step was taken, as I have said, and the preacher of the "Gospel of Economy," as Novalis calls it,* saved his soul for literature. This was his first hardening. He was never after that inclined to let his passion get the better of him, much as he enjoyed the foam and fury of it, and its dainty flavour. The usual criticism on the whole situation is that Goethe was already resolved to make any sacrifice in order to bear "higher the pyramid of his existence." My own belief is that this pyramid-building was an *after-thought*, used by Goethe in fighting with his own sense of moral littleness. The simple truth, as I believe it to have been, is that Goethe's conduct was far less owing to tremendous calculations of self-culture than to simple want of earnestness in any of the concerns of life, added to a tremendous æsthetic horror of that most unpicturesque of all things—matrimony, as practised in modern Germany. Throughout his whole career he never allowed any one feeling to strike deep root. He carefully watered his sentiments, trained his virtues (such

---

* See "Aesthetik und Literatur," p. 183, vol. i. of Tieck and Schlegel's edition of Novalis.

as they were), daintily enjoyed his tastes—made, in fact, a sort of back-garden of his affections, whither he could retire without any danger of being bored by the world, and where all was fine weather and perfect shade. He had celebrated his affair with Annchen in "Die Laune des Verliebten," where he is personified under the affected title of Eridon, and he adopted a similar theatrical attitude after the Frederika episode, took Nature into his confidence, and wrote, besides many less affected lyrics, the wild "Wanderers Sturmlied," of which the two marked characteristics are inordinate self-satisfaction, and utterly heathen affectation :

> Wen du nicht verlässest, Genius,
> Nicht der Regen, nicht der Sturm
> Haucht ihm Schauer über's Herz.
> Wen du nicht verlassest, Genius,
> Wird die Regengewölk,
> Wird dem Schlossensturm
> Entgegen singen,
> Wie die Lerche,
> Du da droben!

And so on, with a great deal of Goethe, Anacreon, Theocritus, and Jupiter Pluvius, with plenty of writing which shows the animal spirits and conceit of a very young man anxious to vindicate bad conduct on the plea of genius, but not one note of genuine feeling throughout, or even a word indicative of conscious "pyramid-building." Nor is there much feeling in the "Farewell,"* supposed to be written about the same time. The fact is, Goethe's very liquid feelings ran always readily into the lyrical glass, and sparkled

---

* These musical verses are to be found among Goethe's lyrics, and begin :
> Let mine eyes the farewell utter
> Which my lips attempt in vain! etc.

there, with ever so light an inspiration. However, he had decided for himself against Frederika and matrimony. The poor clergyman's daughter's real rivals were Clara, Gretchen, Adelaide, Mignon, and the rest of that shadowy troop already existing in embryo. From first to last he hated everything unpicturesque and slovenly, and he knew well, and ever remembered with quite a comical horror, how matrimony takes the bloom even off the freshest cheek, destroys the charming mystery which surrounds a woman as with angelic drapery, and renders even passion tawdry with repeated indulgence. More than most men he loved to sip his honey, and pass on. Cordially would he have enjoyed the criticisms of Balzac on married people, apropos of the nuptial life of Madame and Monsieur Jules :—" A l'amour d'un mari qui bâille, se présente alors une femme vraie, qui bâille aussi, qui vient dans un désordre sans élégance, coiffée de nuit avec un bonnet fripé, celui de la veille, celui du lendemain,"* etc.; for he had Balzac's own love of mysterious elegance and rose-coloured light. When he describes Wilhelm Meister's feelings of lurking dissatisfaction at the personal untidiness of Mariana, whose bower of bliss was adorned with "articles appropriated to personal cleanliness—combs, soap, and towels," and " with water and flowers, needle-cases, hair pins, rouge pots, and ribbons," and when he describes how at one time she would " put aside her boddice that he might approach the piano," and at another, " place her gown on the bed, that he might provide himself with a chair," Goethe himself, in all these details, is evincing his own morbid horror of the revelations of domesticity. He loved pretty

---

* " Histoire des Treize."

women and light women—he would even go to the length of temporarily adoring them to distraction—but his appetite was satisfied with sipping, and he never seemed to desire, like rasher lovers, for full possession. Marriage thus repelled him on the æsthetic side, and we scarcely wonder, seeing what sort of wives would have been made of any of these women typified in his heroines. Fancy Goethe wedded to Mariana, or to Ottilie, or even to Mignon! He had far too curious and fastidious an eye. He would have wearied of Lili's liveliness, and sickened of Frederika's sentiment. Then again he had ascertained at a preternaturally early age (and *this*, by the way, is a fact so unusual and strangely unnatural, that it looks not only like genius, but diablerie), that every additional human tie, however delightful in the forming, is a source of anxiety and irritation. He feared responsibility, not because he lacked strength, but because he was a moral coward. He had a morbid horror of anything which disturbed his equanimity. By what series of bunglings and confusions he resigned himself at last, after full fruition, into the arms of Christiane Vulpius, is a mystery to this hour.

Being naturally of Brother Noyes' way of thinking, and altogether holding that man cannot "exhaust his power of loving in one honeymoon,"* he soon steeled his heart sufficiently to get the very largest amount of pleasure out of the least possible amount of responsibility. He did not often insist on fruition —indeed, he avoided it as dangerous; and he enjoyed a love affair *on paper* with a woman he never saw, quite as much as his flirtations with fair creatures in

---

* " Modern Socialism."

the flesh—*videlicet* his Wertherian epistles to the young Countess von Stolberg.

If we are to trust his own account in the "Wahrheit und Dichtung," he really did love Lili. He describes her as his "*first real love*, and probably his last, for he was afterwards a stranger to such raptures as he then knew." This young lady was Fräulein Anna Elizabeth Schönemann, daughter of a fashionable widow in Frankfort, a lady who received a great deal of society, and was supposed to occupy a far higher sphere than Goethe, although he had then an enormous reputation as the author of "Götz von Berlichingen" and the "Sorrows of Young Werther." After a great deal of trouble, owing to the social pride of the Schönemann family, Goethe was betrothed to Lili; but he appears to have been much frightened by the warnings of Lili's married sister, who predicted all sorts of wretchedness, and, indeed, gave the young lovers clearly to understand, on the score of her own enormous experience, that wedlock was a mistake! All Goethe's old scruples and terrors of responsibility arose, and he behaved like a veritable coward. "First real love" sounds comically in connection with his own narrative. The excitable young gentleman who had composed fiery "Sturmlieder," and was the author of all the frothy sentimentalism and Wertherism of the period, was of so unromantic a disposition as to shrink with horror when Lili proposed that he should fly in her company to America. Instead of doing anything so desperate, he adopted the remedy he had discovered in poor Frederika's case, and withdrew from the scene of his attachment, accompanying the Counts Stolberg to Switzerland, in order to break off the engagement. While *en route*, on the margin of the lake of Zurich, he composed the beautiful lines entitled, "Auf dem See." Hutton's version of this poem is so lovely that I cannot neglect the opportunity of transcribing it here, expressing at the same time a hope that the translator will some day gather together his incidental translations from Goethe and Heine, since they are beyond all comparison faithfuller and finer than any others with which I am acquainted:

> I draw new milk of life, fresh blood,
>   From the free universe;
> Ah, Nature, it is all too good,
>   Upon thy breast, kind nurse!
> Waves rock our boat in equal time
>   With the clear splashing oar,
> And cloudy Alps with head sublime
>   Confront us from the shore.
>
> Eyes, have ye forgot your yearning?
>   Golden dreams, are ye returning?
> Gold as ye are, oh, stay above!—
>   Here, too, is life—here, too, is love.
>
> Host of stars are blinking
>   In the lake's crystal cup,
> Flowing mists are drinking
>   The tow'ring distance up.
> Morning winds are skimming
>   Round the deep-shadow'd bay,
> In its clear mirror swimming
>   The ripening harvests play.

Dainty as this poem is, it contains nothing indicative of special emotion; it is one of those masterly pictures in which Goethe excelled, and which he most excelled in when perfectly tranquil. "I allow objects," he used to say, "to impress themselves *peacefully* upon me; afterwards I observe the impression, and endeavour to reproduce it faithfully; in this lies the secret of what men are accustomed to call the gift of genius." Judging from all the poems supposed to be addressed to Lili, I should conceive his passion never mastered him; they are very lovely and very calm, full of nice pictures of that "Love in a cottage" which the writer dreaded so much in reality. The lines called "Neue Liebe, neues Leben," bear the very slightest traces of excitement, and are for that reason inferior; but nothing can excel the calm and gentle beauty of such poems as the "Wanderer," written and published in the Göttingen *Musen Almanack*, and expressive of his "sorrow" on leaving Frederika. Just after he had cast aside the gentle girl because he was morbidly afraid of marrying her, he could exclaim passionately in the person of the "Wanderer":

> Farewell!
> O Nature, guide my steps!
> Oh, guide the wanderer
> While over sepulchres
> Of holy bygone times
> He passes!
> Guide him to shelter,
> Screened from the North,
> And where the sunlight falls,
> Subdued through poplar trees.
> *And when I come,*
> *At evening, home*
> *To my cottage,*
> *Made golden by the sun's last rays,*
> *Let me embrace a wife like this,*
> *Her infant in her arms.**

The poems to Lili are occupied with similar sentiments. Of the two sets of lyrics, those occasioned by Frederika are the most passionate, take the "Wilkommen und Abschied" as an example; but both break into false notes wherever the real language of fervid love is to be imitated. Goethe exhausted his true enthusiasm very early, quite as early as Wilhelm

---

* Goethe's "Gedichte," vol. II. p. 129 (Kunst).

Meister exhausted *his,* and possibly through a similar circumstance. However, after parting with Lili, and flying to Switzerland, he got no further than the top of Mount St. Gothard, where he suddenly became home-sick. He returned to Frankfort, was forgiven by Lili at once, and seemed about to resign himself to matrimony, when suddenly the old nervous dread came back upon him, and, coupled with the want of enthusiasm on the part of the Schönemann family (who appear to have been quite as inaccessible and high-minded as the "family" of Mrs. Micawber), made him slowly but surely attempt to escape. The engagement was broken off, and, instead of enjoying the honeymoon, Goethe began to write "Egmont."

It would be scarcely worth while to recapitulate these very tawdry love affairs, if my object was merely to repeat the old savage charges against Goethe; but my object is far different. It seems, nevertheless, inconsistent on the part of Goethe's admirers to defend his conduct for one moment, save on the score that no other sort of conduct could possibly have preceded the composition of his great works. If his life was necessary to his works, well and good; only eulogise the works, and admit that his life was bad. So far from being a creature of inexorable will and tremendous perseverance, Goethe was about the most plastic piece of clay that ever came out in the rough shape from Nature's manufactory. His power was the passive power of allowing the world to work upon him, and in him, and out of him, pretty well as it pleased. Susceptible to every impression, he was specially possessed by none. No better illustration of this truth could be found than the episode with Lili. He raves and sings of "love in a cottage," yet he has a morbid dread of living with his wife in her father's comfortable house. He enjoys Lili's society tremendously, while he is in it. He goes to Switzerland, and Nature almost obliterates love, until suddenly, in the Mount St. Gothard, a furious impulse induces him to return home. He hies home to Frankfort, is welcomed passionately, and immediately his mind is driven back into doubt by Lili's relations. Goethe took the impression of the moment like wax, and kept it till another impression obliterated it; and it was this very liability to many influences that constituted his strength against each influence in particular.

Wax is wax, clay is clay; and Goethe's mind was composed of this, not of marble. He had mighty perseverance — in moving from one emotion to another. The same character is illustrated in his literary productions and studies. Their variety was caused by Goethe's eternal vigilance in changing his objects of sympathy, in order that none might grow stale and wearisome. His powers of concentration were so fleeting that he never could manufacture a connected plot or write a dramatic whole, and that it took him a lifetime to patch "Faust" into a great poem. He wandered from one idea to another, from this subject to that, as the slow wind travels over a plain in summer. He was subject to false enthusiasm —of Wertherism, of "Sturmliedism," of mediævalism, of classicism; but all these moods were trivial while they lasted, and brief in duration.

His belief in Art was the nearest approach to a belief that ever lingered with him long; yet even about Art he was sceptical; he never loved it as it was loved by the weather-beaten, ethical, scrap-of-knowledge-crammed soul of Schiller. He went on and on, and up and up, chiefly because the wave of the world floated him up and on. By just a slight change of circumstances we can conceive him deserting literature altogether. He would have made an excellent business man, a first-class artist, a tolerable parson, a successful actor, or a good dancing-master. In either of these professions he would have found a certain play for his flexible genius, and would have succeeded in adapting himself to circumstances.

It was, however, specially arranged by that Providence which had charge of him, that he should go to Weimar, on the invitation of the young Duke; and go he did, at twenty-seven years of age, and remained there, more or less, for the rest of his days. We know a little, but not much, of his life there; he would never publish a description of it, but to all requests that he would do so, replied, "The world may know what I have been, and what I have done, but how it fared with the man Goethe individually, will ever remain my secret." Far better that it should remain a secret, if, as I surmise, its "tranquil happiness" was a mere succession of selfish indulgences and æsthetic ponderings. We all know what the life of Weimar was—how, as Schiller said, every woman had had a *liaison*, and how the young Duke's madcap freaks alarmed even Goethe, who liked to enjoy his wickedness quietly, and never frothed his champagne in the pouring out. In his conversations with Eckermann, the German Boswell, he confessed that he indulged in many love-affairs during his first years at Weimar. Lionised by all, treated as a veritable prince, he had secured the summit of his personal ambition. Henceforth all ran smoothly with him. He had fashioned his heart to supreme polish, so that it reflected all things perfectly, as on a mirror of burnished steel. Few scruples were likely to trouble him now. He was beyond the reach of annoyance from any future Frederika or Lili. The "pyramid of his existence" now occupied his entire attention, and kept him busy till the day of his death, when, in spite of all his pains, it tumbled into pieces like a house of cards.

II.

GOETHE'S TORYISM.

"THE cultivation of my own mind," writes Wilhelm Meister to Werner, "has been secretly, from youth upwards, my wish and my design. This purpose still possesses me; and the means of compassing it are constantly growing more definite. I have seen more of the world than you believe, and have profited by it more than you think. Therefore, take some notice of my words, though they may not quite chime in with your way of thinking. If I were a Nobleman, then would our dispute be at once over; but since I am a Citizen only, I must go my own way, and I only hope that you will comprehend me. I know not how it may be in foreign lands, but in Germany a truly liberal, and, if I may so express it, *personal*, education is possible to a Nobleman only. A Citizen can become distinguished, and, with tremendous labour, cultivate his mind (*Geist*); but his personality is lost to him, do what he may. Since the Nobleman, by constant association with the well-born, necessarily cultivates a well-born manner; which manner of his, seeing no door is shut against him, becomes perfectly natural, and since his figure and his person are valued alike in court and in camp, he naturally learns to think something of himself, and to *show* that he thinks something of himself. A certain stately grace in performing trifles, and a certain easy eloquence in grave and weighty matters, clothe him well, because he ever lets the world feel that he is thoroughly at ease. He is a public character, and the more cultivated his movements, the more sonorous his voice, the more grave and reserved his whole manners, the more consummate he becomes. He may be cold, but he is sagacious; he may be cautious, but he is wise."* And Wilhelm, with that stupendous high-pressure tutorial power which so distinguishes him, goes on to argue that being, unhappily, only a citizen, he has no course open to him consistent with what he calls "the harmonious cultivation of his nature" but *to go upon the stage!* Into these further considerations I cannot follow him; but is it not clear that the above passage contains, as in a nut-shell, pretty much Goethe's own way of thinking on the subject of which he is treating?

He was a Tory by temperament, by intellect, by culture, by all save birth; a man who conceived himself born in a higher and calmer sphere than that of his fellows, and who resented any disturbance of that sphere as a very odious piece of rudeness and violence, to be serenely "put down." The harmonious culture of his nature, on the most aristocratic principles, was the sole aim of his life, the sole subject of his literature. He was never a vain man, in the sense of being hungry for popular applause; so far from that, he walked far over the heads of the multi-

---

* Wilhelm Meister's "Lehrjahre," vol. II. chap. iii.

tude, smiled at their criticism, and took their homage as very interesting and very natural in inferior beings; but the man Goethe, the princely creature who walked in the gardens of Weimar, was to him a far more interesting subject than any of his works. He was for ever posing before the intellectual mirror, with a view to the improvement of his personality. For rank of all sorts he had the highest reverence, and no passages in his writings are more nauseous than those exhibiting his aristocratic predilections.

His manner as a literary Jupiter became, by diligent cultivation, truly great, though verging on pomposity. Here, as elsewhere, in his life as in his works, the tiniest pinch of Shakespearian *humour* would have made him a nobler figure and a mightier poet. If he had but once got a peep at himself from the truly divine point of view, that of human Comedy, he might have been saved. But he was incapable of true humour. As a play-writer he wrote tragedies and farces; never comedies. There is the very tiniest gleam of the true light in the little passage in his Autobiography where he speaks of the stars which presided over his nativity, but even this dies away in a pompous smile; he was not altogether sure but that Jupiter and Venus, or the principles those planets represented, *had* something to do with the matter! Yet Goethe, building up his pyramid, was a sight to make Shakespeare smile—and angels weep.

Forsaking the bourgeoisie for ever, he became a member of the society at Weimar, selling his birthright of genius for a place at the Duke's table and a share of the Duke's pleasures. He speedily completed his aristocratic vocation, and became a veritable

Petronius Arbiter Goethe, tutor and master of the Revels. In course of time, his naturally theatrical nature had finally decided on the part he was to *play* for the remainder of his life—that of Literary Prince —and when he was ennobled, in 1782, he was already the living mirror of dilettante aristocracy.

It seems to me quite confusing confusion to attempt, as all Goethe's apologists attempt, and as even Mr. Hutton, otherwise unsympathetic, is led to attempt, to divide Goethe's character into fragments— to say, for example, that he had the pride of power, but not the pride of ostentation, and that he was generous outside the sacrifice of his own individuality. A man's nature is a man's nature, and cannot in any possible critical crucible be transformed into another metal. Goethe, like all other selfish men, was generous in everything which caused him no serious personal sacrifice; he could give away money liberally, for example, and he was seldom jealous of contemporaries. He had a heart easily moved by suffering of any sort; so easily moved that he steeled himself carefully from the contemplation of all human pain, and gradually, I believe, conquered his natural sensitiveness altogether. He was, in plain words, by nature and by habit, a Pagan, the creator of modern Paganism. So far as he was concerned, the leading lesson of Christianity—that sacrifice for others is a bliss in itself, and the noblest of all human ends— might never have been taught at all.

To all these charges, of course, there is a ready and a trenchant answer—a silent reference to Goethe's great services to humanity as a literary creator; and although this answer has been used so often, it will be used again and again. And naturally Humanity is grateful. But, setting altogether aside, in the meantime, that other argument, tremendous in its strength, of Goethe's literary *offences* against Humanity —of the pernicious influence, as one may think, of the whole Goethe-system of literature and æsthetics—let us ask ourselves whether Goethe did actually sacrifice honestly to Art, and whether, if he had been less of a courtier, if he had blurred the mirror of his mind less by over-polish, he might not have produced far higher literary work, and lived an infinitely nobler life. Here, again, I am compelled to revert to my former definition, and remind the reader that Goethe's nature was a plastic and a theatrical nature, almost always attitudinising to receive the new impressions. Naturally ready to take one impression after another, he was suffered to harden in the bad atmosphere of Weimar until his temporary aristocratic impressions became fixed for life. He isolated himself thenceforward, and the world scarcely reached him—else I can conceive his views indefinitely widening. Note how instantaneously, when he ran into Italy out of Weimar, and beheld the great monuments of antiquity, he changed all his ideas of Art, cast off his Mediævalism in one moment, and embraced Classicism. " I perceive," he wrote, " after many years, that I am like an architect who endeavours to rear a structure on a bad foundation." Indefatigable in fashioning his thought into form, he wrote his " Iphigenia."

Yet this, indeed, was not increasing width of view; it was rather the cat-like faculty of contracting the eye-ball to gain a more microscopic power of vision. From Wertherism to classicism was a step in literature, *perhaps* a step higher, but certainly not a step broader ; and there is far more genius in " Götz," with all its disjointedness, than in the statuesque and almost lifeless imitation of Greek tragedy. What Goethe wanted was not the classicism of Italy, nor the mediævalism of Germany; it was something far more startling and chaotic—the daimonic Liberalism of the French Revolution. This *might* have possessed him, had he ever come truly under its influence; and, had it done so, it would at least have blown his Toryism to the winds, and enabled his soul not only to feel *for* humanity, as he often was capable of doing, but to feel *with* it, as he never did till the day of his death! He had no decided political views, but on the whole inclined to believe in Despotism, beneficent Despotism of his own sort, embellished with all the graces of life, and diligently fostering the Arts. The great wail of the world would never reach his ear. His ear, like his eye, was microscopic; he saw nothing *en masse;* he heard no large volumes of sound. Minister of Art and Science at Weimar, Governor of the Institute, the Library, and the Botanical Garden, what had he to do with Revolutions, save only the revolution of the world on its axis and the revolution of fair faces round his own soul? Politics was a disturbing element, and he waved it aside. "Weak men," he said, "have often revolutionary ideas; they fancy they would be better off ungoverned, and never feel that they are incapable of governing themselves;" and, again, "All men, on attaining liberty, exaggerate their weaknesses — the strong become savage, the weak cowardly." To him, authority was in itself beauty, order of any kind almost sacred. In childhood his hero had been Frederick the Great—the immortal Fritz—but in later years, when he was frozen to dilettanteism, force of any kind repelled him. When Madame de Staël spoke to him of the treason of Moreau, he hurriedly requested her to change the subject, and talk about something more pleasant.

"You young people," he observed, "recover quickly when a tragic explosion has filled you with momentary terror; but we old fellows are right to protect ourselves from impressions which affect us powerfully, and only interfere with the even tenor of our activity." On another occasion, he wrote in his correspondence: —"It matters little in what degree a noble man finds himself, as long as he understands it exactly, and knows how to fill it. All precipitation is fatal; I don't see that we have ever gained anything by leaping over the barriers of degree, and yet nowadays all is precipitation; everybody seems trying to perform only somersaults. Do your best in your place, without troubling yourself about the confusion which, near or far, only *wastes time* in a deplorable way." This is teaching, unfortunately, very familiar to modern readers, from the savage pessimism of Mr. Carlyle, the sweetness and light of Mr. Arnold, and the æsthetics of Mr. Ruskin; and it has a certain foundation in common sense, in so far as mere frothy agitation is useless and disturbing, and as every man should cultivate his own nature as diligently as he can. But Goethe forgot, and Goethe's disciples forgot, that the world would have made small progress indeed if all men had been of their way of thinking. They assume that all men are students, or ought to be; whereas the *curse* of modern civilisation is the growth of the purely Student-class, which threatens, with its isolated Toryism, its narrowness of critical criterion, its indifference to complex human ties, to become as huge an ulcer on the mind of humanity as the Priesthood has ever been. Goethe never went very deep in his criterion of beauty; he was far too " economical " of his thought. As a man he was characterised by false enthusiasm for *forms* of life, particularly in their most superficial aspects; but he never penetrated—no microscope can ever penetrate—to the lovely significance of all life.

His pictures of ordinary humanity are full of false touches—*e.g.* how theatrical is the attitudinising of every character in "Hermann and Dorothea!" Here is a true genre-picture; but the pose, though natural, is thoroughly a pose. During that memorable picnic, which is interrupted by the appearance of the robbers, who seriously wound Wilhelm, and awaken the reader's eager hope that they have silenced the Bore for ever, how instantly does Wilhelm Meister seize on the theatrical side of the situation and "imagine" himself and his companions a wild company of wanderers with (of course!) himself for their leader. "With this feeling he addressed each member of the party, and coloured the momentary fancy as poetically as he could."* Goethe, like Wilhelm, was ever "imagining himself" some one else; but he never went profoundly into that some "one's" nature. What struck him in life was not its pathos and piteousness, not its subtle means of happiness, not its solemnity, not, indeed, its higher beauty; he was fascinated by its *picturesqueness;* and we, too, in our turn, so long as we are reading Goethe, share this fascination. Goethe has been called a great philosopher: and so he may be, if a philosopher can be called great who judges the world only by the æsthetic criterion. I rather prefer to believe that Goethe was the greatest *Stage-Manager* of the literary sort that ever lived; a man whose worldly knowledge was wonderful, whose sagacity was endless, whose power of taking pains has scarcely ever been equalled, but whose chief claim

---

* Vol. I. book iv. chap. v.

to distinction was his power of grouping his company of performers and economising, as Novalis would say, the resources of his establishment. His philosophy is a philosophy of the theatre, his ethics are the ethics of the picturesque, his religion is the religion of the *dénouement*. With all his wondrous resources he never quite completes the illusion of the spectator. We are for ever reminded that the exquisite scenery is only painted, that the characters who utter the most moral platitudes may be the most immoral and unpleasant people in reality, and that a great deal is being sacrificed to the demands of the "situation." There is no chaos, of course; everything is "rehearsed" to perfection; we, nevertheless, grow weary of the elaborate completeness of every detail, of the "so romantic" tone of the leading performers, and we acquire a certain suspicion that even the actresses who fascinate us most are only actresses—Philinas playing tender parts and careful to conceal their mischievousness. It is fine art, and good art; but it is Art only. We long once again to meet with characters whose life is "being," and not "seeming," and who are less conscious of the effectiveness of their parts and attitudes. Goethe is to Shakespeare what Goethe is to Nature; and against Goethe, Nature or Shakespeare is the only antidote. How fresh blows the summer wind of *As You Like It*, after the close "hot-house" air of *Egmont* and *Tasso!* How gladly does not one escape from Faust to Hamlet, from Mephistopheles to Falstaff, from Philina and even Mignon to Rosalind and Cordelia!

This, however, is anticipating. My present object is simply to suggest that Goethe was far too closely closeted in his Weimar days to be affected by the shock of the volcano which was shaking all Europe.

The Revolution impressed him as a horrible tempest from which it was his first concern to screen himself entirely. He would as soon have thought it his duty to go to sea in a storm and be thoroughly sea-sick as to venture into the wild ocean of contemporary politics, and lose one day of his precious time in rocking up and down on the billows. Yet I doubt not that the change, though unpleasant, would have done him good in the end. It never struck him that his conduct was selfish, any more than it might occur to a seaman that stopping in harbour in windy weather was selfish. His business in life, as he conceived, was to compose pictures, and the elements then disturbing the world were too chaotic to supply him with any material. He embodied his first feelings concerning the Revolution in a play, the *Great Cophta*,* and then quietly turned to other matters. His general feelings concerning the revolutionists of the period are best expressed in the course of the Intermezzo of *Faust*, where the "Massive Ones" come stamping down everything, and are sharply rebuked by Puck:

Die Massiven. Platz und Platz; und ringsherum!
So gehn die Gräschen nieder.
Geister kommen, Geister auch,
Sie haben plumpe Glieder.
Puck. Tretet nicht so mastig auf,
Wie Elephantenkälber!
Und der Plumpst' an diesem Tag
Sey Puck, der derbe, selber.

At all events, Goethe would not permit the "young elephants" to dance in *his* garden. When the

---

* Founded on the tale of "Cagliostro and the Diamond Necklace." Goethe, when at Italy, took the pains to visit the parents of Cagliostro, and to interrogate them in his own quiet, searching way.

Revolution broke out in all its fury, he was far too busy with the management of the Weimar theatre to have much time to spare for politics. In 1792, however, when the Prussians began their wretched invasion of France, the Duke of Saxe Weimar accompanied them, and was followed by his privy counsellor. Goethe has left an account of the campaign. He appears to have been busily engaged, during all the horrors of the war, in elaborating his prismatic theory of colours, and paying far less attention to the signs of the times than to the "Physics" of Fischer. Pursued from place to place by the "plague of microscopes," as Emerson calls it, he was not likely to take a bird's-eye view of the vast plain of Europe, then the scene of the direst calamity and mightiest commotion. Not that he was blind to the horrors of war; he was far too easily moved for that; and no man has photographed better than he the sorrowful *details* of War, bit by bit, figure by figure. In his own calm way, too, like all close-seeing men, he deplored its waste and worthlessness. But the idea of a Great War, such as Fichte put before the students of Berlin, was beyond his sympathy; it seemed to him like the horrible Earth-Geist conjured up by Faust — formless, hideous, awakening only terror; and, as a titanic Tory, engaged constantly in detaching the discordant elements from his own soul, he believed that men would do better to occupy themselves in a similar manner, and to weed their natures of false growths of centuries of ignorance, than to shatter the thrones of Europe, and imperil the entire fabric of things. He quite forgot, and wilfully forgot—for no man was better capable of a scientific estimate of Revolution than Goethe—that this detaching of discordant elements and weeding out of false growths is only possible after a people or an individual has gone through the preliminary stage of tremendous emotional agitation; after, in fact, the whole soil has been loosened by the shock of moral earthquake. The days when Goethe loved not wisely, but too well, when he was passing from puberty into Wertherism, and lived a life wherein passion was scarcely distinguishable from affectation—the days when the author of "Werther" swaggered into *salons* clinking his spurs and carrying his riding-whip in his hand, and wearing his green jerkin buttoned up to the throat—the days of dissipation, folly, affectation, excitement—these were not the days of pyramid-building, weeding, and detaching, but they prepared his somewhat over-burthened nature for what was to come. Goethe, having once emerged from a crisis, had no mercy for it afterwards. It was not quite true, though he said it, that Anarchy had *always* been more hateful to him than "even Death." He said so when he had imbibed into his soul the social atmosphere of Weimar, when he had *Tasso* in his mind, and when he was standing amazed, so to speak, before the ancient art of Italy. He had never been constantly a "Massive One;" all his parts were chosen for their theatrical effect, and *that* part did not tempt him; but he had been an "Elephant Calf" for all that, and had trampled down everything in his way quite in the revolutionary spirit. When the social crash came he was beyond its reach, so he heard it comparatively unmoved.

Morally speaking, Goethe was by this time incurable. The habit of "preferences" for women had become his sole inspiration, without which his faculty would scarcely act at all. Never did Fichte, in his glorious Transcendental scheme, make a greater blunder than when he exclaimed that "the One Eternal Idea assumes a new and hitherto unknown form in each individual in whom it comes to life, and this by its own power and under its own legislation, and quite independently of physical nature; consequently in no way determined thereto by sensuous individuality; but, on the contrary, abolishing such individuality altogether, and of itself alone moulding the ideal individuality, or, as it may more properly be called, originality." Goethe's life alone is enough to upset the entire theory. Without preliminary sensuous agitation, the One Eternal Idea seemed to have no legislation over him at all, and his Soul was entirely at the mercy of his physical nature. In his case, as in that of Rousseau, Science alone could have explained the secret of his genius, if Science had been sufficiently advanced to explain sensuous cerebellic action, and consequent cerebral activity. God could not move Goethe, nor could Nature, nor revolution, nor aspiration, nor intellectual love. None of these could directly move him; but put him in the society of a fair woman—of the Fräulein Stein, of Fräulein Schönemann, of Frederika Briou; titillate him ever so slightly by sensuous means—and Goethe moved at once, expanded, soared, found a thousand ways of expending his activity on the world at large. In so far as this activity broke forth sensually, it impaired, paralysed, and limited his mental activity; but where it excited without fruition, where the homunculus, so to speak, agitated the back part of the brain, and the back part of the brain in its turn moved the mighty cerebral mass behind what the hero-worshippers called "that impassive Jupiter-like brow"—this activity so engendered took an absolute form, begot issue as thoroughly in the way of nature as if the actual body had performed its part and directly engendered offspring. To think what puppets we are, and what a slender string it is that moves the mightiest of us! Out of the total virility of that wonderful mechanism called Goethe, not merely out of Goethe's brain, were born Mignon, and Faust, and Clärchen, and Lothario, all the troop of intellectual offspring, good, bad, and indifferent, just as certainly as was born Goethe's only son in the flesh by Christiane Vulpius. This is not so trifling or so obvious a fact as it seems, and it will have to be borne specially in mind by all who would estimate the true nature, extent, and operation of this man's genius.

But to form a Revolutionist out of an individuality like this was obviously out of the question. His Toryism was the direct consequence of his mode of intellectual action. He needed a minute influence, such as can be exerted by woman only, and only by women under the most favourable circumstances; not a massive or turbulent influence, which would quite have destroyed the true source of his strength—that of conceiving calmly, and tranquilly shaping his conceptions into endless forms of positive creation. This, and not coldness of heart, is the true secret of Goethe's eternal Toryism.

III.

SOURCES OF AGITATION.

ROUSSEAU'S seed had borne its fruit at last; and men, in France at least, had gone back to the state of nature, only taking with them, unfortunately, all the passions and all the follies which had been accumulated for them through centuries of unnatural civilisation. A million nameless voices had raved, a hundred famous voices had spoken. Every king in Europe was shaking in his throne; and a cloud, no bigger than the prophet's hand, was threatening even the Czar. The seed which, under Washington's care, had sprung to fiery flower, had been brought from America by Lafayette; in one night (so to speak) it had overshadowed France, and its leaves were falling as red as blood on the banks of the Rhine. Contemporary with the discovery that all monarchs were shams, that most institutions were abominable, that the priesthood were the instruments of a vile and degrading superstition, had arisen the philosophical formula that the whole theory of the world is exhausted in personal existence, that experience is the only criterion of knowledge, and that religious faith is a false thing, because it is reducible to no experience whatever.* Fichte, from the professorial chair, defined his age as "the third epoch in the history of the world, the epoch of liberation, *directly* from the external ruling authority, *indirectly* from the power of reason or instinct, and *generally* from reason

---

* We get the old dish stewed up nowadays piping hot, as if quite novel; but it is only the " hash " of yesterday's idea.

in any form:" the epoch, in other words, of absolute indifference to all truth, and of entire and unrestrained licentiousness; the epoch, in short, as Transcendentalism called it, of "completed sinfulness."

Almost contemporaneously had Philosophy been revolutionised, and the seed of Locke had sprung into a plant of gigantic dimensions and double nature. In France, the school of Condillac had apotheosized Locke's criterion of Sensation, and had wandered to the very confines of despair—through Materialism to the glorification of physical science only, and thence to the open denial of the existence of the Deity; while in England, on the other hand, Berkeley's amazing genius, by simply turning the doctrine of experience *inside out*, had resolved all experience into mere Idealism, a form of procedure which Hume, in the notorious "Essay on Human Nature," revenged by applying Berkeley's method of analysis to Berkeley's ideal phenomena, and cunningly establishing that thought, reflection, consciousness, being no more than the fleeting fabric of a vision, that higher life of man, which we call Religion, had not the faintest plea for existence. When the so-called Scotch school had contributed their quota of "common sense" philosophy, Kant arose in Germany with his gigantic system of "Categories," building up the system which Fichte was to complete, and which may be said to have revolutionised the whole theory of human responsibility.

Both these great waves of progress—the wave of political reorganisation, and the wave of philosophical speculation—passed by Goethe without seriously affecting his development, unless as sources of disturbance and agitation, varying more or less the first business of his life. We have seen how he withdrew

himself as much as possible from the noise of the
Revolution, and how throughout his career he felt a
certain repugnance for all sorts of violent political
action. "We are justly told," he once said to
Eckermann, "that the cultivation in common of
human capacities is desirable, and also the most important
of aims. But man was not born for that;
properly, each one must develop himself as a particular
individual, but also endeavour to gain an apprehension
of what all are collectively." It was precisely
this idea of collective Humanity, and of the aims
which all human beings have in common, that Goethe
was all his life losing sight of more or less, not without
injury to his moral nature. But of a narrower
human sentiment, that of mere *nationality*, which we
men of the latter half of the nineteenth century have
seen apotheosized as perfectly unselfish, although it
obliterates the highest political thought of all—of
this lower sentiment Goethe was quite capable—
capable, that is to say, of party Deutschthum, or
Germanism, which Frederick the Great had begun,
which Lessing and Klopstock in the higher literature,
Stein in politics, Arndt in poetry, and Jahn in practical
life, were creating, fostering, and magnifying,
and which Goethe therefore, in a half serious, half
comic manner, distinctly stamped with his approval.
As Brander sings:

Ein ächter Deutscher Mann mag keinen Franzen leiden!

is a phrase containing this lofty political feeling in a
nutshell! Judged relatively to Goethe's culture,
however, even this must be regarded as a disturbing
influence: his heart was not quite with *Deutschthum*,
and he was driven into it by the contagion of
personal friendship.

Then, again, as to the other disturbing influences —that of philosophy and philosophers.*

Pure abstract speculation was repugnant to Goethe's mind, and he openly, again and again, expressed his distrust of *all* forms of such speculation, especially when they wandered in the theological direction. Personally, indeed, his sympathies were with the glorification of Science, in the widest significance of that word; but he declined to commit himself even there, as the slightest error in phraseology would have brought upon him the charge of mere Materialism. More than once in his life he appeared to feel a positive detestation of philosophy, and it was, as we know, the object of his unsparing satire; and in the "Intermezzo," for example, which he at first intended to publish as a direct contemporary squib in 1798, Orthodoxy,

---

* Spinoza fascinated him, and he welcomed the first gleams of Fichte's spiritual mind. The latter sent him the " Wissenschaftlehre " and received this reply :

"What you have sent me contains nothing which I do not understand—or at least believe that I understand—nothing that does not readily harmonise with my accustomed way of thinking —and I see the hopes which I had derived from the introduction already fulfilled.

" In my opinion you will confer a priceless blessing on the human race, and make every thinking man your debtor, by giving a scientific foundation to that upon which Nature seems long ago to have quietly agreed with herself. For myself, I shall owe you my best thanks if you reconcile me to the philosophers, whom I cannot do without, and with whom, notwithstanding, I never could unite.

" I look with anxiety for the continuation of your work to adjust and confirm many things for me, and I hope, when you are free from urgent engagements, to speak with you about several matters, the prosecution of which I defer until I clearly understand how that which I hope to accomplish may harmonise with what we have to expect from you."

Idealism, and Scepticism, came in equally for his abuse:

> Prophete rechts, Prophete links,
> Das Welt-kind in der Mitten!

This was the situation: and the prophets were a subject of annoyance to the " world-child "—Goethe. With him conception was synonymous with creation. His thought was a Form, his feeling an Image. Science, History, Society, even Politics, were capable of a concrete reflection in the mirror of that still and mighty mind; but Philosophy, since she cast but a vague shadow, only disturbed and overclouded his natural powers of reflection and understanding.

The famous passage in " Faust," thus translated by Mr. Bayard Taylor in his remarkable translation, has been accepted by the world of critics at large as fairly representing " Goethe's Creed :"

Faust. My darling, who shall dare
"I believe in God!" to say?
Ask priest or sage the answer to declare,
And it will seem a mocking play—
A sarcasm on the asker.
Margaret. Then thou believ'st it not?
Faust. Hear me not falsely, sweetest countenance!
Who dare express Him?
Who dare profess Him,
Saying, "I believe in Him!"
Who feeling, seeing,
Deny His being,
Saying, "I believe Him not!"
The All-unfolding,
The All-upholding,
Folds and upholds He not
Thee, me, Himself?
Arches not there the sky above us?
Lies not beneath us, form, the earth;
And rise not, on us shining
Friendly, the everlasting stars?
Look I not, eye to eye, on thee,

> And feel'st not, thronging
> To head and heart, the Force,
> Still weaving its eternal secret
> Invisible, visible, round thy life,
> Vast as it is, fill with that force thy heart,
> And when thou in the feeling wholly blest art,
> Call it then what thou wilt—
> Call it Bliss! Heart! Love! God!
> I have no name to give it!
> Feeling is all in all :
> The name is sound and smoke,
> Obscuring Heaven's clear glow.
>
> *Margaret.* All that is fine, and good to hear it so ;
> Much the same way the preacher spoke,
> Only with slightly different phrases.
>
> *Faust.* The same thing in all places,
> All hearts that beat beneath the heavenly day,
> Each in its language, say ;
> Then why not I in mine as well.
>
> *Margaret.* To hear it thus, it may seem passable,
> And yet, some hitch in't there must be,
> For thou hast no Christianity.

Faust is here expressing the "Immanence" of Spinoza in very loose although beautiful language; but Goethe, although he found much in Spinoza to satisfy the cravings of his nature, was not the man to rest contented merely with Spinoza's theology. Very finely, in 1813, he expressed himself to Jacobi: "As poet and artist I am Polytheist; on the other hand, as a student of Nature, I am Pantheist ; and both with equal positiveness. When I need a God for my personal nature, as a moral and spiritual man, He also exists for me. The heavenly and the earthly things are such an immense realm, that it can only be grasped by the collective intelligence of all human beings." It is needless, however, to observe that this was not the language of a man who had any strong religious cravings. Goethe, in fact, approached religion from the outside, accepting it gratefully as a *subject*, and so far it ministered to his moral development; otherwise, when it forcibly broke upon him in any shape, it became a hindrance and a source of disturbance.*

A still more constant source of disturbance arose from his private personal relations. His habit of cold impassiveness and stately reserve grew upon him at Weimar; and repelled many of his friends who were not slow to express their irritation in words. "Outside relations," he said, "make our existence, and at the same time devastate it; nevertheless, one must withdraw oneself occasionally from study, for I don't think it healthy to be completely isolated like Wieland." Schiller, faithful to him as he was faithful in all things, was rewarded by a certain amount of confidence; much the same as Goethe would have vouchsafed to a clinging mistress, Lili or Frederika; and when Schiller died, the blow went straight home to Goëthe's heart. When the aged and noble-minded Klopstock thought fit to remonstrate on the disorderly living encouraged by

---

* Note also the following from the "Confessions:" "Jacobi's book has deeply grieved me; and how, indeed, can I have any pleasure in finding so dear a friend supporting this thesis: that Nature veils God from our view! Penetrated as I am, by a pure, deep, and innate method, through which I have ever seen God in Nature and Nature in God, and to such an extent, that this conviction is the base of my entire existence, must not so narrow and absurd a paradox separate me for ever, spiritually speaking, from a man whose venerable heart I cherish so deeply? Well! I take care not to be overcome altogether by such discouragement, and have returned again with double ardour to my old refuge—the 'Ethics of Spinoza.'" And still more beautifully Goethe writes elsewhere, that " No being can fall into nothingness. The Eternal stirs in all things. Thou *art*, be happy in that idea. *Being* is eternal, for the laws of being protect the treasures of life with which the universe clothes itself." Compare with these remarks the weird chorus of the Earth-Spirit in "Faust:"
"In Lebensfluten, in Thatensturm?" etc.

Goethe at Weimar, the "privy councillor's" reply was cold and keen as ice. He solicited no confidence and he tolerated no interference. His affectations—for they *were* affectations—alienated his best friends. "What the devil possesses this Wolfgang!" cried Mark, a friend of his childhood; "why on earth will he play the courtier and the valet-de-chambre? Has he nothing better to do?" And the same excitable person said to Goethe himself, "Look here, Goethe! when I compare what you are with what you might have been, all that you have written seems to me contemptible!" But his most troublesome relations appear to have been with Herder. The great ideal philosopher and the great poetic image-former possessed a strange attraction for each other, by virtue of the individual strength of each; yet they never perfectly comprehended one another, and on one side, at least, there was a great deal of irritation. They met for the first time at Strasburg, when Herder was twenty-two years of age, and Goethe seventeen. This was in 1766. Twenty years afterwards, when both were at the zenith of fame, when Goethe's name was a household word with young Germany, and Herder's gigantic ὕλη was delighting all philosophers of the old school, Herder had not yet abandoned the air of patronage which he had affected to his junior student, and Goethe, on his side, had not forgotten Herder's epigram on his name:

Thou! descendant of *Gods*, or of *Goths*, or of *Gutters!* (*Koth.*)

There was no love lost between the two; and their mode of intercourse was rather that of two rival swordsmen than of affectionate friends. On the whole, Goethe seemed rather afraid of Herder's mighty mind, knowing well that its great scheme of the Universal Idea, with all its practical tendencies towards Optimism and the regeneration of Humanity, was exactly the scheme which refused admittance to so shallow and slight a theory as that of mere self-culture and "pyramid building." "It is doubtful," Herder once cried passionately, *apropos* of Goethe's cold-bloodedness and affectation—" it is doubtful if a man has any *right* to raise himself to a sphere where all suffering, true or false, real or merely imaginary, becomes equal to him ; where he ceases to be a Man, if he does not cease to be an Artist ; and whether this right, once admitted, does not imply the absolute negation of human character. No one cares to envy the gods their eternal tranquillity ; they may regard everything on earth as a mere game, the chances of which they direct as they please. But we are men, men subject to all human wants, and we do not care to be amused for ever with theatrical attitudes. You study Nature in all her phenomena, from the hyssop to the cedar of Lebanon. But I should not like you, for all that, to conceal from me the most beautiful phenomena of them all—Man, in his natural and moral grandeur." To the same effect, though with less success, protested others—Wieland, Jacobi, even Schiller. But Goethe, though the criticism struck home, was not to be moved. Affectation and indifference, two elements quite contrary in themselves, had blended together to form the one pose that he kept for the rest of his life : a pose thoroughly theatrical, as Herder's keen eye at once detected, but so long used as to become natural at second hand. An earthquake would not have changed it. The statue stood, in courtier's costume, calm, holding a microscope. A thunderbolt might have dashed the statue to the ground ; but it would have altered nothing. To alter Goethe now, God would have had to obliterate him altogether.

So the volcanoes of Europe thundered, and the philosophers of Europe reillumined the universe of thought, and mistresses wept, and friends protested and sneered, but still the statuesque Titan stood smiling on his pedestal. From the Revolution, Goethe turned to his "Theory of Colours;" from philosophy, to the microscope; and passing friendship aside as a source of constant disturbance, and avoiding a true union for the same reason, he solemnised his marriage with Christiane Vulpius, just as the great battle of Jena was taking place hard by. "In order to cheer these sad days with a festivity," he wrote to Meyer, "I and my little home-friend (*Hausfreundin*) yesterday resolved to enter with full formality into the state of holy matrimony, with which notification I entreat you to send us a good supply of butter and other provisions that will bear carriage." Poor Christiane had been his mistress for seventeen years, and had borne him several children, all of whom died, even the only son and heir. She was very pretty when Goethe first saw her. Latterly she yielded greatly to habits of intemperance. "What is this relation?" wrote Goethe to the Frau von Stein when she remonstrated with him on his liaison; "who is beggared by it? Who lays any claim to the feelings I give to the poor creature? Who to the hours I pass with her?" His friends despised and insulted her, and he allowed his friends to despise and insult her. Schiller never alluded to her. Wieland called her son the son of the servant (*der Sohn der Magd*). Yet she was never weary of waiting on and loving the "privy councillor," as she ever called Goethe.

"Who would think," he said, "that this person had already lived with me twenty years! What pleases me in her is that no change takes place in her nature; she remains as she was." One day as they were driving in the country, Christiane had an apoplectic stroke, and lay as if dead in the vehicle. Goethe ordered the coachman to drive himself home, murmuring to himself, "What an alarm there will be at the house when we draw up, and they see this person dead in the carriage!"

During the great conference of powers at Erfurt, Napoleon Bonaparte made himself acquainted with most of the great men of Weimar. The meeting of the Emperor and Goethe is thus alluded to by the present writer in the "Drama of Kings:"

> But yestermorn the old man Wieland stood
> Enlarging his weak vision for an hour
> Upon the demigod, who of Greece and Rome
> Talk'd like a petulant schoolboy; and this day,
> I beheld Goethe with a doubtful face,
> Part dubious and part eager, proof of thoughts
> Half running on ahead, half lingering,
> Enter the quarters of the Emperor;
> But when he issued forth his features wore
> Their pitiless smile of perfect self-delight,
> His lips already quivered with a pæan,
> His stately march was quicken'd eagerly,
> And all his face and all his gait alive
> With glory that the sun of Corsica
> Had shone upon him to his heart's content.

Goethe was much fascinated by the daimonic power of Napoleon, and from that day forward had a firmer faith in Despotism; nor can we wonder at the fact, when we remember his Napoleonic treatment of politics, philosophy, friendship, and the domestic idea—all alike, sources of disturbance to be repressed at all hazards. He was a Napoleon on a small scale, without the soldier's plea, or the excuse of national necessity. Bonaparte was the child of the Revolution, welded hard and unchangeable by very fire, and pushed upward and onward less by sheer volition than by the vast European wave of political change; he had mounted the popular Monster, and although he seemed to curb and drive it, it took him pretty much where it pleased; and finally, in mercy to the man's immortal soul, God made England pitiless and consigned him to St. Helena. Goethe had less excuse for becoming what he was; indeed, sheer contractedness of soul kept him what he was—a subtle rather than a great European literary power, and of doubtful value to the world. Unfortunately, there was no St. Helena in store for him. He died with a demand for "more light."* Alas! had light been given in full and just measure, it would have withered and blinded him. His life is a melancholy subject for human contemplation, so sadly here and there does it force upon us the truth that growth is not always gain, and that Art works less by giving than by hardening and cruelly taking away.

Here I must pause, not without an apology to the hero-worshipper for the form of some of my remarks on this subject—a subject involving in its treatment not only a critical estimate of the leading literary man of modern times, but an examination of the whole critical theory of modern life. If Goethe was wrong, then much in modern life is wrong; if Goethe's mind was physiologically defective, then is such defect noticeable everywhere in modern society and literature. But let it not be

---

* Goethe's last words, "Dass mehr Licht hereinkomme."

hastily assumed that I am ungrateful to Goethe's work or insensible to Goethe's charm. Before that mighty figure, that "Jupiter-like brow," before the total result of that vast literary life, I bow again and again in homage. I honour Goethe as the greatest literary "worker" of modern times. The character of Goethe I do not honour, as I have shown. But I do not forget—nay, I would emphatically point out at parting—that the last work of the man Goethe's hand was to point in dying acknowledgment at the figure of the man Jesus, the ideal of Christian Altruism. The crowning human joy was at last recognised as self-abnegation—or, as it is expressed in the sublime last pages of the second Faust, "The draining of the Marsh!" Let the reader now turn to those pages, and perceive how at last even he, Goethe, the would-be Apostle of Egoism, was compelled to be absorbed, as every human force is absorbed soon or late, into the divine tendernesses of a sacrificial gospel.

NOTE.—This article, in its first publication some years ago, was vigorously assailed by a certain portion of the press, and my old friend George Henry Lewes made it the subject of an especially severe animadversion. The truth perhaps lies midway between the aggressive Jacobinism of my criticism and the exaggerated Goethe-worship of modern men of letters. It should be remembered, however, that the foregoing does not pretend to be an exhaustive estimate of Goethe as a poet. As a poet, Goethe comes to us, not like Shakespeare in native strength and majesty, but like a first-class master of the ceremonies with excellent credentials. His poems, with the exception of "Faust" and certain of the ballads, have been accepted because they have been strongly "recommended" by the best judges. "Faust" alone has mastered the popular heart by the sheer strength of genius, and "Faust" alone, when all the rest is forgotten, will entitle its author to a place in the world's literary Pantheon.

R. B.

A NOTE ON LUCRETIUS.

"INSTEAD of God, the whirlwind reigns" ('Αντὶ Ζῆνος ὁ Δῖνος βασιλεύει), says Aristophanes, in the "Clouds;" to which may be added, in the words of a sadder and sublimer thinker, "Wo keine Götter sind, walten Gespenster."* According to the philosophers who plume themselves on having annihilated the Deity, Matter is come again, but in the very midst of Matter strut our modern "spectres" of the scientific lecture-room—the ATOMS. What a "whirlwind"! We hold our breath and stop our ears; we shut our Bibles, if we have any, and prepare our instruments; we look this way and that through a great darkness, and watch the fluent Tyndall declaiming, the otiose Huxley intoning, the silent Spencer musing finger to forehead and smiling knowingly at the Unknowable. There is darkness, and a great explosion of gases. The wise ones are imperfectly agreed among themselves. Peripatetic and epicurean dispute on points of detail, as they did long ago. Theologians rush in where laymen fear to tread, and call incontinently on the Unconditioned. Amid the clamour of names and

---

* Novalis.

things, amid the whirlwind which already threatens to blow the roofs off all our churches and carry away one-half of our libraries, one word we hear distinctly pronounced with reverence again and again, one name we hear, almost forgotten by all save students, until eager scientific dreamers recalled it in order to give its owner his apotheosis—one name of a dead poet—LUCRETIUS, the singer and expounder of the Cosmic " Nature of Things."

Just as Democritus has dethroned Plato, Lucretius is dethroning—whom shall we say, when our choice of pagan theogonists is so limited ?—well, Æschylus. We have discovered that the real poet after our own hearts is not one who can sing to us in noble numbers of superhuman endurance and the wrath of gods, of mighty ideals shattered or upraised by divine destroyers and demi-divine intercessors; nay, that we infinitely prefer a poet who can tell us in voluminous numbers how "nothing was ever begotten out of nothing by divine aid," how flesh is grass, and all things, like the flowers, must disappear; how and in what measure we may conduct the breed of the human species ; and how, finally and chiefly, we can give the liliputian ATOMS their just due as the creators of both protoplasm and poetry, substance, sense, and Soul. We wanted just such a poet for this period, and so, going back to B.C. 99, we find him ready made—a "cosmic creature," as musical as need be to ears unattuned to the hexameters of Virgil, and as explicit in his physiological explanations as Walt Whitman ; a great, indeed, and an eminently sincere poet, with the splendid qualification of never even having heard of that "obstruction," Christianity; just, in fine, such a singer as our own Tyndall would be, if the Professor would only put his ornate periods into the flowery fetters of rhyme. Of course, and as the reader may conceive, he could not be always right, living as he did before the birth of Science, but his book is universally admitted to be wonderfully "correct" in essentials, and a sublime specimen of what is now termed the "scientific" imagination. We know now that the ATOMS, which he dreamed of, are acknowledged facts; and if we only bridge over the gulf between his two first books and the other four by a few scientific links, such as "protoplasm," we shall find in the "De Rerum Naturâ" an admirable exposition of the History of Creation, as far as we can at present understand it. If the end of the fourth book is expurgated, the book will do to read even in young ladies' colleges. For those who find a poem fatiguing which contains no imaginative pictures of the supernatural, we may point out the memorable dedication to Venus,

Æneadum genetrix, hominum divumque voluptas,

as an admirable substitute (somewhat out of place, it is true, in so precise a production) for any of those absurd religious conceptions with which we are familiar.

It is time to be serious; and lest the critic of the period, ever on the look-out for heresy against the spirit of the laboratory, should accuse me of treating a great and influential poet with irreverence, let me confess at once my deep and profound admiration for the poet in question. So far from grudging him his apotheosis, in which even Bishops cordially assist, I rejoice over it as another token that justice, poetic or non-poetic, is done to all great thinkers sooner or later. I welcome even the Atoms, and the voluminous literature the little *semina* have created. I cordially agree with Dryden, who criticised nothing that he did not illuminate, and who has left us the best criticism of this author extant, that Lucretius possessed a "sublime and daring genius," to which, let me add, no amount of study can do too much honour. Who that remembers the lovely glimpses of nature so frequently given as we traverse the arid track of Materialism over which he leads us, can doubt the "genius," or deny that it is "sublime"? Sometimes, indeed, when I remember such pictures, I am inclined to place Lucretius higher than a final judgment may prove warrantable. As I behold the clouds above me,

> Dant etiam sonitum patuli super æquora mundi ;

and the "cœrulean of the great universe" and the vast tract of the ocean at my feet,

> Maxima qua nunc se ponti plaga cœrula tendit;

and the "dædal Earth yielding up her flowers,"

> Tibi suaves dædala* tellus
> Submittit flores ;

and in dark solitary places beneath the "shadows of Orcus and hateful pools,"

> An tenebras Orci visat vastasque lacunas ;

and the "flaming walls of the world,"

> Flamantia mœnia mundi ;

and beyond that even, the "divine shores of light,"

> Dias in luminis oras ;

so I know by these and many other tokens, beautiful

---

* Mr. Munro translates this into "manifold of works," but surely he might have adopted the actual equivalent so repeatedly used by Shelley. Thus :
> Through thee the dædal Earth
> Brings forth fresh flowers.

and musical exceedingly, that a Poet is guiding me, not a peripatetic Pedant pale with joy of the discovery that the moon is *not* green cheese. Nay, I forget, amid such glimpses, that a Lucretius leads me and not a Virgil, and that I am being guided—dare I say it under the new scientific Inquisition?—through an *Inferno*. It is only when my foot falls on the dark graves beneath it, when my breath inhales the lowest atmosphere of a poem which begins with a parody and ends with a pestilence; it is only when the ATOMS darken the vision and perplex the judgment, that I know I am visiting an *Inferno* indeed, and cry pitifully with Dryden,—our guide "is so bent on making us a materialist, and teaching us to defy an invisible power—in short, he is so much an *Atheist*, that he sometimes forgets he is a *Poet*."

It is perhaps too much to assume in the ordinary English reader, for whom I write, any special acquaintance with Lucretius and his writings; and it has seemed to me likely that a short sketch of the poem, with a few remarks *en passant* on its bearing towards modern thought, may not be unacceptable. Far be from one, whose scientific pretensions are infinitely modest, to wear and tear the reader with another disquisition on the Atomic Theory; even were I armed and ready for such work, I should not attempt it under the Inquisition, when the next unpardonable sin to believing in a Deity is to offer any reasons for so believing, and when even a semi-scientist like Mr. Lewes is listened to with ill-disguised contempt, simply because he has not spent even his suckling-time in a laboratory. My attempt is much humbler on the present occasion. I shall be very respectful to the Atoms, and accept any explanation of their existence which their disciples—I was going to say their creators !—are willing to give me : I shall touch very delicately on Evolution, and not at all, perhaps, on Protoplasm ; and when I have given my brief account of Lucretius and his poem, I shall only suggest, in the most reverential manner possible, that good poetry was never wasted on a worse subject, and that, if this is the most poetic solution of Creation that MATERIALISM has to offer us, the world will feel itself justified, *pace* Professor Tyndall, in resuscitating some Poet of SPIRITUALISM as soon as possible !

Our poet begins, as I have said, with a parody— the memorable address to Venus ; and the picture he draws of her power is very beautiful. She is the divine spirit of things ; all follow her and obey her, the winds, the clouds of heaven, the flowers of earth, the waves of ocean smiling at her advent, and heaven rejoicing in her light. That his picture may not be too insubstantial, he describes her with Mars lying at her feet, looking up at her in passion, while his breath is lingering on her lips ; and—*O si sic omnia!* —he begs her, in her own lovely language, to buy peace for Rome, that he may quietly sing to Memmius of the wonderful Nature of Things. The style of this invocation is at once Homeric and Virgilian ; it is both simple and ornate ; but it is, in the highest sense, a parody, because it is the mere imitative conjuration of a divine entity in whom the singer has no faith. What he really means by Venus, despite all his beautiful prelude, is made explicit enough in Book IV. :—

> Sic igitur Veneris qui delis accipit ictus,
> Unde feritur, eo tendit gestitque coire, etc.,
> Haec Venus est nobis ! hinc autem est nomen Amoris ;
> Hinc illaec primum Veneris dulcedinis in cor
> Stillavit gutta et successit frigida cura.

This "alma Venus," observe, remembering the epigram of Novalis, is the first of the Lucretian "Spectres." We are now at the portals of Chaos; passing which rapidly, we at once see the darkness gathering, but are detained for a moment while the Poet tells us of the curses of religion and the blessings of Epicurus:—

> When human life lay foully desolate,
> Crush'd 'neath Religion, who with hideous head
> Lower'd horribly from all the gates of heaven,
> A man of Greece dared to uplift his eyes,
> And braved the dreadful Phantom to her face!
> Him neither fables of the gods could tame,
> Nor thunderbolts, nor the deep roar of heaven.
> These only raised fresh hunger in his soul
> To be the first to break with mortal hands
> The bars of Nature's yet unopen'd gate.
> He conquered, therefore, by the living will
> Within his soul; and lo! he swiftly passed
> Far out beyond the flaming walls o' the world,
> Traversing with unconquerable mind
> The most immeasurable universe;
> From whence returning victor, he expounds
> What can, what cannot, be, explaining clear
> The principles and boundaries of things.
> Thus, in her turn, Religion is cast down
> And trampled underfoot, and up to heaven
> We soar, exalted by his victory!
>
> Thus singing I am haunted by a fear
> That thou* may'st deem we walk unholy ground,
> And tread upon the wicked ways of sin;—
> Quite otherwise! for 'tis *Religion's* self
> Who is the mother of most damnéd deeds.
> Thus once at Aulis gather'd mighty chiefs,
> The flower of Danai and the first of men,
> Staining with Iphianassa's gentle blood
> The thirsty altars of the Trivian maid.
> Soon as the fillet clasped her virgin hair,
> And dropt in equal length down each pale cheek,
> And she beheld her sire stand sorrowing
> Close to the arch-priests with the hidden knife,

---

* Memmius.

> And all around her weeping countrymen,
> Then, dumb with horror, dropping on her knees,
> She sank upon the ground . . . .
> What could it then avail the luckless Maid
> That first her lips had prattled to the king
> The name of 'Father?' Shrieking, shivering,
> Uplifted in the cruel hands of men,
> She straight was borne, not with sweet bridal song
> And solemn rites of Love's first sacrifice,
> But stain'd while stainless, in her bridal prime,
> There on the bloody altars to be slain
> By that safe father's sacrificial stroke—
> That gods might give the Greeks a favouring wind,
> And prosper well the sailing of the fleet.
>
> Such evils evermore to mortal men
> Religion teaches! *

This passage, perhaps the most striking in the whole poem, is the prelude to the poet's avowal of simple and unvarnished materialism. Beginning with his first and cardinal principle, that nothing was ever begotten out of nothing by Divine intervention,

> Nullam rem e nihilo gigni divinitus unquam,

he proceeds to pile illustration upon illustration of this solemn discovery. I need not follow him through his long catalogue; enough to say that he is entirely at one with Professor Tyndall on such points as the efficacy of prayer. That the laws of Nature are unalterable, that it is absolutely decreed what each thing can do and what it cannot do, that phenomena of all sorts are produced by natural laws, and that nothing whatever can happen without a natural cause,

---

* This and the other metrical renderings in the text make no pretence to constant literal correctness, though they are often pretty close for a free translation. Mr. Munro's unpunctuated prose, though admirable from certain points of view, is, as a rule, very hard to follow, and too full of attempts to get an esoteric and laboured meaning out of single words.

are propositions on which I cordially agree with him,—and so, we presume, would any decently-cultivated Bishop. He proceeds forthwith to prove the imperishability of matter; next, the existence of Void (*namque est in rebus inane*), without which Motion would be impossible; and next, that Matter and Void compose Nature, and that nothing beyond these exists.

All this is expressed very admirably, with as much poetry as the subject is capable of bearing, and moreover, melodiously—the lines making the hard, regular, metallic music of the blows of a smith's hammer on his anvil. We are now face to face with the Atoms, or first beginnings, out of which all other bodies, however simple, are fashioned; no force can affect them, they are indestructible; while all things we behold around us—even iron, stone, brass, marble—are destructible, consisting, as they do, of Matter and Void. Thus, the Atoms are solid, being without void. While ever entering into fresh combinations, they remain the same for ever. They are perfectly hard, indestructible, eternal. To paraphrase Goethe, " the wonderful eternal Atoms are great as in Creation's day." Nevertheless, they are invisible—lying "far beneath the ken of sense;" and yet for all that, they have parts—each part being so small that it has never existed and can never exist by itself, being by its very nature a part of the Atom.*

---

* These first beginnings have parts, but their parts are so small as not to admit of existence separate from the atom. The atom, therefore, has not been formed from a union of these parts, but they have existed in it unchangeably from eternity. Such parts, then, are but one more proof that the first beginnings are of everlasting singleness. Again, without such ultimate least things, the smallest and largest things will alike consist of infinite parts, and thus will be equal. Again, if Nature went in division beyond the atom, such least things

With all the recent literature of the Atomic Theory, newly set before us, with Tyndall's Address, Clark Marshall's Essay on Molecules, Professor Jenkins' "North British Review" Essay on the Atomic Theory of Lucretius, and Professor Veitch's bright little *brochure* under the same name—all, doubtless, fresh in the minds of our readers—it would be supererogatory to describe the Atoms further in detail. Enough to say that the theory of Lucretius, averring the existence of ultimate and indivisible particles of matter, is now universally admitted by modern chemists. It is admitted, too, that there is a limited number of different Atoms, out of each of which is composed an elementary chemical substance. "And therefore," in the words of Newton, "that nature may be lasting, the changes in corporeal things are to be placed only in various separations, and new associations and motions of these permanent particles." This is the secret which keeps Nature for ever fresh and new, this is the unchangeable law of never-changing change; by this the sun shines, and the flowers grow, and the bosoms of love rise and fall; and the world of things, despite its innumerable transformations, is the same world of Genesis, as fresh and fair now as ever.

This, so far as I have described it, is a satisfactory

---

as these parts of the atom could not have the qualities which birth-giving matter must have—weight, motion, power of striking, and clothing, and combining. A passage necessarily obscure, because dealing with one of those questions which utterly elude the grasp of human reason. Epicurus, building up his dogmatic system, and hating all scepticism of first principles, determined that his atoms should have size, shape, weight—in his own words, μέγεθος σχῆμα βάρος—and therefore extension. But, if extension, then parts; and how can that which has parts be indivisible?—MUNRO'S NOTES.

creed, and by no means naturally connected with the poet's other theories.

> The One remains, the Many change and pass;
> Life, like a dome of many-coloured glass,
> Stains the white radiance of Eternity.

Towards the end of Book II., however, we get a glimpse which would satisfy Dr. Cumming. The fruit ripens and falls in its season, man grows and decays in his season, and in its season the earth shall perish—for want, Lucretius explains, of sustenance.

> And in this wise, so storm'd, the walls o' the world
> Shall crumble into ruins and decay.
> E'en now the age grows frail, and mother Earth,
> Out of whose womb all mighty races came,
> With all the bodies of gigantic beasts,
> Grows sick, and scarce can bear her pigmy forms.
> For ne'er methinks by any chain of gold
> Let down from Heaven upon the nether fields
> Came down the races of humanity,
> Nor out of ocean and rock-rending waves
> Were any mortals born,—but the same Earth
> Which bare them in her womb, now with her milk
> Feeds them and suckles them!

With this end of Book II. the reader finds a great darkness growing upon him: and, in fact, such a darkness is necessary, unless he prefers to be led blindfold. Dazzled with the mystery of the Atoms, he moves on, in humble expectation of having the whole further process of Being explained.

No explanation is vouchsafed him. Book III. opens with another eulogy of Epicurus, who, by teaching men that the world was not formed by a Divine Power, but by a fortuitous concourse of Atoms, relieved men from supernatural dread—of the gods, of death, and of post-mortem punishments. It is a great jump from the fortuitous concourse of chemical elements to the mind and soul of man—a jump which could never be forgiven in a theologic poet, but is highly eulogised in one whose "scientific imagination" favours modern Materialism. *Animus*, or mind, resides in the heart, while *anima* is diffused throughout the whole body; and both *animus* and *anima* are simply combinations of minute atoms. We are thus gradually led to the main argument of the book, that what is called the soul perishes with the body:

> Quid dubitas, tandem quin extra prodita corpus
> Imbecilla foras, in aperto, tegmine dempto;
> Non modo non omnem possit durare per ævum,
> Sed minimum quodvis nequeat consistere tempus?

This position, that the soul is born and dies with the body, is sustained in a style of argument worthy, not of a supreme poet, but of the late Mr. Winwood Read or Dr. Draper of New York.*

> Death, therefore, I opine, concerns us not,
> Since the mind is but mortal, and will perish!

For consolation, we are reminded that the best men die as well as the worst—even Epicurus being turned to dust. This may be comfort to Professor Tyndall, who can look forward cheerfully, in his sweet poetic way, to "melting like a streak of morning cloud into the infinite azure of the past." Unfortunately, neither the prospect nor the arguments would satisfy ordinary mortals who are not professional chemists. So far as our human guide is concerned, he has, I repeat it, led us into an *Inferno*, and already we seem to hear the wail of the lost—an infinite ululation. For all that, the poet contains such an abundant

---

* This, however, is not the position sustained by Dr. Draper in his "Physiology."

happiness within himself, that he sings figuratively to dispel our fears:

> The pathless tracks of the Pierian springs
> I tread, before untrodden, and with joy
> Approach the waters, stooping down to drink.
> Gladly I pluck fresh flowers, and for my brow
> Enweave a chaplet from those secret spots
> From whence the Muses never yet have given
> A wreath to cover any mortal head!

His task it is, he adds, to free the mind from superstition, and to set forth a dark subject in the most lucid verses possible. He proceeds, still following the ideas of Epicurus, to treat of Images—how they are discharged from the surfaces of things, how these images affect the eyes, and are in a certain subtle sense corporeal, as well as taste and sound. After a variety of striking illustrations, he comes back to Venus, and treats very physiologically of the nature of love and desire.

Book V. is chiefly devoted to proofs that the world is not eternal, because as the chemic elements are changeable and perishable, the world is changeable and perishable too. The world began and the world will end.

> Therefore, not closèd is the gate of Death
> Against the sun, the skies, the earth, and sea,
> But ever yawning with wide open'd maw
> It looketh on them, waiting for their coming!

He proceeds, as explicitly as possible, to explain the world's beginning; and to show, recurring here to his main point, that nothing was originally done by Divine Wisdom or Understanding. "The first beginnings of things, many in number in many ways impelled by blows for infinite ages back, and kept in motion by their own weights, have been wont to be carried along and to unite in all manner of ways, and thoroughly to test every kind of production possible by their mutual combinations; therefore it is that spread abroad through great time, after trying unions and motions of every kind, they at length meet together in these masses, which suddenly brought together become often the rudiments of great things, of earth, sea, heaven, and the race of living things."* He then describes creation according to the cosmogony of Epicurus—the birth of the earth, the uprising of the fiery ether, and of the sun, moon, and stars; and of course he is not to be censured for placing the earth in the middle of the world. Of day and night, of eclipses, of plants, animal life, and man, he discourses with "scientific" eloquence. Here certainly he gives us an inspired fore-glimpse of the doctrine of Evolution and the survival of the fittest:

> And many living things have died away,
> Too weak to procreate and save their seed.
> For wheresoe'er the breath of life is drawn,
> By cunning or by courage or by speed
> Each race has saved itself from the beginning.
> And many things, through use to mortal men,
> By us protected, prosper and endure.
> By courage, lions fierce and savage races
> Have been protected; foxes by their craft;
> And by their flight, swift stags. But faithful dogs,
> Light-sleeping, and all seed of burthen'd beasts,
> And all the woolly flocks and hornèd herds,
> Have thriven, O Memmius, by the help of man.

He proceeds to describe the early state of Nature, and soon, in a passage of surprising eloquence, he describes the condition of primitive Man himself:

> Then was the race of men a hardier race,
> Like to the hard, strong earth from which they sprang,
> And on the ground-work of their mightier bones
> Strong thews and sinews knit the frame of flesh.

---

* Munro's translation.

Not then, by quick extremes of heat or cold,
Or food unfit, or any malady,
Did mortals sicken. While the sun thro' heaven
Rolled on thro' many lustres, they prolonged
A life as roving as the life of beasts.
No hand then guided the sharp crooked plough,
Or dug the fields, or sowed i' the earth new seeds,
Or cut old boughs away with pruning-hooks ;
What had been given by the sun and showers,
What green Earth freely on her bosom bore,
Was ample then to satisfy their needs.
Mostly on acorn-bearing oaks they fed,
Or berries of the wild arbutus-trees,
Which now thou seest in winter-time grow red,
And which were then more large and plentiful ;
And many wholesome fruits and foods beside,
More than enough for miserable men,
The flowery freshness of the green earth bare.
Then rivers and soft fountains called to them
To come and quench their thirst ; as, nowadays,
The torrent waters rushing from their hills
With bubbling murmur echoing far and wide,
Summon the thirsty tribes of savage beasts.
Within the silvery temples of the nymphs
Then, too, they rested after wandering,
And watched the quiet waters creeping forth,
Bathing with limpid flow the dripping rocks,
Trickling all silvery o'er the emerald moss,
Or bubbling brightly o'er the level plain.
And yet they knew not how to work with fire,
To tan wild hides, or clothe about their frames
With skins of beasts ; but deep in glades they dwelt,
In hidden forests, under mountain caves,
Sheltering their rugged limbs among the boughs
From the wild beating of the winds and rains.
They knew no common use nor common weal,
No common law nor custom ; for himself
Each struggled, taught to think of self alone,
And whatsoever he by fortune found
Each to his own lone cavern bore away.

* * * * * *

And, marvellously swift of hands and feet,
With stones and great clubs fashioned out of trees,
They hunted down the forest-ranging beasts ;
And some they conquered, and from some they fled,
Crouching and hiding ; and when night-time came,
They rolled themselves like swine upon the ground,
And cover'd up their limbs with boughs and leaves.

A NOTE ON LUCRETIUS.

> Yet never wailed they for the day to come,
> Nor wandered through the shadows of the night
> With terror stricken ; silent, sunk in sleep,
> They waited, till the sun with flaming torch
> Illumed the heavens ; for they had ever known
> Such alternations of the light and dark,
> And so no wonder fell upon their souls,
> Nor any fear that an eternal night
> Might come upon the earth and cover it,
> Veiling the golden sun for evermore !

This is quite in the spirit of Sir John Lubbock, and yet it has also a flavour of Rousseau. What follows is much in the same vein, and quite *en rapport* with modern science. How men learnt the uses of fire, and sheltered themselves from the cold ; how men softened, and leagues of friendship were formed ; how speech was learned, and human intercourse increased ; how more and more every day those who excelled in intellect kindly showed men new methods—till, at last, kings were elected, towns built, wealth accumulated, and the worship of the gods began. Finally, civilisation came. " Ships and tillage, walls, laws, arms, roads, dress, and all such things, all the prizes, all the elegances, too, of life without exception, poems, pictures, and the chiselling fine-wrought statues,—all these things practice, together with the acquired knowledge of the untiring mind, taught men by slow degrees as they advanced on the way step by step. Thus Time by degrees brings each several thing forth before men's eyes, and Reason raises them up into the borders of light ; for things must be brought to light one after another and in due order in the different arts, until these have reached the highest point of development."* So ends the fifth book.

Book the sixth and last opens with an eulogium

---

* Munro.

of Athens, first teacher of agriculture and useful arts to suffering men, and the thrice-honoured birthplace of Epicurus. Lucretius then elaborately explains the nature of thunder, and of those luminous portents which from time to time affright the world. He shows that thunder is simply the collision and clashing of clouds, and that lightning is the fire struck out by such collisions. Recurring again to his main point, he heaps derision on those who attribute storms to the instrumentality of gods.

> If Jupiter and other gods above
> Can shake the glittering regions of the sky
> With awful sound, and wheresoe'er they will
> Hurl down avenging fires, why spare they those
> Who fear not to commit atrocious crimes?
> Why scorch them not with lightning thro' and thro',
> Making a sign to teach us mortal men?
> And why is he whose conscience knows no sin,
> Tho' he be stainless, wrapt about with flame,
> And caught into the fiery arms of heaven?
> Why aim the gods at solitary spots,
> Wasting their labours and their thunderbolts?
> Is it to exercise their arms and thews?
> Why does the Father suffer this Himself,
> And not reserve it for His enemies? etc.

In the same spirit he explains earthquakes, the secrets of the sea, the volcanic flames of Etna and the inundation of the Nile, the temperature of wells and springs; and, finally, coming to the loadstone or magnet, he recapitulates all that he has said, in the first part of his poem, on the rarity of bodies. "It is necessary to establish that nothing comes under sense save body mixed with void. For instance, in caves, rocks overhead sweat with moisture, and trickle down in oozing drops," etc. This being understood, magnetism is a stream of atoms being pulled back to fill the vacuum in the middle of the loadstone. By a somewhat abrupt transition, Lucretius next treats of diseases " and, from what causes the force of disease may suddenly gather itself up and bring death, dealing destruction on the race of man and the troops of wild beasts." The air is full of seeds, some salubrious, some noxious to man; and as these predominate in the air, health or sickness prevails. This last part of the poem resolves itself less into an explanation of diseased phenomena than a mere catalogue of diseases. We are told of the Egyptian leprosy, of the Attic gout, and, finally, as a crowning picture, of the Athenian plague. No detail is spared us of the horrors of that pestilence. The poet, as if determined to deepen into horrid certainty the mental dread within us, and to save us from mad belief in Divine Beneficence, piles horror upon horror, mingles a hospital with a shambles, and shames the Muse out of her own natural joy. These are the last lines of the entire poem—

> And some were seized with such forgetfulness,
> Themselves they knew not ; and though corpses lay
> Piled upon corpses tombless on the earth,
> No bird or beast of prey came nigh the stench,
> But hovered far away ; and if by chance
> One came and tasted, it grew sick and perish'd.
> Yea, wild birds hung aloof, and savage beasts
> Hid in the dark recesses of the woods.
> Many dropped down in death ; hounds in the street
> Lay stretch'd, scarce struggling, and turn'd o'er and died.
> Then silently passed hurried funerals,
> Followed by none that mourn'd. And mortal men
> Knew for this evil thing no certain cure ;
> For what to one man gave new life and health,
> And suffered him again to see the sun,
> Struck down another into fatal death.
> In these sad days this was most pitiful,
> Most quick to rend the heart :—when any man
> Found himself prisoned in the fatal folds,
> He struggled not, but, lost to life and use,
> Lay on the ground awaiting certain death,
> And yielded up his spirit as he lay.

Ever and ever, like to flocks and herds,
They caught the direful plague from one another!
And death was heaped on death, for those that fled,
Fearing to tend their kinsmen stricken down,
Were dreadfully pursued in turn and slain,
To direful death condemned by dread of death,
Unpitied, doomed, and in their turn forlorn.

* * * * * *

Then every herd and shepherd in the hills,
And every mighty guider of the plough,
Sickened, and in their huts were left to rot,
Dead, slain by poverty and fell disease!
And so dead parents over their dead young
Lay scattered, and upon their parents dead
Dead children; and from country into town
The peasants, driven by the fatal plague,
Came ever, bringing horror in their train,
In all the public places sheltering,
Until Death drifted them in direful heaps
One on another; and impell'd by thirst,
Many crept forth, and crawled along the street,
Until they reached the fountains, stooped to drink,
And even in drinking died! * * *
And all the blessed sanctuaries of the gods
Were piled with corpses, and the heavenly shrines
Were brimful, for the guardians of the places
Had thrown them open to the coming guests.
And no man worshipt now to any god,
For each man's heart was full of present ill.
And gentle rites of burial were forgotten
Which all that pious town had used before,
And men ran hither and thither wringing hands,
And burying their dead as best they might.
And out of horror and of poverty
Were born dark deeds; for many, shrieking loud,
Upon the funeral pyres of strangers placed
Their kinsfolk, setting torches to the same.
And there they fought, with flowing streams of blood,
Sooner than quit their places by their dead!

It is veritably the last circle of the *Inferno*, whence emerging at last, to our infinite relief, we "again behold the stars."*

Brief and insufficient as my glimpse has been of a

---

* Dante, "Inf." XXXIV.

A NOTE ON LUCRETIUS.

work which stands solitary in the literature of antiquity, as the one great poem explaining the phenomena of nature, I have sufficiently expressed its spirit to show what attraction it has for modern materialists. Utterly in revolt against the Alexandrian philosophy and poetry, then so fashionable, Lucretius determined to be terribly non-ideal and realistic. "His poem is indeed," as Professor Veitch has admirably expressed it, "a type in the world of thought of the irrepressible Roman spirit of absolute sovereignty, and love of orderly rule in the world of practical life and action." He himself stands sovereign and centre of things, with no doubts and prevarications, but with a precision of conception which supplies the place of actual verification. Yet they have learned little of Lucretius, they have penetrated but little into his arcana, who aver, like many modern writers who would fain make him a mere enemy of the ancient polytheistic religion, that this poet had a divine consciousness of "something more than Matter." To hint as much is to misconstrue Lucretius completely. He is a materialist pure and simple, solemn and staunch; as bigoted in his creed and as certain of his gospel as the veriest divine that ever thumped a cushion; as anxious to proselytise as any other more popular Apostle; with all the zeal of a missionary, and all the pomposity of a Bishop. He leaves no room whatever for that Unknowable in which our later prophets, such as Mr. Spencer, have so much faith. His individual knowledge may be inadequate, but all things are ascertainable by the human mind—and why?—because there is so little to ascertain. A Void and a fortuitous concourse of Atoms; a Creation and a Change; a march of elements, for ever destroying and for ever renewed—this is what he has to show us, pointing upward. Pointing downward, the earth rolling on to some fiery end, and ever growing weaker and weaker; Man in countless generations passing from primæval simplicity to stages of degeneracy, decay, and death; gods fading away like wreaths of morning cloud, while pestilence and famine complete the doom of each benighted race. His ideas and pictures, like his language, are vivid and grandiose. One feels a certain sense of vastness, of expanse, of duration. I cannot, however, agree with his warmest admirers, that his highest characteristic is an extraordinary feeling for the Limitless. On the contrary, I am acquainted with no poet who confines our conceptions so specifically within a given area; who so persistently weighs and appraises the finite with so feeble a conception of the Infinite; who shocks us with so many prophecies of the scientific lecturing-table and the medical dissecting-room; who is, in a word, so supremely and absolutely blind to all the higher phenomena of Mind. His attitude is Napoleonic; he is master of all things, and conquest can no further go. He has the lowest possible conception even of atomic forces, the vilest possible estimation of the nature and destiny of Man. He is courageous, for he can live; he is not hopeless, for he can die. He knows that God is a Phantom, that Love is a physical desire, that Man is a creature of matter, and that both Man and the world must perish. This knowledge brings him no sweet assurance; it is a cup of hemlock, which only the wise may drink, and which *he* therefore drinks with becoming pride, but utterly without joy. He is a materialist, for he believes the world is over-ripe, and is slowly hastening to decay; he is a pessimist, for he believes that civilisation brings no bliss to "miserable men." Passing out with Epicurus beyond the "flaming walls of the world," he has only discovered that there is nothing there. In truth, this passing the "flaming walls" was only a dream. All the time he was standing at his own door, contemplating the Necropolis, and wondering when his time would come.

If modern Materialism had no more philosophy to teach them than we find in the pages of the "De Rerum Naturâ," men should despair indeed; but, fortunately, nothing is more jubilant and self-satisfied than the tone adopted by every demi-god of the modern lecture-room. The "grand old Pagans," as Professor Tyndall cheerfully calls them,* might despair, but our contemporary Pagans mean to do nothing of the kind. The condition of the world is every day growing brighter, the happiness of man is every day growing surer: these are formulas on which they habitually insist; and the inevitable amelioration of things is due, they add, not to Religion, but to Science. What they mean by Science they have never quite explained, any more than many of their opponents have explained what they mean by Religion; but some things are clear: for example, that just as the religion of such men as the Duke of Argyle and the Bishop of Carlisle is scientific, so the science of such men as Mr. Darwin and Mr. Spencer is religious. In the controversial jargon of the day there is a strange confusion of terms. For example, Dr. Draper (in that very superficial book on the "Conflict of Religion and Science," which Professor Tyndall is so fond of rashly praising)

---

* "Crystals and Molecular Force."

means by Religion chiefly the Roman Catholic Church, and by Science many discoveries which we might almost class as purely mechanical. "I have said nothing," he cries, with a mental confusion which would be fiercely reprobated in a theologian, "nothing adequate about the railway system, or the electric telegraph; nor about the calculus, or lithography; the air-pump, or the voltaic battery; the discovery of Uranus or Neptune, and more than a hundred asteroids; the relation of meteoric streams to comets; nothing of the expeditions by land and sea that have been sent forth by various Governments for the determination of important astronomical or geographical questions; nothing of the costly and accurate experiments they have caused to be made for the ascertainment of fundamental physical data. I have been so unjust to our own century, that I have made no allusion to some of its greatest scientific triumphs; its grand conceptions in natural history; its discoveries in magnetism and electricity; its invention of the beautiful art of photography; its applications of spectrum analysis; its attempts to bring chemistry under the three laws of Avogadro, of Boyle and Mariotte, and of Charles; its artificial production of organic substances from inorganic material, of which the philosophical consequences are of the utmost importance; its reconstruction of physiology by laying the foundation of that science on chemistry; its improvements and advances in topographical surveying, and in the correct representation of the surface of the globe. *I have said nothing about rifled guns and armoured ships, nor of the revolution that has been made in the art of war; nothing of that gift to women, the sewing-machine; nothing of the noble contentions and triumphs of the arts of peace—the industrial exhibitions and world's fairs."* *

Nothing, let me add, about the Crystal Palace and the Barnum Hippodrome of New York; nothing of the kaleidoscope and the magic lantern; nothing about the School Board and the workhouse, of the treadmill and the penitentiary! When a scientific pedant writes nonsense like this, it is difficult to be serious. Blindly oblivious of all those enormous tracts of knowledge, both moral and physical, which have been gained solely for us by the religious instincts of man, he seems to be claiming all the victories of Art for peripatetic chemists and quacks of Nature's laboratory. The truth is, Religion and Science cannot be separated on the off-hand assumption, now so generally made, that the one is not "religious," and the other is not "scientific." To my mind, for example, Mr. Spencer is an eminently religious man; not certainly in the sense which confuses Dr. Draper, but as a man in whom, to paraphrase Professor Tyndall's pompous remark concerning him, "the ganglia are sometimes the seat of a nascent poetic thrill." Professor Tyndall himself "goes to church," in a building of his own uprearing; and it is in no irreverent mood, though the irreverent may sometimes laugh at him, that he stands on a magnetic stool, or experimentalises with a raw turnip. No one familiar with his higher ideas can doubt that he is a man capable of the most noble emotions, and as beneficent in his social conceptions as any Christian of this generation. It is unjust, therefore, to call such men irreligious; and it is, moreover, very con-

---

* "The Conflict between Religion and Science." By D. Draper. International Scientific Series. (King and Co.)

fusing. They are doing missionary work of a very fatiguing kind, and their efforts deserve our warmest encouragement, however much we may quarrel with their "ideas."

It was therefore in a truly proselytising spirit that Dr. Tyndall, in his memorable Belfast address, while rapidly surveying the history of the Atomic Theory from Democritus downward, drew special attention to the scientific forecasts of Lucretius. He first called attention to the original propositions of Democritus, that—(1) From nothing comes nothing; nothing that exists can be destroyed; all changes are due to the combination and separation of molecules. (2) Nothing happens by chance; every occurrence having its cause, which it follows from necessity; (3) the only existing things are atoms and void; (4) the atoms, infinite in number and infinite in form, strike together, and the lateral motions and whirling which thus arise are the beginnings of worlds; (5) the varieties of all things depend on the varieties of their atoms, their number, size, and aggregation; (6) the soul consists of fine, smooth round atoms, like those of fire, and in their motions the phenomena of life arise. "The first five propositions," added the Professor, "are a fair general statement of the Atomic Theory, as now held; as regards the sixth, Democritus made his fine smooth atoms to do duty for the nervous system, whose functions were then unknown." Then, tracing the opinions of Epicurus concerning death, he introduces, by way of anecdote, a fallacy of his own, much in favour at the present day, and used as a constant argument by Mr. John Morley. "'Did I not believe,' said a great man to me once, "that an Intelligence is at the heart of things, my life on earth would be intolerable.' The utterer of these words is not, in my opinion, rendered less noble, but more noble, by the fact that it was the need of ethical harmony *here*, and not the *thought of perpetual profit hereafter*, that prompted his observations."

Now, I have already called Dr. Tyndall a religious man, a man of reverent and holy bearing towards all the great mysteries of creation; but here, simply by passing beyond his depth, he is childishly unjust to those who, not without mightier reasons than any he can ever find among the atoms, believe in the infinite possibilities of spiritual existence. Surely the History of Religion, not as set forth by a superficial pamphleteer, by Dr. Draper, but as contained in that aggregation of individual history which we call "Biography," should teach him that Hegel's favourite joke is not worth this repeated reproduction. The religious thirst for future life is quite another thirst than that for the *bonus* for good conduct often sought by so-called Christians, and seeing that it exists most in those who are content to accept life as an interminable labour darkened by sorrow and by suffering, it should not be classed as altogether a selfish hope of reward. From the modern utilitarian point of view, of course all effort is selfish; and from the same standpoint, there is no particular nobility in struggling after truth before astonished Belfast audiences, or experimentalising in the interest of humanity on an electric stool!

>Fame is the spur which the clear spirit doth raise,
>(That last infirmity of noble mind)
>To scorn delight and live laborious days!

Noble as is the Professor's desire for fame, I question his capacity for martyrdom, and his insinuations concerning religion are more in the spirit of a bigoted bishop than of a good philosopher. Would he not consider it rather hard if an opponent—say the Bishop of Manchester—were to say, " This publishing of pamphlets is all very well, if it were not for the thought of personal profit, whether in the shape of fame or money, *here.*" The truth is, the Professor, stirred into polemics by irritating opponents, does himself the injustice to confound " hope of reward " with "a love of service," which love, I am sure, is the animating spirit of his own life. Now, the religious conception is simply this,—that this life, with all its hindrances and imperfections, is infinitely too brief for that divine service, or supreme self-sacrifice, which many creatures love to intoxication. It is not pleasure that is solicited; it is continual hard work, even associated with pain ; and it is not too much to say that this desire to enlarge the vital horizon is the source of nobler sentiments than the conviction that Death merely robs us of sensation. It is the Materialist here, not the Idealist, who clings firm to the vulgar conception of Heaven and Hell. Dr. Tyndall would doubtless affirm of the early Christian martyrs that they were upheld by the conviction that God would justify Himself after death and make them glad, and so in truth they thought; but it requires no very close study of history to see that many of these meant by heavenly gladness only a further series of personal labours, a further purging and purification from human impurity. The insinuations of the materialist would be unjust even if urged against the best forms of Mahomedanism ; as urged against the higher Christianity, they are simply absurd and self-refuting Religion, rightly understood, is the love of holy service. In this sense, as I have suggested, a Materialist may be very religious; but the state of mind

A NOTE ON LUCRETIUS.

with him is generally this—either that a brief life satisfies his activity, or else that the constant contemplation of the infinitesimal destroys the power of his capacity to generalise truly. With one to whom poetic emotion is "the thrill of a ganglion," thought "cerebration," life "molecular force," creation "evolution," crime "cerebral disease," Religion may well become a question of "rewards and punishments;" but it is as unfair to dismiss Religion in this superficial way, as it would be to treat modern science from the point of view of the holy Congregation of the Index.

I have no objection whatever to modern Materialism; it is a vital and it may be an elevating creed. I have the highest objection, however, to its criticism of those ideas which it does not understand, and which, if we accept its own showing, can never be formulated. Doubtless, it is a far higher and holier belief than the crude religions of Epicurus and Lucretius, in so far as it preaches beneficence, under certain limitations, to the inferior races of men and to the inferior races of beasts. It is a creed of continence, of health, of sobriety, of endurance, and perhaps self-sacrifice. But it is not, at least as presented to us by its leading teachers, the creed it professes to be—that is, a creed of Verification. A Christian is more logical in believing his Christian evidences than a Materialist in accepting his theory of the Atoms; for the very existence of the last is postulated as a theory, while the former, whether false or true, are invariably valued in so far as they are evidence—that is, are verification. I accompany Dr. Tyndall through his Universe; I seem to see his atoms falling through infinite space; I hear him crying, "I prolong the vision backward across the boundary of the experimental evidence, and discern in that Matter which we, in our ignorance, and notwithstanding our professed reverence for its Creator, have hitherto covered with opprobrium, the promise and potency of every form and quality of Life."* Very good, I reply; but what right have you to "prolong your vision across the boundary of the experimental evidence"? You laugh at others for doing so. You are an experimental philosopher—you can tell us startling things about the phenomena of light, heat, radiation, and magnetism—but neither you nor any of your school can tell us one fact, can give us one idea, explaining the phenomena of Life itself. Suppose we, in our turn, were to cry to you, "This is our Universe; we know we are, we see what is; we prolong the vision forwards across the boundary of the experimental evidence, and discern in that Spirit of which you, in your ignorance, can give us no explanation, and notwithstanding your professed reverence for the Unknowable, are daily covering with opprobrium, the promise and potency of every form and quality of Life."

It is not right that I should be construed as objecting to Science, or to its leading modern doctrine, that of Evolution. On the contrary, I quite agree with Mr. Darwin (who showed in all his discussions a reverence of tone and a purity of purpose in which he is almost unique) that "it is just as noble a conception of the Deity to think that He created a few original forms, capable of self-development, into other and needful forms, as to believe that He required a fresh act of creation to supply the voids caused by the action of His laws." (It is but just to add that Mr. Darwin is merely quoting with approba-

---

* Belfast Address.

tion an eminent "author and divine," not using his own words.) Here, however, the pupil and the master are hopelessly at war, Dr. Tyndall almost accusing the great Apostle of Evolution of heresy to his own creed. "The anthropomorphism, which it seemed his object to set aside, is as firmly associated with the creation of a few forms as with the creation of a multitude. We need clearness and thoroughness here. Either let us open our doors freely to the conception of creative acts, or, abandoning them, let us radically change our notions of Matter." In my opinion, and doubtless in the opinion of Dr. Tyndall's great master, no such alternative is necessary; for it is not necessary to discuss Creation at all, seeing that all Science can tell us is that it knows nothing whatever on the subject! All that it does is, passing the boundary of the experimental evidence, to find the Atoms—a name given to numberless forces we cannot understand. We reach these organisms which Mr. Spencer compares to drops of oil suspended in a mixture of alcohol and water; we come to the "protogenes" of Haeckel, a type distinguishable from a fragment of albumen only by its finely granular character. We go further, thanks to the Professor: we break a magnet into infinite pieces, and we find that each of the pieces, however small, carries with it, though enfeebled, the polarity of the whole. This experiment is so conclusive to the Professor, that he "at once closes with Lucretius," affirming that Nature is seen "to do all things spontaneously and without the meddling of the gods," and with Bruno, that she is "the Universal Mother who brings forth all things as the fruit of her own womb." What then? Surely these vague generalisations are unworthy of a physicist. Does the breaking of the magnet, "even when we prolong the intellectual vision to the polar molecules," bring us one whit nearer to the Mystery we are investigating? And if it does not, which materialists themselves admit, why make it the basis of an atheistic assumption? In no single instance have vital and physical forces been found interchangeable on the principle of the correlation of force. Protoplasm has never yet been developed from inorganic matter, although Dr. Bastian's experiments show that what he calls Archebiosis is possible—that is, spontaneous generation of life from dead organic matter. Heterogenesis, or the production of life from any form of inorganic matter, is admittedly impossible. Only by doing what is forbidden to the Spiritualist, only by "prolonging the line of the intellect beyond the range of the sense," can Professor Tyndall support Bruno's principle—that from Matter Life originates. In his "Fragments of Science," he affirms that the polarity of magnetism gives a basis for the conception that "atoms and molecules are endowed with definite attractive and repellent poles, by the play of which definite forms of crystalline architecture are produced. Thus molecular force becomes structural. It required no great boldness of thought to expend its play into organic nature, and to recognise in molecular force the agency by which both plants and animals are built up." Elsewhere, in language which all classes of thinkers must recognise as beautiful, he pursues the same investigation:

> I wish, however, to show you the molecules in the act of following their architectural instincts, and building themselves together. You know how alum, and nitre, and sugar crystals are formed. The substance to be crystallised is dissolved in a liquid, and the liquid is permitted to evaporate. The solution soon becomes supersaturated, for none of the solid is carried away by evaporation; and then the molecules, no longer able to enjoy the freedom of liquidity, close up together and form crystals. My object now is to make this process rapid enough to enable you to see it, and still not too rapid to be followed by

the eye. For this purpose, a powerful solar microscope and an intense source of light are needed. They are both here. Pouring over a clean plate of glass a solution of sal-ammoniac, and placing the glass on its edge, the excess of the liquid flows away, but a film clings to the glass. The beam employed to illuminate this film hastens its evaporation, and brings it rapidly into a state of supersaturation; and now you see the orderly progress of the crystallisation over the entire screen. You may produce something similar to this if you breathe upon the frost ferns which overspread your window-panes in the winter, and permit the liquid to re-crystallise. It runs, as if alive, into the most beautiful forms.

In this case the crystallising force is hampered by the adhesion of the liquid to the glass; nevertheless, the play of power is strikingly beautiful. In the next example our crystals will not be so much troubled by adhesion, for we shall liberate the atoms at a distance from the surface of the glass. Sending an electric current through water, we decompose the liquid, and the bubbles of the constituent gases rise before your eyes. Sending the same current through a solution of acetate of lead, the lead is liberated, and its free atoms build themselves into crystals of marvellous beauty. They grow before you like sprouting ferns, exhibiting forms as wonderful as if they had been produced by the play of vitality itself. The *mechanism* of the process is rendered intelligible by the picture of atomic poles; but is there nothing but mechanism here? There is something, in my opinion, which the mind of man has never yet seized; but which, so far as research has penetrated, is found indissolubly joined with matter. I have seen these things hundreds of times, but I never look at them without wonder. And, if you allow me a moment's diversion from my subject, I would say that when standing in the spring-time and looking upon the sprouting foliage, the lilies of the field, and sharing the general joy of opening life, I have often asked myself whether there is no power, being, or thing, in the universe, whose knowledge of that of which I am so ignorant is greater than mine? I have said to myself, Can it be possible that man's knowledge is the greatest knowledge—that man's life is the highest life?*

The Professor, we should think, is almost solitary in seeing any resemblance between a crystal and a life cell. The microscope instructs us that real living germs have the power of motion and proliferation in quite a different measure to that vouchsafed to a

---

* "Crystals and Molecular Force." By John Tyndall, F.R.S. (Longmans.)

crystal; and we should have "to prolong the intellectual vision very far indeed" before we could imagine a crystal transmuting itself into an organic form.

And here, in view of that last quotation from the Professor, I cannot help complaining of a certain inconsistency. Nothing, it is clear, can be more materialistic than the tendency of Dr. Tyndall's general teaching, yet it does not prevent his ganglia, like Mr. Spencer's, from begetting a nascent poetic thrill. "I have said to myself," he cries under such an emotion, "can it be possible that man's knowledge is the greatest knowledge—that man's life is the highest life?" Well, admitting for a moment that the theory of Evolution is strictly correct, may we not prolong the vision so far *forward* as to assume the existence of beings as much our superiors, as we, in our highest thoughts, are the superiors of the primordial germs? Dr. Tyndall, possibly, would smile at this, and refer us to the evidence of the senses; but such beings, if they existed, would be no more apparent to ordinary sight or touch than the primordial germs. Electricity is atomic, yet it is invisible, and moreover it is a force. Furthermore, admitting the theory of crystallisation, would there be a greater invisible leap between that form of matter which is structural and that form of matter which we might call spiritual, than there is between that form which is crystalline and that other which is structural? If a life germ can be developed out of a crystal, why may not a spirit (using that term for want of a better) be developed out of a body? In another and clearer phraseology, made clear to us by the teaching of a Seer whom Dr. Tyndall utterly misunderstands, may not a spiritual body issue in the course of Evolution from a body corporeal; and, further, seeing that the process of evolution has been going on so long, may not such spiritual bodies exist, although they are as unrecognised by us as we are unrecognised by the silkworm in its cone?

Professor Tyndall is very sarcastic on what he calls "psychic" conditions, "obviously connected with the nervous system and the state of the health, on which is based the Vedic doctrine of the absorption of the individual into the universal soul." He cites Plotinus, Porphyry, Wordsworth, and Emerson as being subject to such ecstasies; and as if this confusion of types were not sufficient, he carelessly joins with the rest the name of Swedenborg. Now, in Swedenborg he might have found, up to a certain point, a most powerful ally, as he would discover in a perusal of the "Mechanism of the Intercourse of the Soul and the Body;" where the great thinker clearly shows that the Soul is finite, that it is one of the Body's natural parts, that its seat is in the brain, and that it resides particularly in the cortical substance of the cerebrum, and partly also in the medulla, but is ubiquitous in all parts of the brain. Again, we do not think that Swedenborg prolongs his intellectual vision more unwarrantably than Dr. Tyndall, when he affirms, in his "Economy of the Animal Kingdom," that "should any one of the external spheres of nature be dissolved, the internal nevertheless remains unharmed; thus, where Air ceases Ether is found; when the red blood dies its animal spirits survive; and though death destroys the body the Soul escapes unscathed." It would be wasting time to prolong this allusion to him whom Mr. Emerson calls "one of the mastodons of literature," or specially to enlarge on his superficially mystic but intrinsically scientific conceptions of the Spiritual Body. Nor must I for a moment be understood as preaching Swedenborgianism. I am only suggesting that Dr. Tyndall's sneer at Swedenborg was uninstructed, and that there are some few quasi-scientific suggestions of the Swedish seer which may, after all, come as close to a solution of organic life as an explanation which attempts to connect organic life with crystallisation, and spiritual life with the phenomena of molecular force.

On the whole, one is grateful that the Professor sometimes believes in the possibility of higher types than the human. May I then suggest to him that perhaps that Matter in which he discerns the promise and potency of all earthly life, may in reality be only a phenomenon of spiritual force? and though it is admittedly impossible to tell whence that spiritual force, or life, has emanated, that it is not quite so impossible to guess whitherward it is to grow? The sum of force is indestructible and unchanging, the forms of force are destructible and ever-varying. We find Death universal, but Life omnipotent. We are not so sure that we die, as that Death cannot destroy, but can only change, the sum of force within us. Unless Dr. Tyndall can prove to us that this sum of force, including the basis of consciousness itself, is so redistributed among the elements that no possibility of future existence is tenable, he should cut from his programme of Materialism his dogma of the mortality of the Soul. Unless he can prove to us what consciousness *is*, we cannot accept his dicta that consciousness *dies*. "Old decays," sings the poet, "but foster new progressions;

and this may be as true of the cerebral forces as of what the Professor calls a "hydrocarbon." Again, since the atoms are imperishable, and Thought is assumed as the highest evolution of the atoms, Thought itself is atomic, Thought itself is a form of force, Thought itself, despite its infinite fresh combinations, is indestructible, possibly as much so as any given gas.

In the course of his memorable address at Belfast, Professor Tyndall gave an imaginary dialogue between a Lucretian and Bishop Butler, apropos of the Bishop's position that "our organised bodies are no more a part of ourselves than any other matter around us." I wish I had space for the whole argument, which I am compelled to condense. The Lucretian commences thus:

"You speak of 'living powers,' 'percipient or perceiving powers,' and 'ourselves;' but can you form a mental picture of any one of these apart from the organism through which it is supposed to act? . . . . The true self has a local habitation in each of us; thus localised must it not possess a form? If so, what form? . . . . When a leg is amputated the body is divided into two parts; is the true self in both of them or in one? . . . . What if you begin at the other end and remove, instead of the leg, the brain? . . . . Or, instead of going so far as to remove the brain itself, let a certain portion of its bony covering be removed, and let a rhythmic series of pressures and relaxations of pressure be applied to the soft substance. At every pressure the faculties of perception and of action vanish; at every relaxation of pressure they are restored. . . . Where is the man himself during the period of insensibility? You may say that I beg the question when I assume the man to have been unconscious, that he was really conscious all the time, and has simply forgotten what has occurred to him. . . . . I do not think your theory of instruments goes at all to the bottom of the matter. A telegraph operator has his instruments, by means of which he converses with the world; our bodies possess a nervous system, which plays a similar part between the perceiving power and external things. Cut the wires of the operator, break his battery, demagnetise his needle; by this means you certainly sever his connection with the world; . . . . but the operator survives, *and he knows that he survives.* . . . Another consideration. . . . the brain may change from health to disease, and through such a change the most exemplary man may be converted into a debauchee or a murderer. . . . Can the brain or can it not act in this distempered way, without the intervention of the immortal reason?"

And the Bishop, whose arguments we also condense, replies:

"You are a Lucretian, and from the combination and separation of insensate atoms deduce all terrestrial things, including organic forms and their phenomena. Let me tell you, in the first instance, how far I am prepared to go with you. I admit that you can build crystalline forms out of this play of molecular force; that the diamond, amethyst, and snow-star are truly wonderful structures which are thus produced. I will go further and acknowledge that even a tree or flower might in this way be organised. Nay, if you can show me an animal without sensation, I will concede to you that it also might be put together by the suitable play of molecular force. . . . Now comes my difficulty. Your atoms are individually without sensation, much more are they without intelligence. May I ask you, then, to try your hand upon this problem? Take your dead hydrogen atoms, your dead oxygen atoms, your dead carbon atoms, your dead nitrogen atoms, your dead phosphorus atoms, and all the other atoms, dead as grains of shot, of which the brain is formed. Imagine them separate and sensationless, and observe their running together and forming all imaginable combinations. This, as a purely mechanical process, is seeable by the mind. But can you see, or dream, or in any way imagine, how out of that mechanical act, and from these individually dead atoms, sensation, thought, and emotion are to arise? . . . . I am able to pursue to the central organ the motion thus imparted at the periphery, and to see in idea the very molecules of the brain thrown into tremor. My insight is not baffled by these physical processes. What baffles and bewilders me, is the notion that from these physical tremors things so utterly incongruous with them as sensation, thought, and emotion can be derived. . . . Your difficulty, then, as I see you are ready to admit, is quite as great as mine. You cannot satisfy the human understanding in such demand for logical continuity between molecular processes and the phenomena of consciousness."

All this is very admirable, if we can only imagine any one admitting offhand, that "trees and flowers" might be organised out of the play of molecular force; and Professor Tyndall honestly exclaims, " I hold the Bishop's reasoning to be quite unanswerable." He might, had he read his Swedenborg, have constructed for the Bishop a train of still more unanswerable arguments; or turning to a contemporary writer, he may find in Mr. Allanson Picton's ingenious essays* a still further series of proofs that Matter is in its ultimate essence spiritual, and that we are certain of one thing only, the existence of spiritual life.

I have left Lucretius far behind me, gazing still with a sense of complete mastery on his primordial universe, where there is no room, not even an intermundia, where the gods, or a God, may dwell. In investigating the creed of his representative modern followers, of him to whom the torch of Lucretian illuminative genius has been passed on, I have found more comfort combined with far less coherence. Professor Tyndall is certainly a materialist, though he has no particular affection for the name, and he is also, but in no offensive sense, an atheist, though he refuses to put that word upon his banner. In days when so much heat is still introduced into popular controversy, his caution is perhaps necessary; yet I should admire him more if he showed more completely the courage of his convictions. His theory of organic matter is destructive to any sort of Deism; indeed, so far as I see, it leaves no room whatever for even the higher Pantheism, though it is full of that Lower Pantheism which sees in every clod and stone the potency of universal life. He disclaims anthropomorphism, but he cannot free his "ganglia"

---

* "The Mystery of Matter." By Allanson Picton. (Macmillan.)

altogether of mysterious "thrills." His tone is one of quiet insinuation, rather than of formal avowal; but his highest mood is poetic, not scientific. If he would only express his ideas in poetry, much of his writing would be as valuable as much of Lucretius, and he could soar to sublime flights of delicious uncertainty by his admirable plan of "prolonging the intellectual vision beyond the region of the senses!"

FREE THOUGHT IN AMERICA.

I.

ROBERT INGERSOLL.

THERE is a notion even in refined circles in America that the influence of a man like Colonel Robert Ingersoll may be an influence for good. I altogether fail to see it. While doing full justice to the honesty, the courage, and the good humour of this remarkable orator, I am convinced that he is precisely the sort of teacher—I had almost written devil's advocate—to whom Americans should just now shut their ears. Free thought should be distinguished from the offences against common intelligence committed by a Philistine of the Philistines. Ingersoll enters the temples of religion with his hat on one side, a cigar in his mouth, and a jest upon his lips. No matter who the god may be—Vishnu, Buddha, Apollo, or Jesus—he is ready to tackle him in his own peculiar vocabulary. His philosophy may be summed up in the words of Burns:

> To make a happy fireside clime
>   To weans and wife—
> That's the true pathos and sublime
>   Of human life!

This philosophy is all very well in its way, just as well as eating and drinking, dancing, marrying and giving in marriage, and infant-dandling; but if it were all-sufficient, George the Third would have been a great king, and Voltaire would have been a great poet. To take Colonel Ingersoll seriously, of course, would be like asking for reverence from Mark Twain. He represents the natural reaction of American Bohemianism against the Puritanism of Boston and the overstrained Transcendentalism of Brook Farm. But he is just the sort of person of whom America does *not* stand in need. The predominant vices of America, especially as represented by its great cities, are its irreverence, its recklessness, its impatience—in one word, its Materialism. A nation in which the artistic sense is almost dead, which is practically without a literature, which is impatient of all sanctions and indifferent to all religions, which is corrupt from the highest pinnacle of its public life down to the lowest depth of its journalism, which is at once thin-skinned under criticism and aggressive to criticise, which worships material forces in every shape and form, which despises conventional conditions, yet is slavish to ignoble fashions, which, too hasty to think for itself, takes recklessly at second-hand any old or new-clothes philosophy that may be imported from Europe, yet, while wearing the raiment openly, mocks and ridicules the civilisation that wove the fabric—such a nation, I think, might be spared the spectacle of an elderly gentleman in modern costume trampling on the lotus, the rose, and the lily in the gardens of the gods. The exhibition can do no good; it may do no little harm. If the science of mythology did not exist, if the old gods or the new had any bloody altars left, if the tongue of free thought had not been loosened once and for ever, it might be another matter; but the danger now is, not that men may believe too much, but that they may believe too little; that in due time scepticism, which has demolished all religions and fatally discredited the divine religion of poetry itself, may turn the Temple of Mystery into a bear-garden or a beer-garden, exchange the language of literature for the argot of the cheap press, and Americanise even the sentiment of humanity. "I beg to remind honourable gentlemen," said Benjamin Disraeli, on a memorable occasion, "that we owe much to the Jews." I beg to remind the Colonel Ingersolls and Mark Twains of that continent that we owe much to the gods, without whom, when all is said and done,

> The world would smell like what it is—a tomb!

But for them, Europe would have been Americanised long ago; but for them, Europe would have arrived centuries since at the blessed era of presidential elections, colossal public swindles, races for money-bags, the torturing rack of the interviewer, and the inquisition of the newspaper; but for them, but for the divine tyrants and instructors of mankind, malignant or benignant, terrible or beautiful, the pessimism of Schopenhauer and Leopardi might have been antedated a thousand years. For my own part, I should prefer even to accept hell with John Calvin, rather than to eat cakes, drink ale, and munch hot ginger with Colonel Ingersoll. He is the boy in the gallery, cracking nuts and making precocious comments during the performance of the tragedy of life; blind to the splendour of the scenery, deaf to the beauty of the dialogue, indifferent to the pathetic or tragic solicitations of the players; seeing in Christ or Buddha or

Jehovah only a leading man spouting platitudes, and indifferently dressed for the part he is playing. A great mythus is to him a great "lie," nothing more; a great poetical theology is only an invention of the arch-enemy. Hugely does he enjoy the joke of the garden of Eden or the tree of Iggdrassil; clearly does he perceive, having hung round the stage-door of the world, that the goddesses are only ballet-girls, exhibiting their nudity for so much a night. For him Æschylus has no terror, Sophocles no charm, the author of the Book of Job no pathos; everything is leather and prunella, except the performance of Harlequin.

That such a person should have a large following, among a generation so much of his way of thinking, is no matter for surprise; a few centuries ago it might have been a cause for joy; but in the nineteenth century it is truly sad, as showing how little Science has done, after all, to elevate the intellectual condition of the masses. The same uninstructed influence that is thus brought to bear upon religion would speedily be fatal, and already, as I have suggested, threatens to be fatal, to all poetry, all true literature, all great art, and, in the long run, all speculative science. Colonel Ingersoll is very fond of proclaiming his admiration for the great scientific teachers of the age; but in reality he is as far away in spirit from the thought of Darwin as from the vision of Shakespeare, as obtuse to the scientific problems as to the pathetic poetic fallacy. Religion is the grave, elder daughter of Poetry, and to understand religious questions a man must have the heart of a poet. Science, too, is the daughter of Poetry; indeed, her youngest born; while calmer and colder than her mother, she has the same far-away, rapt look into the heaven of heavens;

and her teaching is for poetic hearts also, not for those who confound her with her sordid and hard-working handmaid, Invention. Science ranges the universe, touches the farthest suns, reaches the farthest cloud confines, and cries honestly and loudly, " Thus far—no farther—here I pause;" and then even she begins to *dream*. Invention squats on the ground, sets her little water-wheel, lights her little lamp, pieces her mechanical puzzles, does homely work, delightful and useful to everybody. But Invention-worship is fetish-worship, and Colonel Ingersoll is a fetish-worshipper—that is to say, an individual exactly at the savage stage where neither religion nor science begins. To go to him for religious guidance, is like asking a native of the kingdom of Dahomey to favour us with his ideas on Free-will, the Incarnation, the philosophy of Plato, the art of Raphael, the poetry of Æschylus, the music of Beethoven, and the philosophy of Comte or Spencer.

The Christian stage, whatever objection we may take to it, is higher than the fetish-stage, and the lowest form of anthropomorphism is infinitely superior to totem-worship. The mass of mankind do not need to be told that it is well to fill their bellies, to love their children, to live amicably with one another, to accept no guidance but their own very questionable "common-sense;" all that is taught to them of right and of necessity by the conditions of that period of evolution which they have already attained. What they require to learn is, that life necessitates divine sanctions as well as cheery conditions ; that the gods are not dead, but living—imperishable ideals fashioned by the sublimest and supremest conceptions of mankind; that the truth of any religion lies not in its dogma, but in its moral beauty or poetical imperishability, because just so far as it is beautiful is it fundamentally and actually true; that our sharpest hours of suffering contain our clearest moments of insight; and that human love and sympathy are born, not of common junketing, but of common despair and sorrow. The gospel of hot ginger, as preached by Colonel Ingersoll, would soon make of New York another Sodom. Fortunately, such a man as Octavius Frothingham is hard by, to vindicate the poetry of religion against the champions of cakes and ale, and to prove that free thought, even in America, does not necessarily imply free permission to outrage your neighbour's most sacred convictions.

II.

OCTAVIUS FROTHINGHAM.

MR. FROTHINGHAM is well known to most readers of religious literature as one of the most brilliant and enlightened apostles of free thought or radical religion in America. Until quite lately, I believe, he preached every Sunday in New York; with the field of his present labours I am unacquainted; but my knowledge of him is altogether based on his writings and on Mr. Stedman's little monograph— one of those admirably lucid bits of crystallisation for which the writer is distinguished. Of course, a man educated like myself in the school of English Jacobinism finds in Mr. Frothingham a not very novel type of thinker, uttering sentiments with which the world of free thought has long been familiar; but the author of "Transcendentalism in New England" has a distinct individuality, often perfervid, occasionally convincing, and never tiresome. His style is admirable, even where his matter is questionable, as it now and then is; and, on the whole, America is to be congratulated on the privilege of listening to such a man. But does America listen to him? It would very much astonish me to hear that it did. His faith is far too filmy, his foothold much too unsteady, to carry conviction to the hearts of a hasty generation. His tolerance to all religions, all opinions, all orthodoxies and heresies, is beautiful and welcome, but his infinite patience lacks, to my mind, the shaping power of conviction. He has set his soul free of every bond and shackle, but he leaves it to beat the empty air. With all this, it must be clearly understood that his written works have the highest of all literary merits, that of directly stimulating thought in the reader; they are full of grave, wise, tender, even profound things, expressed in perfect language; they are reverent to the very extremes of their gentle audacity; and there can be no doubt whatever that they have had a deeply beneficent influence whenever and wherever they have been studied. But the fatal spirit of a self-destructive latitudinarianism, which has paralysed the will of every transcendentalist from Hegel downward, possesses Mr. Frothingham also. His message to men carries no conviction, for it has neither the hate of hate nor the love of love; it lacks the fertilising energy and superb bigotry of a logical belief.

Mr. Frothingham, for example, utterly repudiates Anthropomorphism. The universe, in his conception, is, as it was to Spinoza, as it has been to every true transcendentalist, a system of universal Law, entirely divorced from personality. From one point of view, this conception is rational and impregnable; from another, it is inexpedient, not to say trivial. No sane man doubts the profundity of the current ideas on which Mr. Frothingham sails so cheerfully; of the "stream of tendency" and the "power beyond ourselves which works for righteousness;" but many men doubt, as I do, the scientific necessity, or the mental possibility, of divorcing the idea of God from the idea of personality. The poetical image of the magnified non-natural man at least hits the mark better than the preposterous images of "streams" and "tendencies" and impersonal working "powers" beyond humanity. Very instructive it is to observe, in this connection, how the apostle of blind law, taken off his guard, appropriates the anthropomorphic metaphors:

> The Radical has no definition; he does not venture on a written definition. He will not define or confine the infinite. He has no interpretation which he can accept or impose upon anybody else; but the substance of the idea he holds in a manner so transcendental, grand, vast, and beautiful that the others dwarf themselves into utter insignificance. The Hebrew Jehovah seems to him a fanciful and fantastical idea; the Christian's triune deity is limited; and the theist's conception of the personal God is bounded. The Radical believes in the *universal law*, omnipotent, omnipresent, sweeping through the world, administering the least things, controlling the greatest, holding close relations between you and me, *holding in the hollow of its hand* all the affairs of all the nations of the globe. *This idea of law*—material, intellectual, spiritual—comprehends everything, all the domain of reason, all the domain of hope, so vast that no faith can scale its heights, *so tender that one can lie like a child on its bosom*, so mighty and majestic that nobody need be afraid that it cannot overcome every obstacle in the way of the highest and noblest advance. ("The Mission of the Radical Preacher." By O. B. Frothingham.)

Which, after all, is the most illogical and fantastic, the idea of a Hebrew Jehovah, or of a Christian triune deity, or the picture of a Universal Law that "administers" and "controls," holds affairs in "the hollow of its hand," and is so "tender that one can lie like a child on its bosom"? Every one admits that God, in the Absolute, is unknowable and inconceivable; but the consensus of human experience has established that the only image that can represent His *relation* to conditioned creatures is the human or anthropomorphic one, though it has made modern scientists so angry. After all, is not the rejection of the popular image made in the most "crass" spirit of transcendentalism? Where is the wisdom of a criticism that would endow blind law with "hands" and a "bosom," and in the same breath object to the terminology of the Lord's Prayer?

Elsewhere in the same book from which I have quoted, Mr. Frothingham's language becomes less contradictory, but even more extraordinary — so extraordinary, indeed, that, if it came from any other pen, one might presume that the writer had no spiritual claim to speak *in cathedrâ* on religious topics at all. In proclaiming his revolt from the Christian religion, and his rejection of the Christian idea, he admits, regretfully, that the Christian faith still prevails, that it keeps alive the potent activities that sustain the life of Christendom. Nevertheless, he adds, "it is a superstition; it is not grounded on history, on knowledge, on science, on fact, but it is a fancy, an imagination, a tradition;" and now, in the natural course of things, it is dissolving away before the breath of science. People, he naïvely affirms, reject it in the great centres of activity—in Paris, in Berlin, in London, in New York! Among other reasons for the long permanence of this false faith, and its still surviving power, he gives the following: 1. The exceeding antiquity of the system; 2. The hindrances so long thrown in the way of Biblical criticism; 3. *Mirabile dictu*, the persistence with which the faith is taught. The last reason is a superb *non sequitur;* it is simply affirming that the zeal with which an army fights its battles is in direct ratio to the weakness of its cause! But, not content with so wonderful an affirmation, Mr. Frothingham goes on to arraign Christianity because it is the "religion of sorrow." He quotes both Jesus and Paul in illustration of his statement. Then he adds, not without eloquence :

> Through the chinks we can see the light. The condition of man becomes more comfortable, more easy; the hope of man is more visible; the endeavour of man is more often crowned with success; the attempt to solve the darkest life-problems is not so desperate as it was. The reformer meets with fewer rebuffs; the philanthropist does not despair as he did. The light is dawning. The great teachers of knowledge multiply, bear their burdens more and more steadily; the traditions of truth and knowledge are becoming established in the intellectual world. It is so; and those of us who have caught a vision of the better times coming through reason, through knowledge, through manly and womanly endeavour, have caught a sight of a Christendom passing away, of a religion of sorrow declining, of a gospel preached for the poor no longer useful to a world that is mastering its own problems of poverty and lifting itself out of disabling misery into wealth without angelic assistance. This is our consolation; and while we admit, clearly and frankly, the real power of the popular faith, we also see the pillars on which a new faith rests, which shall be a faith not of sorrow, but of joy. ("The Rising and the Setting Faith, and other Discourses." By O. B. Frothingham.)

Is it necessary to demolish this cumbrous snow-heap of misconception, to point out the fallacy that confuses the Christian sentiment with the utilitarian philosophy of loaves and fishes? If all that Jesus meant was that the poor should become the rich in another world, and the suffering become the joyful; if the kernel of His teaching was merely, as narrow logicians have suggested, the notion that bad luck here would of necessity ensure a bonus elsewhere, Christianity would stand but a poor chance at the hands of either the higher or the lower criticism. What Jesus did teach, or what we have learned at least by the Divine Ideal that He afforded, was, and is, that worldly knowledge, worldly prosperity, worldly success and happiness, are poor things compared with the heaven of sin vanquished, the other world of supreme love and insight. If the triumph of the political economist were quite secure; if the earth were equally divided among men according to some such scheme as that of Henry George; if there were no workhouses in it, and no prisons, the poor would still inherit the kingdom of heaven; for the true poor of the Christian idea are those who despise ignoble prizes, who are indifferent to vain knowledge, who have found in the certainty of human failure the sublimity of sympathetic love and insight. It must be borne in mind, too, that Jesus could sit down with the rich man as well as the poor, when the rich man was poor "in spirit." To refute Mr. Frothingham here would be to refute the whole argument of utilitarianism, which has already been done, or attempted, and is of course far beyond the scope of this paper; nor am I in any way holding a brief for the Christian religion, or speaking from the point of view of the orthodox believer. But let us have fair play on both sides, nor attempt to answer the proposition that one may be multiplied into three by an assertion that two and two are four. Elsewhere Mr. Frothingham clearly expresses his conviction that perfect happiness is simply impossible under mundane conditions, and that mere knowledge and power may be, and generally are, in the nature of vanity. As long as these things are true, there is room in our dialectics for the Christian argument that the compensations of a higher and nobler life are precisely what is needed for the settlement of the complex human problem. It is melancholy to find a thinker like Mr. Frothingham, among Americans, of all people in the world, arguing that there is to be a millennium of inexhaustible dry goods and of physical prosperity, compared with which the coming of the Messiah would be but an ineffective performance.

Mr. Frothingham writes very eloquently on evolution; accepts all its splendid suggestions, both in the material and in the moral world; shows clearly that cause follows effect in the social as well as the physical sphere, and that out of evil must come evil, and out of good must issue good. He accepts, if I understand him rightly, the Comtist notion of the perfectibility of Humanity, and infinitely prefers the *Grand Être*, or divine adumbration of the genius of man, to either Jehovah or Jesus, Buddha or Balder. He does not, however, imitate Colonel Ingersoll in treating any of these gods with disrespect, but he nevertheless measures them with his free-thought foot-rule, and finds them, at the best, only a cubit high. What, after all, is this *Grand Être* of which we hear so much? Not the Son of Man transubstantiated, but the Spirit of Man glorified; not the Paraclete, the Redeemer, or the Divine Ideal, but the vague, impersonal, stupendous, and overpowering outcome of all human intelligence, effort, suffering, limitless struggle, and despair. His other names are Science, Knowledge, Intellectual Victory, Moral Supremacy; his other name will be Happiness, or

Summum Bonum, by-and-by. Well, when our *Grand Être* looks forward, what will be his prospect? A reign of indefinite but not endless length, cut short inevitably, sooner or later, by the cataclysm of our solar system. In the far future, then, inevitable Death. When he looks backward, what must be his retrospect? Far away as the first beginnings of life he traces the progression from pain to pain, marks the graves of the generations, from the tomb of the pterodactyl in the chalk to the sepulchre of Franklin among the Arctic snows. Far backward then, Death too; æons of agony, vistas of the types that have perished to fashion the *Grand Être* for his short ecstatic reign. Science may smile at the thought of compensation; but surely the *Grand Être*, with his supreme potentialities of pity, must say to himself, "Alas and alas! though my children now rejoice, like motes in the sunbeam, what of those who have been destroyed, tortured, and obliterated in the long darkness that preceded this splendid dawn of day?" And so, after all, the *Grand Être*, with all his good intentions, finds his poor feet slipping and sinking in the arid sands of pessimism, and the only gospel left for his worshippers to preach will be the old weary gospel of the materialist, "Eat, drink, and be happy, for tomorrow we die!"

III.

THE HOPE OF THE HUMAN RACE.

But to do Mr. Frothingham justice, he is not a pessimist. In one of the very finest of his essays, the sermon on "Immortality," a piece of writing that can be read and re-read for its marvellous clearness of exposition and its consummate beauty of expression, he echoes, though somewhat half-heartedly, the great hope of the human race for an individual existence after death. But in scrutinising his argument closely, we perceive that, while he welcomes with enthusiasm the conception of the *Grand Être*, and states that chimerical Being's case with splendid eloquence, he is lost in amazement that Humanity ever contained that other idea of a personal immortality; can see no rational excuse for it; fears, indeed, that it is altogether too shadowy to be at all tangible. All he can venture to say in plea for it is that its very audacity favours it, its very wildness is its guarantee. Here, again, we get frank confession, but bad logic. How a faith can be vindicated by its own sheer improbability, how a belief may be true because it goes in the teeth of all experience, I leave for the transcendentalists of free thought to decide. I believe the evolutionists have clearly explained how the notion of life after death "developed" easily out of the first superstitions of the human race, and how its permanence in all communities and most individuals proceeds from the permanence of other instincts seemingly imperishable. But where I join issue with Mr. Frothingham is at the one point where issue is possible—that the idea of immortality is irrational and opposed to common experience; for if it were so, there can be no doubt that it would have been "obliterated" long ago in the process of evolution. It is not because it is preposterous, but because it is probable, that it has kept its strenuous hold on the hearts of mankind. Jesus, in His supreme practical wisdom, in His relentless logic, perceived this fully, perceived that this very idea was the natural, indeed the only, escape from between the horrors of our mundane dilemma. And forthwith (for I hold that this Man, whatever His credentials, was scientific or nothing) He proceeded to verification. Opening the human heart, He found that it demanded ampler life on account of the infinite possibilities of love without it. Examining the social organism, He saw that its structure was welded together by the blood of human martyrdom, that every hope and every aspiration within it were based upon the certainty that consciousness, and all its consequent affections, must be permanent, and therefore immaterial. The law of growth was absolute, the indestructibility of force was sure, and the permanence of force was the certainty of the Soul. As for His creed being one of sorrow, that is not strictly true; it is the world that is sorrowful, not the creed that redeems it, which, after all, has never until now had a fair trial. Christianity in its essence, apart from its miraculous pretensions, is, like the mind of its founder, strictly simple and scientific. It may not be feasible, we may be altogether unable to believe it, its history is a long chapter of horrors and enormities, and for some inscrutable reason its priests and paid professors have almost invariably been the enemies of human progress; but, compared with any other creed that has been offered in God's name to men, it has the solitary merit of logical truth and common-sense. If we admit its fundamental proposition, that spiritual personality is permanent, and is at the same time directly conditioned by unselfish love and brotherhood, all the mystery and pain, all the struggle of the ages, becomes clear. Moral salvation, being independent of dogma or of worldly happiness, was as possible for the first half-savage human product as it is possible now for the highest and the meanest of mankind. Knowledge is nothing, power is nothing, material success is nothing; the insight of love is everything, and looks right up into the heaven of heavens, crying, "O grave, where is thy victory? O death, where is thy sting?"

In saying so much, perhaps, concerning one or two points of Mr. Frothingham's teaching, I may seem to be carping at what I came to praise. Let me repeat, then, that the said teaching is in the main as wise as it is beneficent, as beautiful as it is just. For every flower that grows in the gardens of the gods, Mr. Frothingham has reverent admiration; he is Pharisaic to no creed, but tolerant toward all. With his faith in the teaching of science I can find no fault, except that it blinds him now and then to the subtler issues of life and experience; it is, indeed, a kind of faith that must grow in the hearts of all men, and ultimately, I believe, lead to the triumph of the Christian ideal. The star of a holy purpose shines at all times, more or less brightly, through the clouds of the writer's transcendentalism. For with all his scientific leanings he is of the race that produced Emerson and Theodore Parker; he possesses by temperament their vagueness and haziness of logic, leading sometimes to that universal tolerance which makes religion blow neither hot nor cold, but lukewarm. Mr. Frothingham has done noble work in negativing the pretensions of still rampant dogmatisms and special Providences, in asserting the supreme right of private judgment, in bearing testimony from the pulpit that the teachings of Science, instead of narrowing, enlarge the heavenly horizons, and in following the divine thread of meaning to be found in all creeds and all theologies. His teaching has the one cardinal defect, that it lacks the consecrating touch of *pathos* that accompanies the highest kind of spiritual solicitation, which we feel as certainly in the Buddhist books as in the Jewish Testament, in the tragedies of Sophocles as well as in the moralities of John Bunyan, and in the prophecies of Walt Whitman (despite all the Emersonian leaven) as well as in the child-like songs of Whittier. For this is the fatal tendency of Transcendentalism—to soften the lines of conviction, and to strain the anguish out of sentiment. There is no pathos in Emerson; never once does his gentle hand, grasping its soothsayer's wand, touch the fountain of tears; yet even such a man as Spurgeon can stir that fountain, if only with the mere breath of a phrase. And no creed without pathos will ever justify the great human hope, or conquer the great human heart. So I part from Mr. Frothingham with no lack of respect and admiration, but with some little sadness, feeling that the tale he has to tell is one already twice told, and misses the charm of the fairy stories of God, which will continue to add to human happiness so long as the heart of man is as a child's and some glimpses of a heavenly dream remain.

A NOTE ON DANTE ROSSETTI.

> "Some positive, persisting fops we know,
> Who, if once wrong, will needs be always so ;
> But I, with pleasure, own my errors past,
> And make each day a critic on the last."
>
> POPE'S *Essay on Criticism.*

In the early spring of the present year there passed away at Birchington-on-Sea, in Kent, one of the most original painters and most gifted poets who was ever sent to lend light and leading to a perverse generation. A man unique in this particular—that he passed through good and evil report with serene indifference to mercenary reward or social successes ; and that, while exercising an unusual influence on the higher culture of his age, and living in the very midst of a busy and somewhat pertinacious artistic circle, he remained personally unknown to most of his contemporaries, as well as to the public at large. He painted pictures, which I can neither blame nor praise, for I know them too little, but which those well fitted to judge have classed as masterpieces. He wrote poems, which have been both lavishly praised and harshly judged, and which remain, after all is said and done, among the spiritual productions of the present generation. Even fairer than his artistic or literary fame was the love and admiration he awakened in all who knew him. He not merely founded a school, he created a kind of artistic religion, which is fast spreading, through the labours of loving disciples. A man remarkable for his intellectual gifts, he was still more remarkable for his unique power of awakening artistic faith and literary fervour. Missed now by his own circle, he will ere long be missed more by the world which least appreciated him while living; for, when the true æstheticism has indicated itself, and the false æstheticism, which still overshadows it, has withered like an unwholesome weed, the name of Rossetti will be sadly remembered, as that of one of those veiled spirits who sometimes walk the earth to make men pure, and literally to " brighten the sunshine."

When I remember how truly great he was—in that best greatness of modesty and meekness of soul ; when I think how patiently he laboured at his beautiful art and how little golden praise men gave to him ; when I contrast his gentle life with the strenuous lives of noisier and more prosperous men, it seems strange to think that, at any period of his career, any writer could be found blind enough or hard enough to criticise him adversely. Yet, that cruel things were written of him, and by one who should have looked longer and known better, we all know. He has been called a "fleshly" person, a sensuous, even a sensual poet ; he who, more than perhaps many of his contemporaries, was the least objective, the least earthly, and the most ideal. Not even after his death is the cry suffered to abate; and a recent writer in a religious review,* takes occasion to repeat at second-hand, for a wiser generation, all the hasty expressions and uninstructed abuse that I published in hot haste ten years ago, and have since, as my readers know, repented. It is so easy to create a nickname that will stick; so difficult to write a

---

* *The British Quarterly.*

criticism that will endure! Perhaps it may be worth while to endeavour, in the short space at my disposal, to show the readers of this book how false a judgment it was, how conventional, and Pharisaic a criticism, which chose to dub as "fleshly" the works of this most ethereal and dreamy—in many respects this least carnal and most religious—of modern poets.

But let me confess at the outset that, to understand poems like these, the reader must bring something of the sympathy he receives. If he approaches in the wrong mood, or in an antipathetic one, the poems may at first repel him. The magnetism is for magnetic people, under what the mediums call "test" conditions. I myself, being then in a non-receptive mood, once regarded Rossetti's work balefully, disliked his subjects and his workmanship; even thought him sensuous in the bad sense, and was capable of "cutting him up" (how easy it is to "cut up"—even a rose or a lily!) when the occasion served. Afterwards, reading him again less coldly, I began to understand the purity of his meaning and the delicacy of his art. That art has been called mosaic, and so it is; but it is a mosaic made of precious stones of speech, always radiant, and sometimes exquisitely chosen, forming, indeed, an ornate style *sui generis*, in which Latinisms are employed with rare felicity. Some people may prefer simpler styles, though it may be said in passing, that Rossetti could be simple enough when he chose, as in his fine reproductions of old ballads; but that is neither here nor there; the fact being that Rossetti's style was *his own*, and wonderfully adapted to express his sibylline meaning. His method, like that of Jacob Boehmen, was symbolic; and he sometimes used a phrase, as Jacob used a flower, to express whole worlds of recondite mysticism. With such a writer, therefore, to complain that he did not call a spade a spade, or carol songs about buttercups and daisies, was to mistake the whole drift of his meaning. He was one of those who found, as many an old necromancer would have found, an infinity of suggestion in the mere sound of "Mesopotamia." So he came to love music for its own sake, finding a luxury of delight in using sweet sibilants, delicate elisions, and musical alliterations. Proceeding further, he constructed a phraseology quaint, archaic, involved, and involuted, yet only so as are flowers, leaves, bells, and blooms, obeying some intricate caprice of nature.

> A primrose on the water's brim,
> A yellow primrose was to him,
> But it was something more;

it was maiden modesty and virgin pallor, a star in the earth's firmament, a letter in the golden Book of Beauty, a symbol, an abstraction of something stranger and fairer than itself. For the man was a magician, of the tribe of Kubla Khan; and at his bidding there rose a stately pleasure dome, every precious stone of which had a name and a mystery, and, when he entered it to weave his strange verse, he was within his right in using the language of incantation, and in conjuring with such names as "Abracadabra." Those who assert that he loved this Art "for its own sake," know nothing of his method; he loved it because it expressed the almost inexpressible, and supplied him with an occult terminology. If he was wrong, all the mystics have been wrong; Boehmen was a blunderer, Richter was a proser, Novalis was no poet. There is room, surely, in the world for Rossetti as well as Burns, for the poetry of enchanted symbolism as well as for the poetry of kicking up one's heels and rolling with milkmaids in the hay.

The adverse critic has complained that our magician had no humour, was incapable of honest laughter; in other words, he never grinned through a horse-collar, as even poor Heine could do; but neither did Wordsworth or Shelley, nor many another man whom the world calls great. He knew, in fact, that life was no laughing matter. Yet grave humour, of a celestial kind, he certainly possessed, if we are to trust certain memoranda which have been handed about, but never openly published. It was no fault of his that God intended him for a Wizard; it was his destiny, and certainly our gain; for, in these days of garish daylight, of popular science, it needed such a man to show us that geometry is occult as well as simple, that the stars have "influences" as well as rays to be dissolved in the spectrum, and that the flowers may be put to other uses besides the manufacture of cowslip-wine. *You* think that speech is current coin, to be passed freely from hand to hand; *he* knew that it was magical, and, by a simple arrangement of sounds, could be made to figure forth flowers, stars, and astrological portents. Words of strange colour coiled like snakes about his wand, turned into flowers and leaves, turned again into precious stones, and rained as pearls and emeralds on the grass beneath his feet. He wore neither homespun cloth nor sober black, but a robe wrought with Runic letters and signs of the Zodiac—a wizard's robe, in fact. It was not the sort of dress to please prosy people, or to go junketing in; but it suited his purpose and expressed his extraordinary function. The style is the man; and, in this case, no style could possibly be better.

There are people in the world who imagine that

poetry should be easy as A B C, and who tell us that it should deal only with the approven facts of life. In this case, Shakespeare was a bad poet, and Hamlet's soliloquy a vile, roundabout business—as, indeed, simple Goldsmith was eager to show on one occasion. It does not seem to me, however, that poetry is necessarily either simple or occult; it either is or is not *poetry*, and may be as far off in its range as Saturn's ring, or as near to us as cakes and ale. It is surely worth while to strain the eyes a little in gazing at the heavens, and to listen with some attention if we expect to catch the music in the sea-shell. Those who complain that certain great poets are incomprehensible, are simply lazy persons, who want to be tickled with a straw—companions, indeed, of our old friend Bottom, who could conceive of no use for Titania's fairies but to scratch his ears. All deep thought is difficult, *however expressed*—in the crystalline phrase of Dante, or in the jargon of Jean Paul; and there is no easy road to Parnassus. The right question, indeed, to ask in taking up a poet's work, is not whether it is easy, but whether it is difficult *enough*—whether it awakens that thought which concerns the beauty and mystery of life, or whether it goes down like a lollipop, and leaves us none the wiser or the better. A more serious charge against Rossetti's writing, if sustained, would be that it *is* only of the lollipop or *bonbon* order—a luscious thing for very young people; and it is curious that this charge is made by the same critics who complain of its difficulty, its artificiality. The inconsistency is remarkable. If all Rossetti had to tell us was that lollipops are sweet, and sensual pleasure agreeable, and women kissable, why should he have gone in such a roundabout way about it? Why should he have used the language of the spheres, and the machinery of all the necromancers, to express to us the height of foolishness and the depth of apple pie? In simple fact, he does nothing of the sort. He uses amatory forms and carnal images, just as he uses mere sounds and verbalisms, to express ideas which are purely and remotely spiritual; and he takes the language of personal love to express his divine yearning, simply because that language is the most exquisite quintessence of human speech. I do not mean to imply that his forms and images represent *mere* abstractions; in that case, he would be a sort of mathematician, not a poet. But flesh and blood, in his eyes, are sacramental.

Is there any honest man that doubts that Love, even so-called "fleshly Love," is the noblest pleasure that man is permitted to enjoy; or that the sympathy of woman for man, and of man for woman, is in its essence the sweetest sympathy of which the soul is capable? Only one thing is higher and better than Love's happiness, and that one thing is Love's sorrow, when there comes out of loss and suffering the sense of compensation, of divine gain. Well, Rossetti's poetry expresses at once the pleasure, the sympathy, the happiness and the sorrow, the loss and the gain. It has been called the poetry of personal passion; but it is more than this—it is passion transfused into *religion*, into a religion which glorifies grief and peoples the empty heavens with shapes of loveliness and love. Take the opening of what is perhaps his best, and best-known poem:

> The Blessed Damozel leaned out
>   On the gold bar of Heaven:
> Her eyes were stiller than the depths
>   Of waters still'd at even;
> She had five lilies in her hand,
>   And the stars in her hair were seven!

Something vaguer might have contented other poets, but this poet has a necromancer's precision, can *count* each star and lily of the vision, with a sense of their individual signification. The result is, we have not merely a poetical image, but a painted picture; something dreamlike, but with the strange definition *only* known in dreams. As he goes on, the picture changes, but the realism remains—we see the very hues, and hear the very sound, of heaven; and at each wave of the grave wizard's wand, at each measured cadence from his lips, the azure seems bursting open further and further, until we see, in an extraordinary image,

> Time like a pulse shake fierce
> Thro' all the worlds!

If this be not necromancy, I know none in poetry. Pathos there is also in the poem, as when the Blessed Damozel weeps, and we "hear her tears," a gentle sound of rain on the parched universe. But the magician is too sure of his power, too conscious of the supernatural powers which are shaping the spell, to break down and moan. A poet of the earth, earthy, may do that, and set us weeping with him—as Burns does when he hears the bird-song from his place in the ploughed field.

> For pity's sake, sweet bird, nae mair,
> Or *else my heart is broken!*

But the spiritual poet, with his eyes fixed on so celestial a vision, is master of himself. He knows that his glimpse is real, and that, sooner or later, the enchantment will draw him upward—to the Blessed Damozel's embrace—as, indeed, it has already done, since such aspirations are truly sent of God.

The same mood of perfect vision and grave assurance inspires all the best work of Rossetti. He has no questions to ask, no problems to trouble him ; he is sibylline, not from being puzzle-headed, but because he has looked behind the curtain of the Sibyl. He *sees* the trees walk, he hears the flowers speak, with a sober certainty of waking bliss. When an angel passes him, he can feel the very texture of his robe, and tell the colour of his eyes. He is as sure of Heaven and all its white-robed angels as ordinary men are of each other. Something of this certainty he doubtless learned from Blake, though he lacked Blake's childish simplicity and sweet garrulousness. So he "weaves his spell of strange device" in a way bewildering to those who dislike being mesmerised, and who would have sent Paracelsus to prison for fortune-telling.

The finest of his finished works is the "House of Life," which the *British Quarterly Reviewer* calls a "House of Ill Fame." It is, to a certain extent, monotonous, and the sacrament of flesh and blood has a constant place in it ; but out of this sacrament rises the ghostly vision of the Host, and ere we have ended, we hear the voices of all the angels praising the Lord of Heavenly Love. And of this strange texture, of this starry woof, is the so-called "fleshly" poetry. Is it a reproach to this poet that the divinest thing he has seen and known, humanly speaking, is the face and form of a living woman ; that out of *her* eyes, and from *her* lips, he has learned to understand the processions of the stars and the spheric music of the world which, to so many, is unknown ? The stairs of the earthly Love reach to the heavens ; he ascends them step by step, that is all, hand in hand with his sweet guide—who is a bright, earthly maiden at the beginning, then a bride, then a shining creature, winged and marvellously transfigured ; the rest in order; last, an amethyst! You can transfigure Love, but you can never transfigure Lust; this last never made an angel, or inspired a true poem, yet.

And so, when all is said and done, the friendly criticism remains the best and wisest. Those who have read Mr. Swinburne's eulogy of his master, and thought it, perhaps, a little strained, may admit, at least, that it was strained, like all eulogy of love, in the right direction. My own abuse was and is, like all hasty contemporary abuse, nothing. Mr. Swinburne's honest praise was, and is, like all honest praise, something. The poet of the "House of Life" is beyond both; but his fame will remain, when all detraction is forgotten, as a golden symbol, *ære perennius*, of much that was best and brightest in the culture of our time.*

---

* I have given the above as my final and revised opinion on a writer to whom I once stood in strong antipathy. The only suspicious thing I know about some of Rossetti's poetry is the facility with which it can be *imitated*. During a recent competition for a prize given by the *Pall Mall Gazette*, a number of sonnets by various hands was contributed, reproducing in a striking manner the manner, or trick, of Rossetti's verbal style and imagery. Generally speaking, I believe, the merit of a style is in proportion to the difficulty of actual reproduction. Great thought in great language cannot well be imitated. Mannerisms of every kind can. The best of Rossetti's work is beyond the re-rendering of the poetaster.—R. B.

THOMAS LOVE PEACOCK.

A PERSONAL REMINISCENCE.

In the neighbourhood of the picturesque village of Chertsey, close to which the Thames winds broad and clear between deep green meadow-flats and quiet woods, still stand the ruins of Newark Abbey. Situated in a lonely field, eight miles from the village, and near to the Weybridge canal, they lie comparatively unknown and little visited; a mill murmurs close at hand, turned by a small fall; and all around stretch the level fields and meadows of green Surrey. Here, at the beginning of the present century, when these ruins stood as now, a young man and maiden, betrothed to each other, were accustomed to meet and exchange their quiet vows; and here, half a century afterwards, a gray-haired old man of seventy, beautiful in his age as the old Goethe, would wander musing summer day after summer day. The lovers had been parted; the maiden had married and died young, while the man had also married and become the father of a household; but that first dream had never been forgotten by one at least of the pair, and that surviving one was Thomas Love Peacock, known to general English readers as the author of "Headlong Hall."

With a constancy and a tenderness which many more famous men would have done well to emulate, he clung to the scene of his first and perhaps his only love: a love innocent, like all true love; and far preferable, to quote his own words, to—

" The waveless calm, the slumber of the dead,

which weighs on the minds of those who have never loved, or never earnestly." Looking on the face of Peacock in his old age, and knowing his secret, well might one remember in emotion the beautiful words of Scribe: " Il faut avoir aimé une fois en sa vie, non pour le moment où l'on aime, car on n'éprouve alors que des tourmens, des regrets, de la jalousie ; mais peu à peu ces tourmens-là deviennent des souvenirs, qui charment notre arrière-saison. Et quand vous verrez la vieillesse douce, facile, et tolérante, vous puissez dire comme Fontenelle—*L'amour a passé par-là!*"

Yes, Love had passed that way, and set on the old man his gracious seal, which no other deity can counterfeit ; so that, looking upon the old man's face, one read of gentleness, high-mindedness, toleration, and perfect chivalry. These may seem odd words to apply to one whom the world knew rather as a retrograde philosopher and satirical pessimist than a lover of human nature, as a scholar rather than a poet, as a country gentleman of the old school rather than a humanitarian of the new ; but they can be justified ; and it may be questioned, moreover, whether he had not learned of the eighteenth century certain modest virtues which the nineteenth century has incontinently forgotten. To children he was gentleness itself, and all children loved him ; and there could be no prettier sight in the world than the picture of him, as I saw him first, and as in my mind's eye I see him now, sitting one summer day, seated on his garden lawn by the river, while a little maiden of sixteen rested on his knees the great quarto *Orlando Innamorato* of Bojardo, and, following with her finger the sun-lit lines, read soft and low, corrected ever and anon by his kind voice, the delicate Italian he loved so well. Who that looked at him, then, could fail to perceive, to quote Lord Houghton's words, "that he had gone through the world with happiness and honour"? But the secret of his beautiful benignity lay deeper. "L'amour a passé par-là!"

While a student in Scotland, I had known him as the friend of Shelley, and had read his delightful works with pleasure and profit; until at last I was prompted to write to him, expecting (I remember) to receive but a cold response from one who, to judge him by his works, was too much of a Timon to care for boy's homage. I was agreeably disappointed. The answer came, not savage like a wrap on the knuckles, but cordial as a hand-shake. Afterwards, when I was weary "climbing up the breaking wave" of London, I thought of my old friend, and determined to seek him out. Mainly with the wish to be near him, I retreated to quiet Chertsey; and thence past Chertsey Bridge, through miles of green fields basking in the summer sun, and through delightful lanes to Lower Halliford, I went on pilgrimage, youth in my limbs, reverence in my heart, a pipe in my mouth, and the tiny Pickering edition of Catullus (a veritable "lepidum libellum," but, alas, far from "novum!") in my waistcoat pocket. And there, at Lower Halliford, I found him as I had described him, seated on his garden lawn in the sun, with the door of his library open behind him, showing such delicious vistas of

shady shelves as would have gladdened his own
Dr. Opimian, and the little maiden reading from the
book upon his knee. Gray-haired and smiling sat the
man of many memories, guiding the utterances of one
who was herself a pretty two-fold link between the
present and the past, being the granddaughter (on the
paternal side) of Leigh Hunt, and also the granddaughter (on the maternal side) of the Williams who
was drowned with Shelley. Could a youthful
student's eyes see any sight fairer?

> "And did you once see Shelley plain,
> And did he stop and speak to you? . . .
> How strange it seems, and new!" *

And this old man had spoken with Shelley, not once,
but a thousand times; and had known well both
Harriett Westbrook and Mary Godwin; and had
cracked jokes with Hobhouse, and chaffed Proctor's
latinity; and had seen, and actually criticised,
Malibran; and had bought "the vasty version of a
new system to perplex the sages,"† when it first came
out, in a bright, new, uncut quarto; and had dined
with Jeremy Bentham; and had smiled at Disraeli,
when, resplendently attired, he stood chatting in
Hookham's with the Countess of Blessington; and
had been face to face with that bland Rhadamanthus,
Chief Justice Eldon; and was, in short, such a living
chronicle of things past and men dead as filled one's
soul with delight and ever-varying wonder. "How
strange it seemed, and new!"

The portrait prefixed to the collected edition of
his works‡ conveys a very good idea of the man as I

---

* Robert Browning.
† Byron's description of Wordsworth's "Excursion."
‡ Peacock's Works, 3 vols. (Bentley, 1875.)

first saw him—a stately old gentleman with hair as white as snow, a keen, merry eye, and a characteristic chin. His dress was plain black, with white neckcloth, and low shoes, and on his head he wore a plaited straw hat. One glance at him was enough to reveal his delightful character, that of his own Dr. Opimian. "His tastes, in fact, were four: a good library, a good dinner, a pleasant garden, and rural walks." This was the man who, as a beautiful boy, had been caught up and kissed by Queen Caroline; who, when he grew up to manhood, had been christened "Greeky Peeky," on account of his acquirement in Greek; and who had been thus described, in a passage I have not seen quoted before, by Shelley, in the "Letter to Maria Gisborne":

> You will see P—, with his mountain Fair *
> Turned into a Flamingo . . .
> When a man marries, dies, or turns Hindoo,
> His best friends hear no more of him; but you
> Will see him and will like him, too, I hope,
> And that snow-white Snowdonian antelope,
> Marched with the cameo-leopard. His fine wit
> Makes such a wound, the knife is lost in it!

Age had mellowed and subdued the "cameo-leopard," but the "fine wit," as I very speedily discovered, was as keen as ever. His life had been passed in comparative peace and retirement. He spoke French with the good old-fashioned English accent, and he had never been to Paris or up the Rhine; Italy he knew not, nor cared to know; and much as he loved the sea, he had sailed it little. His four tastes had kept him well anchored all his life. In his youth he had had a fifth, the Italian Opera, but the long modern performances, and the decadence of the

---

* Peacock's wife.

ballet, had alienated him. He had his "good library," and it *was* a good one—full of books it was a luxury to handle, editions to make a scholar's mouth water, bound completely in the old style in suits as tough as George Fox's suit of leather. The "good dinner" came daily. "He liked to dine well, and withal to dine quickly, and to have quiet friends at his table, with whom he could discuss questions which might afford ample room for pleasant conversation, and none for acrimonious dispute."* In the "pleasant garden" he was sitting with the clear winding Thames below him and his rowing-boat swinging at the garden steps. And the "rural walks" lay all around him, on the quiet river side, through the green woods of Esher, down the scented lanes to Chertsey, by winding turns to Walton and Weybridge—scenes familiar to him since boyhood and hallowed with the footprints of dead relatives and departed friends. For the old man was, so to speak, alone in the world—his wife and best-loved daughters lay asleep in Shepperton churchyard, his son was somewhere abroad, and the cries of the children around him were not those of his own family. His gifted daughter Rosa, who died in her prime, was gone before, but another daughter, not of the flesh, had risen in her place. Many years before, when she was grieving sorely for the loss of a little child, Margaret, his wife had noticed, on Halliford Green, a little girl in its mother's arms, and seeing in it a strange likeness to her own dead child, had coaxed it into her own house, and dressed it in the dead babe's clothes. Peacock, returning from the India House, looked in through the dining-room window, and seeing the child within was almost stunned

---

* "Gryll Grange."

by its resemblance to Margaret. This little girl, Mary Rosewell, had been adopted by the Peacocks; and now, when all the rest were dead, she remained—a bright, loving foster-daughter, whose baptismal name of "Mary" had long ago been sweetened into "May." I cannot describe her better than in Peacock's own words when describing Miss Gryll: "The atmosphere of quiet enjoyment in which she had grown up seemed to have steeped her feelings in its own tranquillity; and still more, the affection which she felt for her foster-father, and the conviction that her departure from his house would be the severest blow that fate could inflict on him, led her to postpone what she knew must be an evil day for him, and might peradventure not be a good one to her." She has never married, but she has fulfilled her woman's mission perfectly, and the final years of Peacock owed much of their tranquil sunshine to her tender and pathetic care.

Knowing Peacock only from his books, I was not prepared to find in him that delightful *bonhomie* which was in reality his most personal characteristic, in old age at least; and when we became acquainted, and read and talked together, I was as much astonished at the sweetness of his disposition as amused and captivated by his quaint erudition. In that green garden, in the lanes of Halliford, on the bright river, in walks and talks such as "brightened the sunshine," I learned to know him, and although he was so much my senior he took pleasure (I am glad to say) in my society, partly because I never worried him with "acrimonious dispute," which he hated above all things.

There was for the moment one dark cloud of misunderstanding between us—a cloud of smoke; for,

like Hans Andersen's parson,* I "smoked a good deal
of tobacco, and bad tobacco," and to Peacock tobacco
was poison. He forgave me, however, on one condition, that I never smoked within five hundred yards
of his house—an arrangement which, I am ashamed
to say, I violated, for well I remember one night
stealthily opening the bedroom window in the house
at Halliford, and "blowing a cloud" out into the
summer night. I am not sure that much of his hate
of tobacco did not arise from his morbid dread of fire.
He would never have any lucifer matches in his house,
save one or two which were jealously kept in a tin
box in the kitchen. Morning after morning he arose
with the sun, lit his own fire in the library, and read
till breakfast, laying in material for talk which flowed
like Hippocrene—as crystal, and as learned! His
chief, almost his only, correspondent was Lord
Broughton, who had been his friend through life.
The two old gentlemen interchanged letters and
verses, and capped quotations, and doubtless felt like
two antediluvian mammoths left stranded, and yet
living after the Deluge—that Deluge being typified
to them by the submersion of Whig and Tory in one
wild wave of Progress, and the long career of Lord
Brougham as a sort of political Noah. The old landmarks of society were obliterated. Lord Byron was
a dim memory, and the stage-coach was a dream.
The poetry of Nature had triumphed, and the poetry
of Art had died. Germany had a literature, and it
was part of polite education to know German. Beards
were worn. Rotten boroughs were no more. The
Times, like a colossal Podsnap, dominated journalism,
but the *Daily Telegraph* was stirring the souls of

---

* *At være eller ikke at være.*

tradesmen to the sublime knowledge of Lemprière's Dictionary and Bohn's "Index of Quotations." Special correspondents were invented, competitive examination was consecrating mediocrity, and a considerable number of Englishmen drank bad champagne. What was left for an old scholar, but, like the Hudibrastic Mirror of Knighthood,

> To cheer himself with ends of verse,
> And saying of philosophers!

For the rest, the world was in a bad way; best keep apart, and let it wag. ψῦξον τὸν οἶνον, Δωρι! Quaff a cool cup in the green shade, and drink confusion to Lord Michin Mallecho and the last Reform Bill!

It must be conceded at once that Peacock was no friend to modern progress—the cant of it, hoarsely roared from the throats of journalistic Jews and political Merry Andrews, had sickened him; and he was not for one moment prepared to admit that the world was one whit wiser and happier than before the advent of the steam-engine. The pessimism which appears everywhere in his books was the daily theme of his talk; but to understand it rightly we must remember it was purely *satiric*—that, in truth, Peacock abused human nature because he loved it. Genial at heart as Thackeray, he delighted to condemn man and society in the abstract. Hence much of his writing must be read between the lines. In the clever little sketch of Peacock, prefixed to the new edition of the works, Lord Houghton errs to some extent in trying to construct Peacock out of his books.* The "unreasoning animosity" Lord

---

* " In the same spirit he clung to the old religious ideas that haunted all early Roman history, and indeed went far into the Empire, and thus *he liked to read Livy, and did not like to read Niebuhr.*"—LORD HOUGHTON'S PREFACE. The words in italics

Houghton speaks of was purely ironic. For example, so far from having "an indiscriminate repugnance to Scotland and to everything Scotch," he was very fond of Scotchmen, having many correspondents among them; but he could not spare them for all that, any more than Thackeray could spare the Irish, whom he loved with all his heart. When, in "Gryll Grange," he makes Dr. Opimian say of the Americans: "I have no wish to expedite communication with them. If we could apply the power of electric repulsion to preserve us from ever hearing any more of them, I should think we had *for once* derived a benefit from science!"—he is merely, in a mood of what Lord Houghton felicitously called "intellectual gaiety," in an after-dinner mood, expressing a comic prejudice with no deep root in reason. The animosity is Aristophanic. No one reverenced Socrates more than his unmerciful "chaffer," and no man knew the benefit of science better than Peacock. He tried to shut out humanity, but he felt it very intensely. He could fain have resembled the gods of Epicurus—thinking, feeling nothing, as Cicero expresses it, but "Mihi pulchre est," and "Ego beatus sum"—but in reality, he felt for human suffering very acutely. He would fain have had the world one vast Maypole, with all humanity dancing round it, or one mighty Christmas-tree, with all humanity waiting to get a prize from it. Every year, on May Day, he crowned a little May Queen—generally one of his grandchildren—as Queen of the May, and all the little children of the village flocked in to her with garlands,

---

are put by Peacock into the mouth of a young lady in "Gryll Grange," and by no means express his own sentiments; indeed, Niebuhr was regarded by him with the highest admiration, as having almost unique intuition.

to be rewarded, as the case might be, with a bright new penny or a silver coin. He loved the old times for their old customs, and he loved the old customs because they made men gentle and children glad. "He had no fancy," he said, "for living in an express train; he liked to go quietly through life, and to see all that lay in his way." His life, indeed, might be described as one long rural walk, in company with Dr. Opimian, occasionally diversified by a visit to London, and a night at the Italian Opera. He belonged, as Lord Houghton says, "to the eighteenth century," and I may add that he had every one of its virtues without one of its vices.

His literary tastes were very interesting; although they, too, belonged to the eighteenth century. His favourite classical authors were Aristophanes and Cicero. His knowledge of the latter was extraordinary; there was scarcely a passage of any force which he had not by heart. As to Aristophanes, he simply revelled in that quaint satire so akin to the keen writings of his own modern Muse. At a time when he was reading "Pickwick," and delighting in its extravagances, he cried characteristically, with a delicious twinkle of his eye, at dinner, "Dickens is very comic, but—not *so* comic as Aristophanes!" His mind was not so much attracted by the Greek tragedians, though of course he knew them well, as by the comic writers and the satirists; and, on the whole, I fancy he preferred Euripides to Sophocles, for the very reasons which make critics like him less. His sympathies, indeed, were less with the grand, the terrible, and the sublimely pathetic, than with the brilliant, the exquisite, and the delicately artistic. Comedy fascinated him more than Tragedy awed him. Although he was a profound student of the mystical hymns of Orpheus, he read them more as a scholar than as a mystic. It must be admitted, moreover, that his mind was in itself a terrible "thesaurus eroticus," and there was to be found in it many a Petronian quibble and Catullian *double entendre* not to be discovered in Rambach. To the last he loved Petronius—a writer who has never yet received justice for his marvellous picture-painting and delicate graces of diction, and who can be vindicated to the moralist far more easily than Rabelais. Rabelais he loved too, of course; who does not? Like Swift, he preferred Plautus to Terence:

> Despite what schoolmasters have taught us,
> I have a great respect for Plautus,
> And think our boys may gather *there* hence
> More wit and wisdom than from Terence!

From these tastes of his in the classical direction, the reader may readily guess what authors and what books he selected from more modern fields. It will readily be understood that he was partial to Molière, to Voltaire's satirical works, and to the dramatists of the Restoration; that he admired "Sir Roger de Coverley" and the *Spectator*, and had by heart "Clever Tom Clinch" and the other sardonic verses of Dean Swift; and that he did *not* care much for the poetic transcendentalism of Coleridge. He esteemed the poetry of Milton, but far preferred Milton's prose. At the time I knew him, he could repeat by heart nearly the whole of Redi's "Bacchus in Tuscany"— a bibulous masterpiece which had been admirably translated by Leigh Hunt. Of modern non-poetical works, I should say his three favourites were Monboddo's "Ancient Metaphysics," Drummond's "Academical Questions," and Horne Tooke's "Diversions of Purley"; to which may be added, with a reservation, Harris's "Hermes." He was always very fond of philosophic philology, and one of the last works of his life was to issue to his private friends a new interpretation of the *Aelia Lælia Crispis*.

But the above brief catalogue of his favourites affords no glimpse of his true attainment. In reality he had not read so many books as many less masterly men; but his peculiarity was that he had so read and re-read his favourite ones that he had completely attained the interior of them. Thoreau used to say that the Bible and Hafiz were books enough for any one man's lifetime; and certainly, a lifetime might be spent on the study of the Bible alone. Peacock had some dozen authors virtually by heart,—and thus, the polyglott of his delightful talk was really surprising. He never forgave a false quantity; Browning's Avat*ar*, in "Waring," would have driven him into a fever, and, in speaking of America, he never forgot the fact that its most popular poet, at that time, had committed the false Latin of "Excelsior."* His tastes in poetry may be presumed; but I ought to mention to his honour that he was one of the few early lovers of Wordsworth, despite his personal dislike to the Lake School. He was never, till the day of his death, quite *en rapport* with Shelley's moonshine-genius; he far preferred such a solid, flesh and blood poet as Burns, and of Burns' poems his favourite was "Tam o' Shanter;" and he had little or no appreciation for John Keats Indeed, he never passed the portico of the green little

---

* Is it possible that Peacock himself is responsible for the translation in the verses to "Gryll Grange" of a passage from the Metamorphoses of Apuleius; wherein "fluctibus educata" is rendered by "the educated in the waves," etc.? There are several errors in the new edition, not to speak of the many unaccentuated Greek quotations.

Temple erected by Keats to Diana, remembering with indignation the barbarous fancies consecrated therein ; for he could prove by a hundred quotations that the sleep of Endymion was eternal, whereas in the modern poem the Latmian shepherd is for ever capering up and down the earth and ocean like the German chaser of shadows.* The ancient conception, as briefly incorporated by Cicero in the passage where Diana is described as watching for ever the sleep of " her beloved Endymion," is certainly very lovely. And here I may remark incidentally that the influence of Peacock on the lurid genius of Shelley, though doubtless chilling on occasion, was certainly beneficial and in the interest of Art. He checked a thousand extravagances, and helped to form Shelley's later and more massive style as exemplified in such pieces as " Alastor, or the Spirit of Solitude." Peacock sugggested the title for this poem, and was amused to the day of his death by the fact that the public, and even the critics, persisted in assuming Alastor to be the name of the hero of the poem, whereas the Greek word Ἀλάστωρ signifies an evil genius, and the evil genius depicted in the poem is the Spirit of Solitude.

Nothing can be more gentle, more guarded, than Peacock's printed account of Shelley. His private

---

* For similar reasons, he was perpetually wroth with Byron. He gives one frightful instance of incongruity in the notes to "Nightmare Abbey."—" In Manfred, the great Alastor, or Κακος Δαιμων, of Greece is hailed king of the world by the Nemesis of Greece, in concert with three of the Scandinavian Valkyriœ, under the name of the Destinies ; the astrological spirits of the alchemysts of the middle ages ; an elemental witch, transplanted from Denmark to the Alps ; and a chorus of Dr. Faustus's devils, who came in at the last act for a soul. It is difficult to conceive where this heterogeneous mythological company could have met originally, except at a *table d'hôte*, like the six kings in " Candide."—" Nightmare Abbey," p. 332, vol. i. of collected edition.

conversation on the subject was, of course, very different. Two subjects he did not refer to in his articles may safely be mentioned now—Shelley's violent fits of passion, and the difficulty Peacock found in keeping on friendly terms with Mary Godwin. Many were the anecdotes he told with a twinkling eye, of Shelley's comic outbursts. One I particularly remember. When the two friends were rowing one day on the Thames, as it was their constant custom to do, they came into collision with a flat-bottomed boat moored in the centre of the stream, in which an old tradesman and his wife were contentedly seated, bottom-fishing. Remonstrances and strong expressions from the "lady" ensued; and, as the friends pulled away from the scene of the encounter, Shelley shrieked out, in his peculiarly unmusical voice, "There's an old woman angling for unfortunate fishes, as the Devil will angle for her soul in H——!" As for Mary Godwin, I fancy Peacock never really liked her; and this fact, of course, must be weighed in estimating his opinions relative to her and her predecessors. On one occasion, at least, he refused to enter Shelley's house while "she was in it," and was only constrained to do so by an entreaty from Mary herself. On the whole he is just, even generous, to her memory; but he certainly preferred Harriett, if only on the ground of her surpassing beauty.

It is well known that Peacock portrayed Shelley in the "Scythrop" of "Nightmare Abbey," and it is pleasant to remember that Shelley admitted the truth of the portrait, and was amused by it. Specially pointed was the passage wherein Scythrop, who loves two young ladies at once, tells his distracted father that he will commit suicide:—There is no doubt that if Shelley could have kept *both* Harriett and Mary he would have been happy; for he, more than most men, needed the triple wifehood so amusingly described in " Realmah." Seriously speaking, the picture of the man Shelley, as depicted by Peacock, directly in his " Memorials," and indirectly in the novel, is far more lovable and fascinating than the "divine" characterless humanitarian whom hero-worshippers love to paint.

I do not propose to attempt, on the present occasion, any estimate of Peacock's novels, although I believe they are entitled to a far higher place in literature than Lord Houghton seems inclined to give them; but they are full of opinions which he expressed even more admirably in conversation. His detestation of the literary class lasted until the end. "The understanding of literary people," he affirmed, "is exalted, not so much by the love of truth and virtue, as by arrogance and self-sufficiency; and there is, perhaps, less disinterestedness, less liberality, less general benevolence, and more envy, hatred, and uncharitableness among them, than among any other description of men." In his young days he had cut and slashed at his brethren, especially at the Lake Poets, whom he appreciated very much notwithstanding. Latterly he was wont to affirm, as in " Gryll Grange," that "Shakespeare never makes a flower blossom out of season, and Wordsworth, Coleridge, and Southey are true to nature in this *and in all other respects.*" He hated Moore as much as he loved Burns. " Moore's imagery," he makes Mr. MacBorrowdale say, " is all false. Here is a highly applauded stanza :

> " The night dew of heaven, though in silence it weeps,
> Shall brighten with verdure the sod where he sleeps ;
> And the tear that we shed, though in secret it rolls,
> Shall long keep his memory green in our souls.

But it will not bear analysis. The dew is the cause of the verdure, but the tear is not the cause of the memory—the memory is the cause of the tear." I am sorry to say he could never be persuaded to appreciate Tennyson. Specially offensive to him was the laureate's picture of Cleopatra as " a queen with swarthy cheeks and bold black eyes, brow-bound with burning gold." "Thus," he writes, "one of our most popular poets describes Cleopatra ; and one of our most popular artists has illustrated the description by a portrait of a hideous grinning Ethiop . . . . Cleopatra was a Greek, the daughter of Ptolemy Auletes and a lady of Pontus. The Ptolemies were Greeks, and whoever will look at their genealogy, their medals, and their coins, will see how carefully they kept their pure Greek blood uncontaminated by African intermixture. Think of this description and this picture applied to one who, Dio says—and all antiquity confirms him—was 'the most superlatively beautiful of women, splendid to see, and delightful to hear.'*. For she was eminently accomplished : she spoke many languages with grace and facility. Her mind was as wonderful as her personal beauty. There is not a shadow of intellectual expression in that horrible portrait." For the rest, the Cleopatra of Shakespeare delighted him, as having not one feature in common with that other abominable "Queen of Bembo."

He was a great believer in Greek painting, with its total absence of perspective ; nevertheless, he abhorred pre-Raphaelism, though it loves perspective as little as the Greeks ! But in fact, he was generally

---

* Περικαλλεστάτη γυναικῶν . . . λαμπρά τε ἰδεῖν καὶ ἀκουσθῆναι οὖσα.—DIO. xlii. 34.

inclined to cry with his own Gryllus, in " Aristophanes in London " :

"—All the novelties I yet have seen,
Seem changes for the worse."

New schools of painting and poetry attracted him as little as new science. One of his prejudices was amusing in the extreme, and it is foreshadowed, like so many of his latter peculiarities, in " Gryll Grange." Great as was his knowledge of Greek, Latin, Italian, and French—which Horne Tooke calls "the usual bounds of a scholar's acquisition"—and considerable as was his interest in Goethe and the Weimar circle, he disliked everything German, and never attempted to learn that wonderful language, which may be said to be the key to the golden chamber of modern poetry and philosophy. Mr. Falconer observes in " Gryll Grange," quoting a dictum of Porson's, that " Life is too short to learn German ; meaning, I apprehend, not that it is too difficult to be acquired within the ordinary space of life, but that there is nothing in it to compensate for the portion of life bestowed in its acquirement, however little that may be!" He used to quote with a chuckle Porson's doggerel:

"The Germans in Greek
Are sadly to seek ;
Save only Hermann,
And Hermann's a German ! "

It is strange that he was not curious in this direction, for his literary appetite was unbounded. When we first met, and when he was approaching his eightieth year, he was studying Spanish, in order to read the *Autos* and other masterpieces of Calderon. Conceive the literary vitality, in an old man of that age, which would urge him on to the study of a tongue almost new to him! The task was a comparatively easy one, of course, from his consummate knowledge of other kindred tongues, but it still possessed difficulties enough to daunt a less earnest lover of learning. His cry for more light, like that of the old Goethe, was heard till the very last.

As I write of him, and look again upon the photograph of his genial features, I am reminded, by a certain general resemblance to the portraits of Thackeray, that the author of "Vanity Fair" was one of his greatest admirers, and wrote to him several pleasant letters, in one of which, which I saw, he promised to pay a long visit to Lower Halliford. I do not think the visit was ever paid; but it is pleasant to think of those two men in company, for they possessed many characteristics in common. What evenings there would have been in the old house at Halliford if Thackeray had come! What capping of quotations, what mellow music of eighteenth century voices, while these two kindred spirits drank their after-dinner wine! For Thackeray's heart was with the eighteenth century too; and either one or the other of these two white-headed "old boys" would have been quite at home, if suddenly translated back in time, and set down by Temple Bar with the Dean of St. Patrick's, or with Pope in his villa at Twickenham, or in a Whitefriars hostelry with Dick Steele. On such an evening, when the old heart was warm with wine, and after Thackeray, perhaps, had trolled out to his host's delight the ballad of "Little Billee," or "Peg of Linavaddy," I can conceive the author of "Gryll Grange" reciting, in that rich, mellow voice of his, his own lovely verses called "Love and Age:"

> I played with you 'mid cowslips blowing,
>   When I was six and you were four;
> When garlands weaving, flower-balls throwing,
>   Were pleasures soon to please no more.

Through groves and meads, o'er grass and heather,
　　With little playmates, to and fro,
We wandered hand in hand together;
　　But that was sixty years ago.

You grew a lovely roseate maiden,
　　And still our early love was strong;
Still with no care our days were laden,
　　They glided joyously along;
And I did love you very dearly,
　　How dearly words want power to show;
I thought your heart was touched as nearly;
　　But that was fifty years ago.

Then other lovers came around you,
　　Your beauty grew from year to year;
And many a splendid circle found you
　　The centre of its glittering sphere.
I saw you then, first vows forsaking,
　　On rank and wealth your hand bestow;
Oh, then I thought my heart was breaking,—
　　But that was forty years ago.

And I lived on, to wed another:
　　No cause she gave me to repine;
And when I heard you were a mother,
　　I did not wish the children mine.
My own young flock, in fair progression,
　　Made up a pleasant Christmas row:
My joy in them was past expression,—
　　But that was thirty years ago.

You grew a matron plump and comely,
　　You dwelt in fashion's brightest blaze;
My earthly lot was far more homely;
　　But I too had my festal days.
No merrier eyes have ever glistened
　　Around the hearthstone's wintry glow,
Than when my youngest child was christened,—
　　But that was twenty years ago.

Time passed. My eldest girl was married,
　　And I am now a grandsire gray;
One pet of four years old I've carried
　　Among the wild-flowered meads to play.
In our old fields of childish pleasure,
　　Where now, as then, the cowslips blow,
She fills her baskets ample measure,—
　　And that is not ten years ago.

> But though first love's impassioned blindness
>   Has passed away in colder light,
> I still have thought of you with kindness,
>   And shall do, till our last good-night.
> The ever-rolling silent hours
>   Will bring a time we shall not know,
> When our young days of gathering flowers
>   Will be a hundred years ago.

And we know that this was the very sort of music to fill the great guest's eyes with tears, though it spoke only, like his more sad prose muse, of "Vanity, Vanity!" Thackeray touched the same note repeatedly—it was an habitual one with him—but he never touched it more delicately, or with a truer pathos. A little longer, and both were at rest, the veteran worn out with years, and the great good man struck down in the prime of his powers.

Ignorant of the world as it is, circumscribed in his vision like all students of books, narrowed to the knowledge of a good library and a few green walks, thus Thomas Peacock passed away. He lived to see the curious theories which he developed so wonderfully in "Melincourt," and to many of which he was indebted to Lord Monboddo, assuming an importance in the history of science which fairly startled him. The generalisations made by quidnuncs from Darwin's facts, and which, rather than Darwin's own teaching, constitute "Darwinism," were sufficiently portentous to fill an eighteenth century satirist with comic wonder. What Peacock's own views were as to the origin and destiny of Man, I cannot tell: on such subjects he was reticent; but his sympathies were with the antique world, and I dare say he would not have discountenanced a proposal once entertained by Mr. Ruskin, to revive the worship of Diana. At any rate, he was quite pagan enough to astonish conventional people. Miss Nichols, in her excellent and thoroughly sympathetic little sketch of her grandfather, prefixed to the collected works, tells a striking anecdote illustrative of his pleasant paganism. Shortly before his death, a fire broke out in the roof of his bedroom, and he was taken to the library, which lay at the other end of the house. "At one time it was feared the fire was gaining ground, and that it would be needful to move him into one of the houses of the neighbourhood, but he refused to move. The curate, who came kindly to beg my grandfather to take shelter in his house, received rather a rough and startling reception, for in answer to the invitation, my grandfather exclaimed with great warmth and energy, 'By the immortal gods, I will not move!'"

Smile as we may at the formality and pedantry of the eighteenth century, there were giants in those days; and Peacock resembled them in intellectual stature. His books will live, if only for their touches of quaint erudition; but they abound in delicious little pictures, such as that of Mr. Falconer and his seven Vestal attendants in "Gryll Grange," or those of Coleridge and Shelley in "Nightmare Abbey." Sir Oran Haut-ton is perfect, a masterpiece of characterisation, and as for Dr. Opimian, he is as sure of immortality as "my Uncle Toby" himself. But the true glory of Peacock was his delicious personality. To have known and spoken with such a man, is in itself part of a liberal education. I shall not soon forget that we sipped "Falernian" together, though the "Falernian" was no stronger than May Rosewell's cowslip-wine. Circumstances called me back to Scotland, and during the short period preceding his decease, we did not meet. Only a few days before his death he dreamed of his "dear Fanny," the maiden who had been his first love, and for weeks together she came to him in his sleep, gently smiling. Thus the Immortal Ones, call them by what names we may, were good to him until the very end; and while that first and last dream was bright within him, he sank to rest. Let us fancy that, though life parted him from his first love, in death they were not divided; nor shall be, even when—

> The ever-rolling silent hours
>   Have brought a time they do not know,
> When their young days of gathering flowers
>   Will be a hundred years ago!

SYDNEY DOBELL,
AND
THE "SPASMODIC SCHOOL."

A SOUVENIR.

IN the winter of 1860, as I sat alone, writing, in what David Gray described as the "dear old ghastly bankrupt garret at No. 66," Lucinda from the kitchen came panting upstairs with a card, on which was inscribed the name of " Sydney Dobell ; " and in less than five minutes afterwards I was conversing eagerly, and face to face, with a man who had been my first friend and truest helper in the great world of letters. It was our first meeting. David Gray, whom Dobell had assisted with a caressing and angelic patience, never knew him at all, but was at that very moment lying sick to death in the little cottage at Merkland, pining and hoping against hope for such a meeting. "How about Dobell?" he wrote a little later, in answer to my announcement of the visit. "Did your mind of itself, or even against itself, recognise through the clothes *a man—a poet?* Has he the modesty and make-himself-at-home manner of Milnes?" What answer I gave to these eager inquiries I do not remember, nor would it be worth recording, for I myself at that time was only a boy, with little or no experience of things and men. But even now, across the space of dull and sorrowful years, comes the vision of as sweet and shining a face as ever brought joy and comfort this side of the grave; of a voice musical and low, "excellent" in all its tones as the voice of the tenderest woman; of manners at once manly and caressing, bashful and yet bold, with a touch of piteous gentleness which told a sad tale of feeble physical powers and the tortured sense of bodily despair.

I saw him once or twice afterwards, and had a glimpse of that fellow-sufferer, his wife. He was staying with some friends on the hills of Hampstead, and thither I trudged to meet him, and to listen to his sparkling poetic speech. I recall now, with a curious sense of pain, that my strongest feeling concerning him, at that time, was a feeling of wonder at the gossamer-like frailness of his physique and the almost morbid refinement of his conversation. These two characteristics, which would be ill comprehended by a boy in the rude flush of health and hope, and with a certain audacity of physical well-being, struck me strangely then, and came back upon my heart with terrible meaning now. Combined with this feeling of wonder and pity was blended, of necessity, one of fervent gratitude. Some little time previous to our first meeting, I had come, a literary adventurer, to London; with no capital but a sublime self-assurance which it has taken many long years to tame into a certain obedience and acquiescence. About the same time, David Gray had also set foot in the great City. And Sydney Dobell had helped us both, as no other living man could or would. For poor Gray's wild yet gentle dreams, and for my coarser and less conciliatory ambition, he had nothing but words of wisdom and gentle remonstrance. None of our folly daunted him. He wrote, with the heart of an angel, letters which might have tamed the madness in the heart of a devil. He helped, he warned, he watched us, with unwearying care. In the midst of his own solemn sorrows, which we so little understood, he found heart of grace to sympathise with our wild struggles for the unattainable. At a period when writing was a torture to him, he devoted hours of correspondence to the guidance and instruction of two fellow-creatures he had never seen. To receive one of his gracious and elaborate epistles, finished with the painful care which this lordly martyr bestowed on the most trifling thing he did, was to be in communication with a spirit standing on the very heights of life. I, at least, little comprehended the blessing then. But it came, with perfect consecration, on David Gray's dying bed; it made his last days blissful, and it helped to close his eyes in peace.

No one who knew Sydney Dobell, no one who had ever so brief a glimpse of him, can read without tears the simple and beautiful Memorials, now just published, of his gracious, quiet, and uneventful life. Predestined to physical martyrdom, he walked the earth for fifty years, at the bidding of what to our imperfect vision seems a pitiless and inscrutable Destiny. Why this divinely gifted being, whose soul seemed all goodness, and whose highest song would have been an inestimable gain to humanity, should have been struck down again and again by blows so cruel, is a question which pricks the very core of that tormenting conscience which is in us all. Ill-luck dogged his footsteps; sickness encamped wherever he found a home. His very goodness and gentleness seemed at times his bane. At an age when other men are revelling in mere existence he was being taught that mere existence is torture. We have read of Christian martyrs, of all the fires through which they passed; but surely not one of them ever fought with such tormenting flames as did this patient poet, whose hourly cry was of the kindness and goodness of God. From first to last, no word of anger, no utterance of fierce arraignment, passed his lips.

> The best of men
> That e'er wore earth about him was a sufferer—
> The first true Gentleman that ever lived.

And like that "best of men," Sydney Dobell troubled himself to make no complaint, but took the cup of sorrow and drained it to the bitter dregs. Such a record of such a life stops the cry on the very lips of blasphemy, and makes us ask ourselves if that life did not possess, direct from God, some benediction, some comfort unknown to *us*. So it must have been. "Looking up," as a writer * on the subject has beautifully put it, "he saw the heavens opened." These pathetic glimpses seemed comfort enough.

Doubtless to some readers of this book the very name of Sydney Dobell is unfamiliar. To all students of modern poetry it is of course more or less known, as that of one of the chief leaders of the school of verse known by its enemies as "the Spasmodic." With Philip James Bailey and Alexander Smith, Dobell reigned for a lustrum, to the great wonder and confusion of honest folk, who pinned their faith on Tennyson's "Gardener's Daughter" and Longfellow's "Psalm of Life." His day of reign was that of Gilfillan's "Literary Portraits" and

---

* Matthew Browne, in the *Contemporary Review*.

of the lurid apparition, Stanjan Bigg; of the marvellous monologue, and the invocation without an end; of the resurrection of a Drama which had never lived, to hold high jinks and feasting with a literary Mycerinus who was about to die. It was a period of poetic incandescence; new suns, not yet spherical, whirling out hourly before the public gaze, and vanishing instantly into space, to live on, however, in the dusky chronology of the poetic astronomer, Gilfillan. The day passed, the school vanished. Where is the school now?

> Where are the snows of yester-year?

Yet they who underrate that school know little what real poetry is. It was a chaos, granted; but a chaos capable, under certain conditions, of being shaped into such creations as would put to shame many makers of much of our modern verse. As it is, we may discover in the writings of Sydney Dobell and his circle solid lumps of pure poetic ore, of a quality scarcely discoverable in modern literature this side of the Elizabethan period.

Sydney Dobell was born at Cranbrook, in Kent, on April 5, 1824. Both on the paternal and maternal side he was descended from people remarkable for their Christian virtues and strong religious instincts; and from his earliest years he was regarded by his parents as having "a special and even apostolic mission." The story of his child-life, indeed, is one of those sad records of unnatural precocity, caused by a system of early forcing, which have of late years become tolerably familiar to the public. He seems never to have been strong, and his naturally feeble constitution was undermined by habits of introspection. It is painfully touching now to read the extracts from his father's note-book, full of a quaint Puritan simplicity, and an over-mastering spiritual faith. Here is one:

> I used frequently to talk to him of how delightful and blessed it would be if any child would resolve to live as pure, virtuous, and holy a life, as dedicated to the will and service of God, as Jesus. I used to say to him that if one could ever be found again who was spotless and holy, it was with me a pleasing speculation and hope that such a character might even in this life, be called as a special instrument of our Heavenly Father for some great purpose with His Church, or with the Jews.

The seed thus sown by the zealous parent bore fruit afterwards in a disposition of peculiar sweetness, yet ever conscious of the prerogatives and prejudices of a Christian warrior. Out of the many who are called Sydney Dobell believed himself specially chosen, if not to fulfil any divine mission "with the Church or with the Jews," at least to preach and sing in the God-given mantle of fire which men call genius. In his leading works, but especially in "Balder," he preached genius-worship; of all forms of hero-worship, devised by students of German folios, the most hopeless and the most hope-destroying. Thenceforward isolation became a habit, introspection an intellectual duty. With all his love for his fellow-men, and all his deep sympathy with modern progress, he lacked to the end a certain literary robustness, which only comes to a man made fully conscious that Art and Literature are not Life itself, but only Life's humble handmaids. He was too constantly overshadowed with his mission. Fortunately, however, that very mission became his only solace and comfort when his days of literary martyrdom came. He went to the stake of criticism with a smile on his face, almost disarming his torturers and executioners.

When Sydney was three years old his father failed in business as a hide merchant, and, removing to London, started as a wine merchant. "About this time," says the biographer, "Sydney was described as of very astonishing understanding, as preferring mental diversion to eating and drinking, and very inventive with tales." Strange moods of sorrow and self-pity began to trouble his life at the age of four. At eight, it was recorded of him that he " had never been known to tell an untruth." From seven years of age he imitated the paternal habit, and used "little pocket-books" to note down his ideas, his bits of acquired knowledge, his simple questions on spiritual subjects. For example: " Report of the Controversy of Porter and Bagot. Mr. Porter maintains that Jesus Christ lived in heaven with God before the beginning of the world." At the age of ten, he was an omnivorous reader, and the habit of verse-writing was growing steadily upon him. I know nothing more pitiful in literature than the story of his precocity, in all its cruel and touching details. At twelve years of age he was sufficiently matured to fall in love, the object of his passion being Emily Fordham, the lady who only nine years afterwards became his wife. By this time his father had removed to Cheltenham, and had set up in business *there*. Sydney and the rest of the children still remained at home, and thus missed all the invigorating influences of a public school; for the father belonged to the sect of Separatists which holds as cardinal the doctrine of avoiding those who hold adverse, or different, religious views.

The account of that dreary life of drudgery and over-work at Cheltenham may be sadly passed over; it is a life not good to think of, and its few gleams of sunshine are too faint and feeble to detain the reader long. From the date of his removal to Cheltenham he acted as his father's clerk. The account of the period extending from his twelfth year to the date of his marriage is one of hard, uncongenial toil, varied by scripture-readings of doubtful edification, and a passion morbid and almost pedantic in the old-fashioned quaintness of its moods. The biographer's record may form, as we are told, "a one-sided and painful picture," but we suspect that it is a true one, truer, that is to say, than the idea in its author's memory of "light, buoyant, various, and vigorous activity." The truth is, the parents of the poet blundered in blindness, a blindness chiefly due to their remarkable religious belief. His father especially, despite all his kindness of heart, was strenuous to the verge of bigotry. One can scarcely remark without a smile the inconsistency with which one who was "a publican," and by profession a vendor of convivial and intoxicating liquors, held aloof from the non-elect among his fellow-creatures. "Business is not brisk," he wrote; "I can't account for it, except, as usual, in our retired life and habits." The idea of a sad-eyed Separatist dealing in fiery ports and sherries, shutting out the world and yet lamenting when "business was not brisk," is one of those grim, cruel, heart-breaking jokes, in which Humanity is so rich, and of which the pathetic art of the humourist offers the only bearable solution.

At the age of twenty, Sydney Dobell was married to an invalid like himself, and one like himself of a strong Puritan bias. The humourist must help us again, if we are to escape a certain feeling of nausea at the details of this courtship and union, with its odd glimpses of personal yearning, its fervent sense of the "mission," and its dreary scraps from the Old Testament. The young couple settled down together in a little house at Cheltenham; and though for a time they avoided all society and still adhered to the tenets of the elect, this was the beginning of a broader and a healthier life. All might perhaps have been well, and the poet have cast quite away the cloud of his early training, but for one of those cruel accidents which make life an inscrutable puzzle. Just as Sydney Dobell was beginning to live, just as his mind was growing more robust, and his powers more coherent and peaceful, he was struck by rheumatic fever, caught during a temporary removal to a Devonshire farmhouse. As if that were not enough, his wife, always frail, broke down almost at the same time. From that time forward, the poet and his wife were fellow-sufferers, each watching by turns over the attacks of the other. It may be said without exaggeration, that neither enjoyed one day of thoroughly buoyant physical health. Still, they had a certain pensive happiness, relieved in the husband's case by bursts of hectic excitement.

By this time, when Dobell was four-and-twenty years of age, the great wave of '48 had risen and fallen, and its influence was still felt in the hearts of men. It was a time of revolutions, moral as well as political. Dobell, like many another, felt the earth tremble under him; watched and listened, as if for the signs of a second advent. Then, like others, he looked across France, towards Italy. Thus the "Roman" was planned; thus he began to write for the journals of advanced opinion. He had now a wine business of his own, and had a pleasant country house on the Cotswold Hills. Having published a portion of the "Roman" in *Tait's Magazine*, he was led to

o

correspond with the then Aristarchus of the poetic firmament, the Rev. George Gilfillan. Gilfillan roundly hailed him as a poetic genius, and he, not ungrateful, wrote : " If in after years I should ever be called ' Poet,' you will know that my success is, in some sort, your work." Shortly after this, he went to London and interviewed Mr. Carlyle. " We had a tough argument," he wrote to Gilfillan, "whether it were better to have learned to make shoes or to have written ' Sartor Resartus.' " At the beginning of 1850 he published the " Roman." This was his first great literary performance, and it was tolerably successful : that is to say, it received a good deal of praise from the newspapers, and circulated in small editions among the general public.

The subject of this dramatic poem was Italian liberty, and the work is full of the genius and prophecy of 1848. The leading character is one Vittorio Santo, a missionary of freedom, who (to quote the author's own argument) " has gone out disguised as a monk to preach the cause of Italy, the overthrow of the Austrian domination, and the restoration of a great Roman Republic." Santo, in the course of the poem, delivers a series of splendid and almost prophetic sermons on the heroic life and the great heroic cause. As an example of Dobell's earlier and more rhetorical manner, I will transcribe the following powerful lines :

> I pray you listen how I loved my mother,
> And you will weep with me. She loved me, nurst me,
> And fed my soul with light. Morning and even
> Praying, I sent that soul into her eyes,
> And knew what heaven was, though I was a child.
> I grew in stature, and she grew in goodness.
> I was a grave child ; looking on her taught me
> To love the beautiful : and I had thoughts
> Of Paradise, when other men have hardly

Looked out of doors on earth. (Alas! alas!
That I have also learned to look on earth
When other men see heaven.) I toiled, but even
As I became more holy, she seemed holier;
Even as when climbing mountain-tops the sky
Grows ampler, higher, purer as ye rise.
Let me believe no more. No, do not ask me
How I repaid my mother. O thou saint,
That lookest on me day and night from heaven,
And smilest. I have given thee tears for tears,
Anguish for anguish, woe for woe. Forgive me
If in the spirit of ineffable penance
In words I waken up the guilt that sleeps,
Let not the sound afflict thine heaven, or colour
That pale, tear-blotted record which the angels
Keep of my sins. We left her. I and all
The brothers that her milk had fed. We left her—
And strange dark robbers with unwonted names
Abused her! bound her! pillaged her! profaned her!
Bound her clasped hands, and gagged the trembling lips
That prayed for her lost children. And we stood,
And she knelt to us, and we saw her kneel,
And looked upon her coldly and denied her.

* * * * *

You are my brothers. And my mother was
Yours. And each man amongst you day by day
Takes bowing, the same price that sold my mother,
And does not blush. Her name is Rome. Look around
And see those features which the sun himself
Can hardly leave for fondness. Look upon
Her mountain bosom, where the very sky
Beholds with passion; and with the last proud
Imperial sorrow of dejected empire
She wraps the purple round her outraged breast,
And even in fetters cannot be a slave.
Look on the world's best glory and worst shame.

The "Roman" is full of this kind of fervour, and is maintained throughout at a fine temperature of poetic eloquence. Its effect on the ardent youth of its generation must have been considerable. Perhaps now, when the stormy sea of Italian politics has settled down, it may be lawful to ask oneself how much reality there was in the battle-songs and poems that accompanied or preluded the tempest. It is quite conceivable, at least, that a man may sing very wildly about "Italy" and "Rome" and "Freedom" without any definite idea of what he means, and without any particular feeling for human nature in the concrete. This was not the case with Dobell; every syllable of his stately song came right out of his heart. For this Christian warrior, like many another, was just a little too fond of appeals to the sword; just a little too apt to pose as "an Englishman" and a lover of freedom. He who began with sonorous cadence of the "Roman" wrote, in his latter moods, the wild piece of gabble called "England's Day." The "Roman," however, remains a fine and fervid poem, worthy of thrice the fame it is ever likely to receive. What Mazzini wrote of it in 1851 may fully be remembered at this hour, when it is pretty well forgotten:

> You have written about Rome as I would, had I been born a poet. And what you did write flows from the soul, the all-loving, the all-embracing, the prophet-soul. It is the only true source of real inspiration.

Meantime the air was full of other voices. Carlyle was croaking and prophesying, with a strong Dumfriesshire accent. Bailey had amazed the world with "Festus," a colossal Conversationalist, by the side of whom his quite clerical and feebly genteel "Devil" seemed a pigmy. Gilfillan had opened his wonderful Pie of "Literary Portraits," containing more swarms of poetical blackbirds than the world knew how to listen to. Mazzini was eloquent in reviews, and George Dawson was stumping the provinces and converting the *bourgeoisie*.

> The world was waiting for that trumpet-blast,
> To which Humanity should rise at last
> Out of a thousand graves, and claim its throne.

It was a period of prodigious ideas. Every literary

work was macrocosmic and colossal. Every poet, under his own little forcing glass, reared a Great Poem—a sort of prodigious pumpkin which ended in utter unwieldiness and wateriness. No sort of preparation was necessary either for the throne or the laurel. Kings of men, king-hating, sprang to full mental light, like fungi, in a night. Quiet tax-paying people, awaking in bed, heard the Chivalry of Labour passing, with hollow music of fife and drum. But it was a grand time for all the talents. Woman was awaking to a sense of her mission. Charlotte Brontë was ready with the prose-poem of the century, Mrs. Browning was touching notes of human pathos which reached to every factory in the world. Compared with our present dead swoon of Poetry, a swoon scarcely relieved at all by the occasional smelling-salts of strong æsthetics, it was a rich and golden time. It had its Dickens, to make every home happy with the gospel of plum-pudding; its Tennyson, to sing beautiful songs of the middle-class ideal, and the comfortable clerical sentiment; its Thackeray, to relieve the passionate, overcharged human heart with the prick of cynicism and the moisture of self-pity. To be born at such a time was in itself (to parody the familiar expression) a liberal education. We who live now may well bewail the generation which preceded us. Some of the old deities still linger with us, but only " in idiocy of godhead," nodding on their mighty seats. The clamour has died away. The utter sterility of passion and the hopeless stagnation of sentiment nowadays may be guessed when some little clique can set up Gautier in a niche: Gautier, that hairdresser's dummy of a stylist, with his complexion of hectic pink and waxen white, his well-oiled wig, and his incommunicable scent of the barber's shop.

What an apotheosis! After the prophecies of '48; after the music of the awakening heart of Man; after Emerson and the newly-risen moon of latter Platonism, shining tenderly on a world of vacant thrones!

Just as the human soul was most expectant, just as the Revolution of '48 had made itself felt wherever the thoughts of men were free, the Sullen Talent, tired of the tame-eagle dodge, perpetrated his *coup d'état*, stabbed France to the heart with his assassin's dagger, and mounted livid to his throne upon her bleeding breast. It is very piteous to read, in Dobell's biography and elsewhere, of the utter folly which recognised in this moody, moping, and graceless ruffian a veritable Saviour of Society. The great woman-poet of the period hailed him holy, and her great husband approved her worship. Dobell had doubts, not many, of Napoleon's consecration. But Robert Browning and Sydney Dobell both lived to recognise in the lesser Napoleon, not only the assassin of France political and social, but the destroyer of literary manhood all over the world. Twenty years of the Second Empire, twenty years of a festering sore which contaminated all the civilisation of the earth, were destined to follow. We reap the result still, in a society given over to luxury and to gold; in a journalism that has lost its manhood, and is supported on a system of indecent exposure and black-mail; in a literature whose first word is flippancy, whose last word is prurience, and whose victory is in the orgies of a naked Dance of Death.

Be all that as it may, those were happy times for Sydney Dobell. In one brief period of literary activity, he wrote nearly all the works which are now associated with his name. To this period belongs his masterly review of "Currer Bell," a model of what such criticism should be. The review led to a correspondence of singular interest between Miss Brontë and Dobell. "You think chiefly of what is to be done and won in life," wrote Charlotte; "I, what is to be suffered . . . If ever we meet, you must regard me as a grave sort of elder sister." By this period the fountain of Charlotte Brontë's genius was dry; she knew it, though the world thought otherwise, and hence her despair. She had lived her life, and put it all into one immortal book. So she sat, a veiled figure, by the side of the urn called "Jane Eyre." The shadow of Death was already upon her face.

Dobell now began to move about the world. He went to Switzerland, and on his return he was very busy with his second poem, "Balder." While labouring thus he first heard of Alexander Smith, and having read some of the new poet's passages in *The Eclectic Review*, wrote thus to Gilfillan: "But has he [Smith] not published already, either in newspapers or periodicals? Curiously enough, I have the strongest impression of *seeing the best images before*, and I am seldom mistaken in these remembrances." This was ominous, of course, of what afterwards took place, when the notorious charge of plagiarism was made against Smith in *The Athenæum*. Shortly afterwards he became personally acquainted with Smith, and learned to love him well. He was now himself, however, to reap the bitters of adverse criticism in the publication of his poem of "Balder." In this extraordinary work, the leading actors are only a poet and his wife, a doctor, an artist, and a servant. It may be admitted at once that the general treatment verges on the ridiculous, but the work contains passages of unequalled beauty and sublimity. The public reviews were adverse, and even personal friends shook their heads in deprecation. At the time of publication he was in Edinburgh, having gone thither to consult Dr. (afterwards Sir James) Simpson on the illness of his wife, and there he was to remain at bay during all the barking of the journals. A little cold comfort came from Charlotte Brontë.

"There is power in that character of *Balder*," she wrote, "and to me, a certain horror. Did you mean it to embody, along with force, many of the special defects of the artistic character? It seems to me that those defects were never thrown out in stronger lines."

Despite the ill-success of his second book, Dobell spent a very happy season in Edinburgh. If not famous, he was at least notorious, and was well enough in health to enjoy a little social friction. Alexander Smith, the secretary to the University, was his bosom friend; and among his other companions were Samuel Brown, Blackie, and Hunter of Craigcrook Castle. "Smith and I," he wrote, "seemed destined to be social twins." Just then there appeared in *Blackwood's Magazine* the somewhat flatulent satire of "Firmilian," written at high jinks by the local Yorick, Professor Aytoun. The style of Dobell and Smith was pretty well mimicked, and the scene in which Gilfillan, entering as Apollodorus, was killed by the friends thrown by Balder from a tower, was really funny. The poets satirised enjoyed the joke as much as anybody, but they little guessed that it was a joke of a very fatal kind. From the moment of the appearance of the "spasmodic" satire, the so-called spasmodic school was ruined in the eyes of the general public. A violent journalistic prejudice arose against its followers. Even Dobell's third book, "England in Time of War," though full of fine lyrics, entirely failed to reinstate the writer in public opinion. He was classed, though in a new sense, among the "illustriously obscure," and he remained in that category until the day he died.

Perhaps the pleasantest of all his days were those days in Edinburgh, when, in conjunction with Smith, he wrote a series of fine sonnets on the war, which won the warm approval of good judges, like Mr. Tennyson. There was something almost rapturous in Smith's opening sonnet to Mrs. Dobell—

> And if we sing, I and that dearer friend,
> Take *thou* our music. He dwells in thy light,
> Summer and spring, blue day and starry night.

A friend wrote that he could love "Alexander" for that sonnet; and, indeed, who could not love him for a thousand reasons? The story of Smith's martyrdom has yet to be told—nay, can never be told this side of the grave. But let this suffice—it *was* a martyrdom and a tragedy. How tranquilly, how beautifully, Smith took the injustice and the cruelty of the world, many of us know. Few know the rest. It was locked up in his great gentle heart.

When I have mentioned that, immediately after the War Sonnets, Sydney Dobell issued independently his volume of prose, "England in Time of War," his literary history is told. Though he lived on for another quarter of a century, he never published another book. Three works, "The Roman," "Balder," and "England in Time of War," formed the sum total of his contributions to literature while alive; and all three were written at one epoch, in what Smith called "the after-swell of the revolutionary impulse of 1848." For the last half of his life he was almost utterly silent, only an occasional sonnet in a magazine, or a letter in a journal on some political subject, reminding the public that he still lived. Of this long silence we at last know the pathetic cause. Sickness pursued him from day to day, from hour to hour, making strenuous literary effort impossible. Never was poet so unlucky. Read the whole heart-rending story in his biography; I at least cannot bear to linger over these tortures. He had to fight for mere breath, and he had little strength left him to reach out hands for the laurel. How meekly he bore *his* martyrdom I have already said.

When I met him he had the look of one who might not live long, a beautiful, far-off, suffering look, wonderfully reproduced in the exquisite picture by his younger brother, an engraving of which faces the title-page of his biography. Many years later, not long indeed before his death, he sent me a photograph with the inscription "*Convalescens convalescenti*;" but all photographs reproduce the man but poorly, compared with the picture of which I have spoken. Even then, in the joyfulness of his eager heart, he thought himself "convalescent," and was looking forward to busy years of life. It was not to be. No sooner was his gentle frame reviving from one luckless accident, than Fate was ready with another. "The pity of it, the pity of it!" It is impossible to think of his sufferings without wondering at the firmness of his faith.

When Death came at last, after years of nameless torture, only a few cold paragraphs in the journals told that a poet had died. The neglect, which had hung like a shadow over his poor ruined life, brooded like a shadow on his grave. But fortunately for his fame, he left relatives behind him who were determined to set him right, once and for ever, with posterity. To such reverent care and industry we owe the two volumes of collected verse, the exquisite volume of prose memoranda, and lastly, the beautiful Life and Letters. Thus, although only a short period has elapsed since Dobell's death, though it seems only yesterday that the poet lay forgotten in some dark limbo of poetic failures, the public is already aware of him as one of the strong men of his generation, strong, too, in the sublimest sense of goodness, courage, and all the old-fashioned Christian virtues. He would have been recognised, perhaps, sooner or later, though I have my doubts; but that he has been recognised so soon is due to such love and duty as are the crown and glory of a good man's life. The public gratitude is due to those who have vindicated him, and made impossible all mistakes as to the strength of his genius and the beauty of his character. His music was not for this generation, his dreams were not of this earth, his final consecration was not to be given here below.

> Vex not his ghost : oh, let him pass ! He hates him much
> That would upon the rack of this rough world
> Stretch him out longer.

But henceforth his immortality is secure. He sits by Shelley's side, in the loneliest and least accessible heaven of Mystic Song.

THE IRISH "NATIONAL" POET.

On Wednesday, the 28th May, 1879, the citizens of Dublin, with that enthusiasm which so distinguishes them in matters considered national, celebrated the centenary of Thomas Moore. The house where the poet was born was illuminated, perfervid speeches were delivered by Lord O'Hagan and others, an ode from the pen of Mr. Denis Florence MacCarthy was recited in public, a procession marched to the tunes made familiar by "Moore's Melodies," and Moore's words were sung with a spirit at once patriotic and bacchanalian. It appeared to be agreed on all hands that Moore was the representative poet of Ireland, and that he occupied the same position in relation to his country as that filled by Burns in relation to Scotland, and Béranger in relation to France. If this be really the case, so much the worse, in my opinion, for Ireland and Irish literature. Thomas Moore was no doubt what his countrymen would term an "iligant" poet, and he has written some verses which go brilliantly to music and are well adapted to the atmosphere of drawing-rooms in all parts of the world. He evinced, moreover, in his arrangement of words for the exquisite national melodies, a most refined taste and a well-nigh perfect judgment. To have seen him seated at the piano, his white hands rambling over the keys, and his voice warbling forth the best of his own compositions, must have been a treat of no common order; as a refined entertainer, indeed, he seems to have been without a peer. But seen at last in the light of a popular apotheosis, in the rosy and somewhat alcoholic glare of a great nation's enthusiasm, he seems as poor a literary figure as may well be conceived. Nearly every line he wrote is pregnant with platitude and literary affectations; nearly every song he sang is either playfully, or forlornly, or affectedly, genteel; and though he had a musical ear, he was deficient in every lofty grace, every word-compelling power, of the divine poetic gift. Above all, he lacked simplicity—that one unmistakable gift of all great national poets, from Homer downwards. And the cardinal defect of the verse was the true clue to the thoroughly artificial character of the man. Beginning in early life as the friend of Young Ireland, as the born companion of Robert Emmett and other martyrs of the hopeless days of the Rebellion, he ended as the adored "musical wit" of London drawing-rooms, the pet of London publishers, the "agreeable rattle" of fashionable literary gatherings. Handsome, agreeable, courteous, affable, even dignified, he lived to become the friend and confidant of Byron, and most other distinguished men of his age. At the height of his popularity Mr. Murray gave him a princely sum for "Lalla Rookh"—a poem which, as Hazlitt wittily remarked, "he should not have written even for a thousand pounds." There was a period when a patient public found poetry in his " Veiled Prophet of Khorassan," and saw pathos in his episode of " Paradise and the Peri." He was the biographer of Lord

Edward Fitzgerald and of that infinitely greater Lord who died at Missolonghi. Society tittered at his epigrams, and politicians delighted in his political satires on behalf of the Whigs. He dressed well, went everywhere, knew everybody, and wherever he went generally sang for his supper; in a word, he was the parvenu and fine gentleman. If we compare this spruce little courtier, with his enthusiasm of gentility and his sham revolutionary sentiment, with the picture of Burns in his exciseman's coat, or that of Béranger in his old, shabby dressing-gown, we may see at a glance the difference between a playful singer of the *salons* and a true poet of the people.

I have granted the merit of Moore's verses and the amusing nature of his personality; but I must protest in the name of justice against his acceptance as the national poet of Ireland. If Irishmen accept him and honour him as such, so much the worse for Irishmen, since his falsehood of poetical touch must respond to something false and unpoetical in their own natures. I have said that a national poet must be simple—Moore was always ornate in the bad sense. Listen to him when he is "patriotic:"

> Forget not the field where they perished;
> The truest—the last of the brave!
> All gone—and the bright hope we cherished
> Gone with them, and quenched in their grave!

Or elsewhere when he cries in more ringing cadence:

> Let Erin remember the days of old,
> Ere her faithless sons betrayed her;
> When Malachi wore the collar of gold
> Which he won from the proud invader;
> When her Kings, with standards of green unfurled,
> Led the Red Cross Knights to danger;
> Ere the emerald gem of the western world
> Was set in the crown of a stranger!

Compare any of this fustian with "Scots wha

hac," or the "Marseillaise," or "Les Gaulois et les Francs;" compare it even, which is more to the point, with Curran's "Wearing of the Green," or Thomas Davis's "Green above the Red." Another characteristic of a truly national poet is what is termed "local colour." Beyond making a tautological parade of the shamrock (the only trefoil he appears to have ever seen), Moore never even attempts to depict the common objects of the landscape of his country. Even when he sings of Arranmore he can only tell us of "breezy cliffs," "flowery mazes," "skiffs that dance along the flood," "daylight's parting wing," and all the stock phenomena of the albums. His "Vale of Avoca" might be situated anywhere between Ireland and Japan; there are a thousand "sweet valleys" where "dark waters meet," but surely an Irish poet might have conveyed by some felicitous touch or image that the waters in question met in the Wicklow Mountains? As in his pictures of nature, so in his renderings of the transports of love. Who that has read Burns' "Highland Mary," or Tannahill's "Jessie, the Flower o' Dunblane," or Béranger's "Lisette," can tolerate the affectations of "Come rest in this bosom, my own stricken deer," or "Lesbia has a beaming eye"? Again, a national poet should be pathetic. The high-water mark of Moore's pathos is to be found in such lyrics as "She is far from the land," which is the mere twaddle of a keepsake compared with "Ye banks and braes," or "Adieu, charmant pays de France," or (to come back to Ireland again) with Clarence Mangan's "Dark Rosaleen," or Banim's "Soggarth Aroon." Lastly, a national poet should have humour. The humour of Thomas Moore is not even good wholesome "blarney" —it is the mere fluent *persiflage* of a diner-out.

The question which occurs to me, apropos of the present centenary, is not a merely literary one. Criticism has long ago settled the poetical rank of Thomas Moore, and no amount of local enthusiasm, no association of that delightful melody to which his falsest songs are set, will alter the supreme fiat of the critical world. But I cannot help asking myself again whether or not the choice of so shallow and insincere a poet is an indication of shallowness and insincerity in the Irish character itself? I am very unwilling to think so. I would rather believe that the apotheosis of Thomas Moore is the work of an over-zealous minority, and that the great strong heart of the people has no real response for such a singer. A national poet represents his nation, as Burns represents Scotland, as Béranger represents France. I should be sorry to believe that Moore represents Ireland — sorry, I mean, for Ireland's sake. I have heard Irishmen, quite alive to Moore's defects, defend his fame by saying that he is, if not a great poet, at any rate the greatest Ireland has produced. This is a matter of opinion. Judged by the voluminousness of his works, he is perhaps paramount. But do not let us forget that Ireland can boast of such poets as Thomas Davis, John Banim, Gerald Griffin, Callanan, Curran, Samuel Lover, Wolfe, Samuel Ferguson, Edward Walsh, and Clarence Mangan. Where in Moore's tinsel poems shall we find such a piece of wondrous workmanship as Mangan's "Vision of Connaught in the Thirteenth Century," such a heart-rending ballad as Banim's "Soggarth Aroon," such a torrent of native strength as Ferguson's "Welshmen of Tirawley," such a bit of rollicking vigour as Lysaght's "Sprig of Shillelah," or such a thrill of simple pathos as Gerald Griffin's

"The tie is broke, my Irish girl"? John Banim sleeps unhonoured, Clarence Mangan lies forgotten, Gerald Griffin is best remembered for his masterly piece of prose fiction. Yet these men were truly national poets; every word they wrote had an Irish ring, and their simple and noble efforts in Irish minstrelsy have gone right home to the spirits of the people. I am sorry indeed for Ireland, if, with such men for singers, she can persist in crowning as her laureate the ghost of a parvenu gentleman in tights and pumps, who spent his days and nights among the Whigs in London, whose patriotism was an amusing farce, and who, merely to make himself look interesting, pinned a shamrock to the buttonhole of his dress-coat, and warbled cheerful little dirges about the sorrows of the country he had left behind him.

HEINE IN A COURT SUIT.

In all history there could hardly be two figures more violently contrasted or diametrically different than the blameless Prince Consort of England and the inspired Gnome of German poetry; and it goes without saying that the biographer of the one was ill fitted to become the translator of the other. I can hardly conceive, therefore, what species of infatuation possessed Mr. Theodore Martin * when he resolved to employ his leisure, lately so admirably utilised in the editing and preparing dainty documents of the Court, in adapting Heinrich Heine's "Poems and Ballads." I use the word adapting advisedly, for when a Courtier, however refined and cultivated, tries to handle a revolutionary Poet, the result is certain to be adaptation, if not downright misrepresentation and mutilation. As wild and agile as Goethe's Flea, as tricksome as an Elf, as uncertain and misleading as a Will-o'-the-Wisp, gamesome and lachrymose by turns, by turns outraging all the conventions and respecting all the proprieties, now the most doleful German that ever spun ditties to his mistress's eyebrow, and again (what Thiers called him) the wittiest Frenchman that ever lived, Heine is

---

* Now Sir Theodore Martin.

the last spirit in the world to rise to the conjuration of a respectable elderly English gentleman, armed with a German dictionary, a quill pen, and an "expurgating" apparatus. He who poked fun at all authorities, human and superhuman, and was never so happy as when sprinkling crumbs in the beds of the little Kings of Teutonia, would have shuddered at the mere prospect of such treatment. A large portion, say at least a round third, of Heine, is sheer naughtiness. He delights in mischief for mischief's sake. He pushes irreverence to the verge of blasphemy, and he whips the galled jade of sensualism, sometimes, with a vigour which makes one quite in love with virtue. Yet this Gnome of impudence and infidelity was capable of the most maudlin Wertherism. He could weep like any school-girl; nay, he would almost deluge you with sentimental milk and water. Curiously enough, this contrariety of mood constitutes his literary fascination. We never know where to have him; it is impossible to predict his temper from one moment to another. Just as he has posed like a philosopher, just as he has touched a note worthy of Hegel in the dumps, a note planetary, speculative, or universal, he "makes a mouth" like a giddy hoyden, skips in the air, and bursts into silvery laughter. In the very midst of his shrill laugh, out comes the pocket-handkerchief, and down fall the tears. Now he gibes at God Himself; anon, he slaps your face for having joined in the gibe. He respects nobody, not even the reader of his books. He introduces the sepulchre and the lupanar as freely as the lyre and the lute, and he is equally matter-of-fact in singing of Herodias with John the Baptist's head under her arm, and of Hortense dying in a Parisian hospital. Nothing comes amiss to him—except obedience to authority. How should he admit the authority of Morality, when he repudiates even that of Art? In the same spirit which makes him shock and outrage social propriety, he now and then deliberately spoils his own poems, wilfully determined not to say the right thing, just because criticism insists that it *is* the right thing, and he *ought* to say it!

Mr. Martin's translations appeared originally in *Blackwood's Magazine*, and they doubtless amused the old-fashioned readers of that somewhat eccentric and antique periodical. Now that they are collected together, one sees more clearly than ever how inadequate they are. It is not that they fail to reproduce Heine's wonderful melody—that, no doubt, was impossible; and it is not that they wilfully misrepresent the general features of their originals. But there is a half-hearted, limping, wooden-legged manner about their lyrical movement which is not rectified by an occasional "hop-step-and-jump" into metrical liveliness. I should do Mr. Martin gross injustice, if I failed to recognise the abundant scholarship, the great conscientiousness, and the busy earnestness, which distinguish his work. He is as just to Heine as he would be to a Prince Presumptive, and that is saying a good deal. He is rigidly fair to him, even too fair, in so much as he will suffer him to say nothing unseemly. But somehow the result is not satisfactory, and Mr. Martin's book is no more like the "Buch der Lieder" than green cheese is like the moon, or the postures of a dancing-master like the leaps of Oberon on the starlit sward.

To descend from general to specific charges, I have first to complain of a good deal of positively bad workmanship. Take, for one example, the first few verses of the weird poem beginning in the original, "Was treibt und tobt mein tolles Blut:"

> What sets my blood *so mad a-spin?*
> Why burns my heart with a fire within?
> My blood *it* boils, it foams, it seethes,
> And a gnawing flame my heart enwreathes.
> My blood *it* foams and seethes *so mad,*
> For I an evil dream have had :
> The Son of Night came, swart and grim,
> And took me away perforce with him.
> He led me to a house was bright, etc.

Really, the "blood it boils" at such a perversion! The awkward repetition of the pronoun is especially disagreeable in its false resemblance to the idiom of the original. Turn, then, to the rendering of the poem beginning " Liebste, sollst mir heute sagen "—a piece certainly not in Heine's best manner, but like all his lyrics, full of verbal felicities, and quite without any affectations :

> Say, love, art thou not a vision—
> Speak, for I to know am fain—
> Such as summer hours Elysian
> Breed within the poet's brain?
>
> Nay, a mouth of such completeness,
> Eyes of such bewitching flame,
> Girl so garner'd round with sweetness,
> Never did a poet frame.
>
> Vampires, basilisks, chimæras,
> Dragons, monsters, all the dire
> Creatures of the fable eras,
> Quicken in the poet's fire.
>
> But thyself, so artful-artless,
> Thy sweet face, thy tender eyes,
> With their looks so fond, so heartless,
> Never poet could devise.

This, surely, is not Heine, but our old friend, Laura Matilda. Who does not recognise at once the cadence of the immortal

> Fluttering spread thy purple pinions,

of the "Rejected Addresses"? In the German poem there is nothing about "fain to know," nothing of the poetaster's jargon about "hours Elysian," a mouth of "such sweet completeness," "a girl garner'd round with sweetness," or "all the dire creatures of the fable eras." Heine merely says, in the simplest possible language: "Dearest, you shall this day tell me, are you not a dream-picture, such as in sultry summer days fills the poet's brain? But no, such a little mouth (Mündchen), such a magic light of the eyes, such a dear, sweet, little darling (Kindchen), was not created by the poet. Basilisks and vampires, dragons and monsters, such horrible fable-animals, *these* are created by the poet's flame. But thee and thy slyness, thy fair face, and the false true look, were not created by the poet." Words and meaning are trifling in the extreme, and only perfect simplicity (shown, for example, in the charming use of diminutives) could make them endurable. But it is precisely this simplicity that enables Heine to produce his most miraculous effects. Just imagine the poet of "Lorelei" using the poetic terminology of the *Family Herald*, the verbal splendours of a young ladies' cardephonia, the gushing verbiage of Julia Mills! Unfortunately, however, one cannot imagine it, nor do I believe that any one will be able to do so—even at Windsor.

All this, perhaps, only amounts to saying that Mr. Martin's translation is no complete representation of Heine's lyrical achievements. In particular cases the rendering is very good indeed, and I might cite the sterling ballad of "The Pilgrimage to Kevlaar" as a specimen of Mr. Martin at his best. He succeeds better with the longer ballads than with the little songs; in the latter the poetic spirit is so volatile and evanescent as altogether to evaporate in the crucible of the translator. Take the tiny lyric beginning " Du liebst mich nicht, du liebst mich nicht," and note the odious transmutation of the first line :

> My love you cannot, cannot brook!
> I don't let that distress me;
> So I but on thy face may look,
> For that's enough to bless me.
>
> You hate, you hate, you hate me ! is
> Your rosy-red mouth's greeting :
> But let me have that mouth to kiss,
> And I'm content, my sweeting.

"That's enough to bless me" is a poor substitute for "Bin ich froh wie'n Konig"; and though the last line of all may be considered a rather felicitous rendering of "So tröst ich mich, mein Kindchen," the general effect is lost. All Mr. Martin's imperfections appear most strongly marked in his version of the marvellous lyric of the "Lorelei," a poem which for strange sibylline charm and sibillant rhythm has never been surpassed. Here are two stanzas :

> With a comb of red gold she *parts it*,
> And still as she combs it she sings ;
> As the melody falls on our *hearts, it*
> With power as of magic *stings.*
>
> *With a spasm* the boatman hears it
> Out there in his little skiff,
> He sees not the reef as he nears it,
> He only looks up to the cliff.

The original, literally translated, is as follows :

> She combs it with golden comb,
> And sings a song meanwhile ;
> It hath a wonderful,
> Powerful melody.
>
> The boatman in his little boat
> Hears it with wild pain,
> He sees not the reef,
> He looks only up to the cliff.

There is nothing about a "*red* gold comb," nothing about "stinging the heart with magic," nothing about the boatman listening "with a spasm." These are mere verbal excrescences ; but, alas ! for the music, for the liquid lapse of sweet syllables, all utterly forgotten or lost ! The reader of such a translation as Mr. Martin's gets no idea whatever of Heine's magic gift of music, but is set actively speculating what the world can mean by calling Heine a great lyrical poet. It is still worse, it is thrice hideous, when the translator, in his despair of simplicity, tries broad Scotch. What provocation was there for such an outbreak as this ?—

> My bairn, we ance were bairnies,
>   Wee gamesome bairnies twa ;
> We creepit into the hen-house,
>   And jookit under the straw, etc.

If the original were written in anything but good genteel German, if a *patois* of any kind had been employed, Mr. Martin would have had a certain excuse. Heine's ballad tales depend chiefly on the excellence of their story and on the quaint originality of their manner, which no translation can altogether spoil. Anything more tender and beautiful than "The Pilgrimage to Kevlaar" can scarcely be conceived, yet the idea is simplicity itself, and the treatment quite free from tricks of style. It is curious to note, by the way, how persistently Heine, as in this poem, broods on the bitterness of life and the supreme piteousness of death. Indeed, a more tautological poet never existed. We really get tired of his repeated conjurations with a wreath of roses, a nude female, and a *caput mortuum*, and his ghosts and skeletons soon fail to frighten us. The one great theme of his Muse, that of Love uniting the quick and dead, and frequently waking up the dead to join the quick, is that of the "Danske Viser" and all kindred groups of ballads. The wild and woeful music made in the wonderful ballad of "Auge und Elsie," which he read in his youth, seems to have reverberated in his brain, and he is never tired of echoing its theme and its cadence.

That cadence and that theme are not for Mr. Theodore Martin. They belong to the wild heart and the wild mood; their region is the lonely greenwood and the dreary sea; and they are not to be "adapted" to the Court or the drawing-room. He who translates Heine must possess something of Heine's nature—free, wild, wicked even, and over bold.

Heine himself carried his wickedness to the extent of hating England and Englishmen with all his heart. His cup of hate would have been full, if he had lived to read Mr. Martin's translation.

A TALK WITH GEORGE ELIOT.

The Priory, North Bank, Regent's Park, London, is a largish, not uncommodious, house, enclosed in its own grounds of about an acre and a half, with trees and shrubs all round, a high front wall facing the street, to which it communicates through a massive doorway. The neighbourhood is quiet, abounding in the cots of those soiled doves who haunt what have been christened (for North Bank is a portion of St. John's Wood) the shady groves of the Evangelist. An actor, Mr. Wilson Barrett, now inhabits the Priory; he has enlarged and altered it to suit his needs, and made it æsthetically resplendent with dados, peacock-papers, and stained glass windows. But in the old days when I haunted it, it was the unpretentious abode of the most famous woman and the cleverest man in England. "George Eliot" dwelt there with her husband, George Henry Lewes; she, known far and wide as the bright genius whose fine creations in fiction began with "Adam Bede"; he, distinguished in many ways as a littérateur, a man of science, and a dilettante.

An afternoon at the Priory, beginning with a modest lunch in the eastern chamber, half study, half drawing-room, and ending with a long chat and tea in the pretty drawing-room, was surely a thing to be remembered. As I look backward, I recall many such afternoons; but one particularly I remember, when the full sunshine of success and happiness dwelt in that little household, and when, to ears eager to listen to me, and hearts full of sympathy, I first told the story of the life and death of David Gray, the young Scottish poet, who came with me to seek his fortune in the great world of London, and on the very threshold of his career was smitten down to die a lingering death.

Conceive a little, narrow-shouldered man of between forty and fifty, with long, straight hair, a magnificent forehead, dark yet brilliant eyes, and a manner full of alertness and intellectual grace. This was George Lewes, whom Douglas Jerrold had once stigmatised as "the ugliest man in London," averring at the same time, that he had caused the chimpanzee in the Zoological Gardens to die "out of jealousy, because there existed close by a creature more hideous than itself!" But George Lewes, though not an Adonis, was certainly not ugly. The great defects of his face were the coarse, almost sensual mouth, with its protruding teeth partly covered by a bristly moustache, and the small retreating chin; but when the face lighted up, and the eyes sparkled, and the mouth began its eloquent discourse, every imperfection was forgotten. Conceive, next, the tenth Muse, or Sibyl, lounging in an arm-chair and shading her face idly with a hand-screen; a powerful-looking, middle-aged woman, with a noticeable nose and chin, a low forehead, a fresh complexion, and full and very mobile mouth. Dress, on this occasion, a plainly cut, tight-fitting dress of blue cashmere, fastened at the throat with a cameo brooch. This was "Mawrian Evans," as Carlyle called her, the George Eliot of the novels. She realised in face and form the description I afterward gave to her in the "Session of the Poets":

> George Eliot gazed on the company boldly
> With the limbs of a sylph and the head of John Locke!

I had been particularly struck by her resemblance to Locke's well-known portrait, engraved as a frontispiece to the famous "Essay." At that time her figure was graceful to elegance. When I last saw her, shortly before her husband's death, she stooped painfully as she walked, and wore an old-fashioned crinoline.

"Tell that story to the public, too," cried Lewes, when I had finished my tale. "Poor fellow! What a pity he ever came to London!"

"Lord Houghton says that your friend was very like the busts of Shelley," said George Eliot, in her deep contralto voice.

"Very like," I answered; "he was curiously feminine in form, and had the most wonderful eyes in the world. Even Tito yonder was not more beautiful," I added, pointing to one of the proof engravings of Du Maurier's illustrations to "Romola," which hung framed over the mantelpiece.

"I don't think, by the way," observed Lewes, "that David Gray can be classed among the true victims of the Babylonian monster, London; at any rate, he was not exactly a literary struggler, at the mercy of what his countryman, Alexander Smith, called

> The terrible city whose neglect is death,
> Whose smile is fame!

He was struck down before he began the struggle at

all; indeed, I have no doubt whatever from your description of him, that the strumous taint, or predisposition, was in him from birth, and that, under any circumstances, his fate would have been the same."

GEORGE ELIOT—"*Quem Di diligunt*, etc. After all, is not Ganymede to be envied? Better to be snatched up suddenly into the heaven of heavens, in all the prime of youth and happiness, than to grow old in a world which is full of sorrow, and in which old age is the least beautiful of human phenomena."

LEWES—"You are quite right there. It is the exaggeration of sentiment which makes the poets give old age a sort of moral halo. There is nothing so pitiful, so horrible, as the slow and certain decay of the human faculties."

MYSELF—"But is not that decay beautiful too?"

LEWES—"Apart from the pathetic fallacy, as Ruskin calls it, not at all. Your favourite Catullus describes it perfectly:

> Cana tempus anilitas
> Omnia omnes annuit!

"In other words, and Scotch ones, 'a' nodding, nid-nid-nodding'; a condition, in short, of ever-increasing inbecility, or vacuity."

GEORGE ELIOT (smiling)—"We are wandering towards deep waters. But it is quite true, I think, that the gradual obliteration of the human faculties and senses, one by one, is the strongest argument against the popular conception of a personal immortality."

LEWES—"Certainly."

GEORGE ELIOT—"Not only do men, under circumstances of physical decay, become feeble and imbecile; when a moral sense remains, it frequently becomes perverted. I have seen an old gentleman, hitherto known as an immaculate and honest merchant, gradually acquire habits of kleptomania, and another, well known for his benevolence, become spiteful, almost homicidal. We are absolutely the creatures of our secretions. So true is this, that the slightest disturbance of the cerebral circulation, say a temporary congestion, will pervert the entire stream of moral sentiment."

MYSELF—"All that is doubtless very correct. I hold, nevertheless, that the soul, the Ego, is invulnerable, despite all temporary aberrations—clouds obscuring the moon's disc, so to speak."

GEORGE ELIOT — "Say rather, disintegrations within the very substance of the moon itself. Where the very substance of the luminary is decaying, what hope is there for the permanence of your—moonlight?"

MYSELF—"The analogy is imperfect; but to pursue it, the lunar elements remain indestructible, and after transformations, may cohere again into some splendid identity."

GEORGE ELIOT—"Moonlight is sunlight reflected on a material mirror; thought, consciousness, life itself, are conditions dependent on the physical medium, and on the brightness of the external environment. *Cogito, ergo sum* should be transposed and altered. *Sum materies, ergo cogito.*"

LEWES—"And yet, after all, there are psychic phenomena which seem to evade the material definition!"

GEORGE ELIOT—"Not one. And science has established clearly that, while functional disturbance may be evanescent, structural destruction is absolute and irremediable. An organism, once destroyed, is incapable of resurrection."

MYSELF—"Then life is merely mechanism, after all?"

GEORGE ELIOT—" Undoubtedly. It is very pitiful, but absolutely true."

LEWES—" But what mechanism! How wonderful, how perfect in its adaptation of means to ends! Even if we hold thought to be a secretion, does that lessen the beauty of its manifestations?"

MYSELF—" Or the mystery of its origin?"

LEWES—" Humph."

GEORGE ELIOT—"The mystery, doubtless, consists only in our ignorance. There was a time, not very long ago, when men knew nothing of that marvellous truth, the circulation of the blood. In time, no doubt we shall discover the precise process by which we think."

So speaking, the Sibyl glanced, not without admiration, at her husband, who was engaged at that very period, as I knew, in experiments concerning the mechanism of thought. He had long before abandoned the metaphysicians, as bewildering and misleading guides, and had completed, in the last edition of his "History of Philosophy," his survey of the progress of thought from its past stage of credulity to its last stage of verification. Now, my sympathies were strongly in the other direction, though I had little or no enthusiasm for what may be termed the *ich* and the *nicht ich* schools of metaphysics. So I shook my head and shrugged my shoulders, saying something to this effect—that if thought was simply mechanism, as they suggested, man was no better than the "beasts that perish."

At this moment there appeared upon the scene another individual, entering quietly through the drawing-room door, which was partly open. The newcomer was a dog, a splendid bull-terrier, who belonged to George Eliot, and generally accompanied Lewes in his walks about the neighbourhood. He came in with a languid wag of the tail, and a general air of importance, glanced patronisingly at me, yawned lazily, and stretched himself on the hearthrug at the feet of his mistress.

GEORGE ELIOT—"'The beasts that perish.' Here is somebody who, if he could speak, would express a strong opinion upon *that* subject; for he is wise in his generation, and magnanimous almost beyond human conception. Do you know what he did once, before he was given to us? The friend to whom he belonged had a little boy, who inherited in full measure the predilections of the archetypal ape."

LEWES (parenthetically)—"The true and only substitute for Plato's archetypal Man!"

GEORGE ELIOT—"One day, our friend had some acquaintances to luncheon. As they sat together they were startled by a sharp cry of pain from underneath the table; and lifting the edge of the tablecloth, they saw the small human monkey squatted on the carpet, in the act of slitting the dog's ear with a large pair of scissors! Out crept the dog, panting and bleeding, followed by his little tormentor. Papa, of course, was very indignant, and seizing the child, who began to sob with terror, announced his intention of administering condign punishment, which he would have done instantly had not the victim interfered. Wagging his tail (just as he is doing now, for he knows I'm telling about him!) the noble fellow rose up, put his paws on the child's shoulders, and affectionately licked his face; then looking at his master, said plainly, in the canine deaf and dumb alphabet, 'Don't beat him! please don't! He's only an undeveloped human being; he knows no better, and — I love him!' Could human kindness and magnanimity go further? Yet I don't suppose you will contend that the poor dog's loving instinct was enough to distinguish him from the other 'beasts that perish.'"

MYSELF—"I'm not sure. Why should not even a dog have a soul like any other respectable Christian?"

LEWES—"Why not, indeed! I have known many so-called Christians who have neither the amiability nor the discrimination of this dog."

GEORGE ELIOT—"Then here we halt on the horns of a dilemma. Every one with a large acquaintance among decent and 'gentleman-like' dogs (as Launce would put it) must admit their share in the highest humanities; and what is true of them is true, to a greater or less extent, of animals generally. Yet shall we, because we walk on our hind feet, assume to ourselves only the privilege of imperishability? Shall we, who are even as they, though we wag our tongues and not our tails, demand a special Providence and a selfish salvation?"

LEWES (laughing)—"Buchanan, like all young men, is an optimist! His spiritual scheme embraces every form of existence, as well as the whole human race."

GEORGE ELIOT—"And why, even, the whole human race? Go into the slums and dens of the city, visit our prisons and inspect our criminals, not to speak of the inmates of our lunatic asylums; and what do you find? Beasts in human likeness, monsters with appetites and instincts, often even the cleverness, of men and women. Are these immortal souls too, independent of physical limitations, and journeying to an eternal Home?"

MYSELF—"Certainly. There is no form of humanity, however degraded, which is beyond the possibility of moral regeneration."

LEWES—"Optimism with a vengeance! Optimism which leaves out of sight all the great physical factors of moral conduct—hereditary disease, cerebral malformations, thought-perverting congestions, all the endless ills that flesh is heir to. I'm afraid, after all, that the dream of a personal immortality is a selfish one. It would come, in the long run, merely to the survival of the fittest, who would build their heavenly mansion on a hecatomb of human failure.... But there, we've talked enough of things at present inscrutable. Come out into the garden, and soothe your mechanism with a cigar."

We left the Sibyl to her meditations, and walked out into the open air. As we strolled smoking along the garden walks, we heard faintly, as from a distance, the murmur of the great city.

"Do you really believe," I said presently, "that the divine thought of Shakespeare was a mere secretion, and that the last word of Science will be one of sheer negation and despair?"

He looked at me thoughtfully, then watched the wreaths of smoke as they curled from his mouth up into the air.

"Man is predoomed to aspiration, as the smoke flies upward. The last word of Science will not be spoken for many a century yet. Who can guess what it will be?"

NOTE.—Although the above sketch is based on memoranda made at the time, I do not give it as a literal report of George Eliot's words, but as a mere transcript from memory of an interesting conversation.—R.B.

THE LITERATURE OF SPIRITUALISM.

"POST MORTEM" FICTION.

It has been suggested by no less (or no greater) an authority than Sir John Lubbock that the earliest ideas of Religion are distinctly traceable to what doctors call dyspepsia, and ordinary people indigestion. During the violent nightmares following a feast of "roasted enemy," our progenitors first saw hideous shapes in dreams, and hence began to suppose that there was a spiritual world surrounding this one, peopled by those pale ghosts of whom even Lucretius himself condescended to give us a glimpse, in his picture of the twilight region of Orcus:

> Quo neque permanent animae, neque corpora nostra,
> Sed quaedam simulacra modo pallentia miris.

Sir John's playful and easy explanation of the great question of the genesis of religious impressions is, of course, only worthy of the young pundits of the *Fortnightly Review*, wits who spell God with a small g, and gladly exchange the poetry of the Old Testament for Holbach's "System of Nature." One of the many answers to the explanation is the simple one that indigestion is a complaint more likely to assail a city banker than a primæval savage. Primitive man, even when he outdid himself cannibalistically, in all probability slept soundly, in supreme defiance of the nightmare. But, although I am compelled to reject Sir John's theory as an account of the dim beginnings of natural piety, I hail it thankfully as supplying a clue to the origin of at least two-thirds of historical apparitions, from the Devil of Luther downwards. Certainly, a large number of ghosts are due to overeating or over-drinking. "A slight disorder of the stomach," said Mr. Scrooge to the grim ghost of Marley, "makes the senses cheats. You may be an undigested bit of beef, a blot of mustard, a crumb of cheese, a fragment of an underdone potatoe!" It would be curious indeed to inquire how far excess in eating and drinking has been a factor in the formation of the phantom-world. Hunger and whisky combined must have created in many Highland Seers the startling phenomena of second sight. Most Irish stories of the "fetches" positively reek of *delirium tremens*. Indeed, it would require the art of a Cruikshank to depict the horrors which imagination can body forth under temporary derangements of the sensory apparatus. But it is in the region of what is known as Spiritualism, in that dark morass where the sad moonshine gleams vapidly through an eternal intellectual fog, that I find Sir John Lubbock's cynical suggestion most useful as a light and a guide. How else explain the existence of apparitions which bear the same relation to respectable, God-fearing —I had almost said church-going—phantoms, that pickled pork and peas-pudding do to wholesome food?

In a spirit of penitence, clad in literary sackcloth

and ashes, I have recently been going through a course of Spiritualistic literature; and now, at its conclusion, I feel almost as dyspeptic as Schiller's "Ghost Seer" himself, and ready to believe in any hobgoblin the imminent festivities of Christmas may devise. If the result is chiefly interesting to a local medical practitioner, the spirits are not to blame; for I have really been most liberally entertained. I now purpose to retail to my readers some of the entertainment I have been taking wholesale. Out of a superfluity of fine things, it is difficult to pick a sample, but I believe I shall not go far wrong if I select a little work which might fairly be entitled "The Spiritualist's Vade Mecum," but which appears with the less pretentious but more touching title of "Rifts in the Veil." It is published, I believe, at the office of the *Spiritualist* newspaper; it is sumptuously got up, I presume under spiritual superintendence; and it is, as the title-page sets forth, "a collection of inspirational poems and essays given through various forms of mediumship, also of poems and essays by spiritualists." A passing examination of some of these "inspirational" productions may lead the reader to discover the true nature of the "inspiration" specified, and may enable him to decide if, after all, the theory of dyspepsia is admissible.

"In the highest forms of inspiration," begins the preface, "the communicating spirit is supposed to give to the medium in a supersensuous state the highest ideas he can then assimilate; presumably, these ideas then flow from the lips of the sensitive, but necessarily somewhat dwarfed and warped by the channel through which they pass, and by the limited powers of the mortal intellects to whose receptive capacity they have to be lowered and adapted. The trance poems given in this book," it is added, "were, in the majority of cases, taken down in shorthand from the lips of the sensitives, as the words were uttered." The first specimen of a " trance " poem—which must by no means be confounded with a poem really " entrancing "—is a splendid utterance by a certain Mr. Thomas Lake Harris, " now the head of a religious community in America." It is in blank verse, verse so blank in its vague magnificence that it makes one feel tenfold " the limited power of the mortal intellect to whose receptive capacity" it has to be " lowered." Here and there it reminds me of Tupper at his highest; more than once it soars to the empyrean of eloquence occupied by the *Rock* newspaper. Take the concluding passage :

> God alone is great.
> He is the primal splendour who illumes
> The full-orbed intellect ; He gave the power
> To plan and execute ; the work is His,
> Its faults grew from our creature finiteness.
> Would it (*i.e.*, the poem) were worthier of its origin.
> 'Tis but a wandering Voice, the harbinger
> Of a great poem that, Messiah-like,
> Shall tread down evil with its feet of fire,
> And clasp all sufferers to its heart of love
> The latchets of whose shoes it may not loose.
> Five years will lead their swift revolving dance
> In choral music round the brightening world,
> Before that Poem shall unfold its form,
> And we will make the Medium worthy it,
> And give it as his spiritual powers
> Wake from their slumber. For the time, farewell.

An unbeliever might wonder why a " heart of love " should wear " shoes " with " latchets," and an unregenerate Fortnightly Reviewer might assert that a Medium " worthy " of such a poem might readily be found in the platitudinous person of Mr. Chadband. But I am not so ill-disposed. What pleases in such poetry is its soothing flow, so easy to follow, so innocent of vulgar mystery. So far, there is no trace of the blue devils, no suspicion of dyspepsia. Ridge's "Food for Infants" is not milder than Mr. Harris's trance poem—so much as I have yet quoted of it. But Mr. Harris does not always remain on the ground; he can soar when he likes. In another specimen of his Muse, entitled "The Translation of Shelley to the Higher Life," he is simply gorgeous in his cloud-compelling flights. Here, through Mr. Harris's trance-mediumship, Shelley himself describes his death by drowning :

> We had gone forth, my friend and I, beguiled
> By summer air and sunshine, and low tones
> Of music from the crisped and crested sea.
> A white flaw struck our barque, and she went down.
> A gurgling, bubbling sound was in my ears.
> White-armed I clipt with sinewy stroke the waves,
> Sank, rose again and sank, and rose and saw
> Returning smiles of sunshine on the sea,
> Then left my languid form upon the deep,
> Borne by its tides and rocking to their swell.

It is quite useless to object to trifling inaccuracies of fact, such as the statement that Shelley and Williams, on that memorable day, were "beguiled by summer air and sunshine." It has been again and again explained by Spiritualists that Spirits, like mortal creatures, are perilously given to lying. All I need remark here is the perfectly Shelleyan movement of this fine fragment. "The thought," says Mr. Harris, "was his (*i.e.*, Shelley's), the thought's word-clothing mine." So perfectly is the nude thought covered, however, that few readers will suspect the existence of any thought at all.

There are more of these "trance poems," and they all present the same characteristics—the fine tenuity of idea and beautiful confusion of images so suggestive of ghostly musings. I should like to quote "The Birth of the Spirit," a piece given through the trance-mediumship of Mrs. Cora L. V. Tappan-Richmond, but it is too splendid for a profane critic. Far more suitable for such a setting is the following "epigram," written, *apropos* of the Slade prosecution, by Mr. Gerald Massey:

> The Apostle bade us "*try the spirits,*"
> And judge them fairly, on their merits,
> But did not clear instructions give
> For catching things so fugitive
> As spirits, in the Lawyer's sieve;
> And possibly, he might retort,
> "*I didn't mean at Bow-street Court!*"

We are not informed whether the above lines were also given through trance-mediumship. If so, I am at a loss which to admire most—the poetry of the Spirits, or their satire.

So far I have proceeded, and have not yet got to the Spirits themselves at all. I have seen them revealed in their "inspirational" poems and epigrams, but that is only through a glass, darkly. I must still linger a little over their works, while I direct attention to their greatest achievement—a *post mortem* work by Charles Dickens. Towards the close of 1873, great excitement was caused in Spiritualist circles by the rumour that a Spirit, "claiming to be Charles Dickens," was completing the unfinished novel of "Edwin Drood." Inquiry showed that the rumour was founded on fact, and that the medium—a medium is always a necessity in such case—was a foreman in the printing office of the *Vermont Recorder and Farmer.* It appears that the matter began through the instrumentality of Dickens himself—that is, of Dickens's simulacrum. One evening, the inspired foreman, at a *séance*, wrote a message addressed to himself, "requesting a sitting," and signed in a plain, bold hand, "Charles Dickens." Several other communications followed, and at last one evening the medium "exclaimed that a *face* was looking down upon him from one corner of the room, with *hands* outstretched towards him." Strangely enough, though the others could see nothing, he "rushed to the spot," and "appeared to *shake hands* (*!*) with the imaginary being." On his relating the circumstance next day to a gentleman, that gentleman stepped to a bookcase, and took down a "Life of Dickens," containing an excellent portrait, and showed it to him. His face, we are informed, "instantly became blanched, as he cried, 'Good God! that's the man I saw last night!'"

All this is ghostly enough in all conscience, but it is so far suggestive rather of *diablerie* than of dyspepsia. If we could suspect a foreman compositor of being a cheat and a liar, there would be room for strong language, but, of course, such a medium was impeccable. The upshot briefly was that Dickens dictated to, or rather through, this individual twelve hundred pages of manuscript, enough to make an octavo volume of four hundred printed pages. Not only did he do this, but he constantly sent brief notes of encouragement and good cheer. These communications have all been preserved, but "are regarded as of a private and personal nature, not for the public eye." Nevertheless, the foreman compositor was permitted to make some extracts. "We are doing finely," wrote Dickens on one occasion. "You have no idea how much interest this matter is *exciting here among the hosts by whom I am surrounded*. . . . When this work is finished, you shall continue to be my amanuensis. *I shall write more after this!*" More astounding still, the Spirit of Dickens gave full directions as to the manner of procedure to secure copyright, and on one occasion sent this note:

> In regard to English publishers: As soon as the first proof sheet is done, address a letter to Sampson Low, Son, and Marston, Milton House, Ludgate Hill, London, England. It is very probable they will negotiate for advance sheets.—Faithfully, DICKENS.

The Spiritualists possess a sort of club, to which ladies are admitted, and which is roundly entitled "The British National Association of Spiritualists." The club, it appears, was founded "for the purpose of uniting Spiritualists of every variety of opinion in an organised body." Attached to it is a library, containing "a large collection of the best works in Spiritualism and occult subjects," and a reading-room, where Spiritualist newspapers and periodicals are regularly supplied. As if this were not enough, well-organised *séances*, to which "a limited number of inquirers are admitted free of charge, are held weekly, under strict test conditions." If privacy is desired, suitable rooms for *séances* may be hired "on moderate terms," and these rooms are supplied with "cabinets." Nay, to crown all, "light refreshments"—in the shape of the toothsome macaroon and the stimulating Bath bun?—"are provided at moderate charges." Connected with this festive place of meeting is a suburban branch, called the Dalston Association of Inquirers into Spiritualism, the "weekly experimental *séances*" of which, I understand, "offer favourable opportunities for the observation of some of the elementary phases of phenomena."

Now, the secretary of the British National Association is a Mr. W. H. Harrison, and it fortunately happens that this gentleman, in one of a series of manuals, called "The Spiritualist's Library," has given us what he calls a "scientifically accurate" description of the sort of performances which go on at most *séances*. Seeing that he has been in the habit of attending at least two or three *séances* every week, "for the purpose" (as he says) "of gaining practical knowledge of the phenomena which take place in the presence of most celebrated media," he may be said to speak with a certain authority. His first experience of Spiritualism was at a lecture given by Mr. D. D. Home, the effect of which, he naïvely remarks, was simply to "puzzle" the strangers present. Shortly afterwards, he called upon Mr. Cromwell Varley, the secretary, electrician, and engineer, to the North Atlantic Telegraph Company, and the first step to conversion seems to have been taken in his astonishment to find that a "secretary, electrician, and engineer," could be a proclaimed Spiritualist. His first *séance* was at Mr. Varley's house. The Spirits gave raps, spelt out sentences (the first of which was "We are glad you are trying to investigate this power!"), and lifted heavy weights. Several other *séances* followed, and at one Mr. Harrison first saw what he calls "writing mediumship"—in other words, Mrs. Varley's hand scribbling messages "under spirit inspiration," while the lady herself was looking at him and talking. But the crowning experience did not come till his introduction to the medium of mediums, Mrs. Mary Marshall, "the younger," then residing at 13, Bristol Gardens, Maida Vale, Paddington. I will give the beginning of this *séance* in his own words :

A TABLE FLOATING UNDER TEST CONDITIONS.

We had no sooner taken our seats than the table gave a jump, and sent my note book and pencil flying over my shoulder. The table then lay down on one side, till its edge touched the ground ; it jumped up again ; then lay down on the other side; after which it began to rotate upon its vertical axis, and to travel about the room, jumping now and then. This was startling; I could not see that our hands were doing it, but I asked Mrs. Marshall whether it was necessary that our hands should touch the table at all. She replied, "Yes, to let the electricity go through, but the slightest touch will do." I did not quarrel with her about the word "electricity," but suggested that we should each of us touch the table with the tip of the middle finger only of each hand, bending up all the other fingers, so that they should be well clear of its surface. We did so. . . . And I again bent down to see if anything was touching the table underneath. Then I remarked, " Now, I am quite satisfied that nothing is touching the table except the tips of our six fingers." Directly I said this, the table rose off the ground slowly to a height of about eighteen inches. Then it fell from our fingers, and was dashed down on to the floor, so that one of its claws was broken off at a place where the solid wood was two or three inches thick; then the table turned itself bottom upwards, and stood rocking upon one of its edges, with its broken foot moving up and down close before my face, as I stood, with my hands on my knees, looking at it. " *There*," said Mrs. Marshall, " *they are showing you the broken leg!*"

A little after, a sheet of paper and pencil was put under the table, for the purpose of producing some spirit-writing. "All our hands were on the top of the table. I heard a scratch on the paper near my feet, then the table, by tilts, signalled out, 'Mend the pencil!'" This being done, the scratching was renewed, lasting about a minute—"when the table began to jump about," which Mrs. Marshall said was a signal the Spirits had finished writing. Mr. Harrison picked up the paper, and found written upon it, "God bless you!" The table next told him that he was a medium, a statement he himself believes to be untrue. Whether or not he expressed his unbelief on that occasion I do not know, but, at all events, the table lost its temper! " I heard a lumbering noise behind me, and on looking round saw the great six-foot table running up to us all by itself; after taking a run of about four feet, it rested with its edge against the edge of the little table round which we were sitting!"

At this memorable *séance*, Mr. Harrison made the acquaintance of the most refractory Spirit that ever made darkness hideous; a truculent, noisy, hectoring, bullying Ghost of the name of "John King," who announced himself "with a great bang which might have been heard in the street." This is how the ruffian of a Ghost conducted himself:

> The first remark I ever heard in the direct voice from the spirits of the departed, from the loved ones gone before, was a bad pun. John King exclaimed: "*Harrison, don't be harassed.*" This remark was rather disappointing to one who supposed that spirits were a kind of archangels, and I suppose my feelings exhibited themselves in my face, for John King next remarked, "You ought to look upon Spiritualism as a jolly thing. I'm jolly enough! Look here, now! I'll sing you a song of my own composition:
>
> > "I wish I had a bird,
> > I would stick it on a spit——"
>
> and so on; I cannot remember the rest of the doggerel. I asked John King "who he was," as I did not remember the name to be that of any departed relative of mine. He replied that he was a Welshman, a native of Carmarthen. I tried to get evidence that he had some local knowledge of Carmarthen, as I knew a little about that town, but *could draw nothing further out of him.*

On another occasion John King recommended Mr. Varley's nephew, who was in bad health, to drink bottled stout, and being asked, "What stout?" he answered promptly, "Guinness's." Then, horrible to relate, the patient took hold of a tube of paper which John King was "using as a speaking tube." "John King seized another, and began to fence with it; I could hear the noise of the two tubes striking against each other." Then, most amazing of all, John King wrested the tube from his adversary; and then, proceeding "to rumple his hair by rubbing the tubes over his head," remarked, "*This is hair-brushing by machinery.*" The imagination which could invent and the impudence which could perpetuate such a ghost as "John King" must possess a strange and not altogether sane physiological basis. Dare I hint at dipsomania as a factor in John King's manufacture? Dare I suggest that John is a distant relation of another touching spirit, "Old Tom"?

There is a sad side to all this folly, to all this pitiful ignorance and moral degradation. A number of poor human creatures, craving for light of some sort in the solemn issues which lie before them, weakened by illness and mental trouble, devour the silly and saponaceous literature of Spiritualism, and are ready to believe, at a moment's notice, in any message from another world. The wish is father to the thought, and your Ghost is already half manufactured when the eye is determined to behold him. If it were otherwise, the existence of so much Spiritualistic trash would be inconceivable. As matters stand, it is the old story of the assumedly blind leading the actually blind. In the words of Mohammed, often quoted by Spiritualists, "One darkness on another darkness; when a man stretcheth forth his hand he is far from seeing it;" and, finally, "he to whom God doth not give light, no light at all hath he!"

THE MODERN STAGE.

I.

NOTES IN 1876.

IT is said, on what I understand to be excellent authority, that on any night during the run of *Hamlet* at the Lyceum Theatre, the occupants of stalls and boxes might be heard whispering between the acts such queries as—Does Laertes fight Hamlet? Is Ophelia going to drown herself? Does the Queen drink the poison? And, does Hamlet succeed his father on the throne of Denmark? Thus, while some gray veteran in the pit was scowling at Mr. Irving, remembering with regret the days of Kean and Macready, and watching with eager eyes and ears for some blasphemous modern corruption of the divine text, the great bulk of the intelligent audience was possibly enjoying Hamlet's adventures with the same sense of novelty they had found in the misfortunes of the *Ticket of Leave Man* and the sorrows of *Formosa*—with this specific additional enjoyment, that they were assured on all hands that seeing *Hamlet* was a very intelligent and creditable thing to do. They had battened to the full on the horrors of Mr. Irving's Matthias; they had wept for hours in sympathy with the sorrows of his

Charles the Martyr; and they were now ready to follow, with the same enthusiasm, the equally interesting and equally unfamiliar episodes in the life of the Danish Prince. An enterprising management, diligent in studying the hearts of audiences, encouraged this disposition to the full; the critics blew their trumpets till the welkin rang again; Shakespeare flourished, and the exchequer of one theatre at least was filled. After all, it was no great drawback to the general success that many of the intelligent audience arrived late, after the first act, or farce, was over; that some few brought with them, as to an opera in some foreign tongue, a "correct book of the words;" that they evinced a more or less decided ignorance of the "plot," and a very unmistakable indifference to the finer lights and shades of the leading characters; that they betrayed a very curious tendency to emphasize by applause the good and novel "sentiments," as they would have done the "good things" of a new farcical piece by Mr. Byron. The one real point was gained, and a large number of *blasé* Londoners flocked to hear the new play of *Hamlet* with an eagerness which seemed highly promising for the future of dramatic art. And what was the general verdict? That *Hamlet* was really a capital play to see, that its leading situations were, at any rate, equal to those of most dramas of the day, and that Mr. Irving acted the leading character in a really creditable and diverting manner.

If the eagerness of these and similar audiences meant little more than the flush of a temporary fashion, having little or no connection with a genuine dramatic taste, it would still afford reasonable hope for a sanguine critic to build upon; since, by due cultivation and fresh encouragement, the ephemeral feeling might be developed into something like intelligent sympathy; but, in point of fact, the eagerness in question is rooted far deeper in the character and nature of the play-going English public. Ignorant as London audiences are of Shakespeare's writings, they have good reasons for believing that Shakespeare's plays surpass most modern productions in continuous human interest. The truth is that the public, though uninstructed, are not unintelligent, and if they have failed to show their sympathy with the highest dramatic art, it is because they have had few opportunities of beholding it. So far as their knowledge goes, their taste is admirable, and their desire to be pleased inexhaustible. They like good strong plays when they can get them, and they adore good strong actors when they know them. They will not go to see Shakespeare or any other author "murdered;" but when a clever actor appears in Shakespearean characters, rendering fair justice to the spirit and letter of the original, they will always encourage him. What they want, and what they might readily get if there were other managers in London equal in energy to Mr. Irving, is a dramatic *education*. Amid the chaos of London theatres, blinded by the flash of tinsel and spangle, deafened by the noise of semi-nude incapables, they stagger in moral intoxication, not knowing whither to turn; but no sooner do they catch one glimpse of a true attraction than they seem eager to support it. True, they want to be humoured by some little specific peculiarity. Mr. Fechter's fair wig, Mr. Jefferson's catchword about his "Dog Schneider," Mr. Robertson's realistic pumps and tea-kettles, Mr. Boucicault's great water-jump, have delighted them in turn. They have rushed to see Mr. Phelps in gaiters and Mr. Irving in a fit. They have enjoyed the weighing-scene in the *Flying Scud*, and the examination-scene in *School*. They have relished Mr. Toole's grimaces and Mr. Lionel Brough's contortions. All these things, however, have been good in their way, or good with a qualification; all the most popular entertainments, even Mr. Burnand's burlesques, having had merit of one kind or another; and the public, with its insatiable appetite for variety of all sorts, has done them ample justice. It may dishearten a lover of the drama to observe the success of a piece of sheer imbecility and vulgarity, like *Dundreary;* but, in taking a bird's-eye view of dramatic affairs for the last ten years, I can call to mind few altogether undeserved successes. The spectacles of Drury Lane and the monstrosities of Mr. Farnie are exceptions to a general rule—that plays succeed on their merits if adequately acted, and that playgoers are not indifferent either to good dramatists or good actors; but Drury Lane is managed under peculiar and disheartening conditions, while the stragglers who support such a theatre as the Gaiety, can hardly be said to belong to the legitimate class of playgoers at all.

It is certainly not my purpose in the present paper to repeat the old stale cry about the decadence of the drama. I believe that people go to the theatre now for the same reasons which took them in Shakespeare's time: they go, primarily, for amusement; and, secondly, for edification. At no period, I believe, did they patronise performances which were edifying and not amusing. In answer to those quidnuncs who wish to apotheosize the drama as the pedagogue of virtue, it can easily be demonstrated that the drama never was, and never has been, a direct educational instrument.* Its chief function is to entertain—to entertain nobly, if possible, but certainly to entertain at all costs. Far from us be the period when it is degraded to the level of a bourgeois Academy presided over by the British Matron, and inspected at regular intervals by the Lord Chamberlain. We have had some pretty specimens of late of how government from above would debase and pauperise the drama. The virtuous functionary who represents an enlightened Court, the leading members of which derive their subtlest theatrical pleasures from the acting of coarse comedians, thought fit, in the interests of respectability, to forbid the performance of the most original productions of Continental dramatic art; he slammed the door in the face of Dumas *fils*, and opened the door wide to *Génévièvre de Brabant*; he denied a hearing to the *Supplice d'une Femme*, and smiled in tender commiseration on the *New Magdalen*. The present writer will certainly not be suspected of a love for *l'école brutale*, as a certain class of dramatic literature is called in Paris; but he would rather see that school flourish on every stage from London to Aberdeen than suffer the spokesman of an illiterate and irresponsible Court, dressed in a little brief authority, to dictate on what terms and under what restrictions the enjoyments of the public are to be admissible. Such interference is another phase of that oppressive legislation which appears

* Previous to the appearance of Mr. Irving as Hamlet, the newspapers contained a paragraph stating that Mr. Tennyson had expressed his opinion that the performance at the Lyceum "would educate the people better than all the School Boards." This delicious nonsense actually went the round of the newspapers. A representation of *Hamlet* is educational in precise ratio to the preparation of the spectator; it had no more effect on Mr. Partridge than that of any other "sensation" drama.

elsewhere in the form of a Contagious Diseases Act; it is intolerable in itself; but that a functionary who incarnates the most degraded superstitions of society, and who presides, so to speak, over the open indecency of a levée crush, when the rank and beauty of our land are transformed like Circe's swine, under the ignoble pressure of degraded ambition—that such a functionary should play Petronius to our pleasures is a hideous farce, a monstrosity, a scandal. Were the great shapes of the past to pass before this Arbiter, how would they fare? Sophocles would be condemned by ears too delicate for calamitous tales of incest; even the marble figure of "Antigone" would awake no awe in the heart of the censor; and as for the "fair heifer" and other kindred naturalisms of Æschylus, they would be pronounced scandalous beyond measure. No hope for Euripides; he has naked Mœnads in his train. Still less for Aristophanes; conceive the British Matron's horror at the recital of the "Ecclesiazusæ!" Plautus is too plain, and Terence is too broad. That smiling, elegantly-dressed fellow must be banished for ever; for is he not Molière, and does he not carry jauntily in his hand the very utensil used as a stage property in *Le Médecin Volant?* Worse still, not one of the crowd of "mighty magicians," who wear the trunk and doublet of our golden age, is fit to be heard. Marlowe and Cyril Tourneur, Massinger and Shirley, must begone from the charmed circle of this scented courtling. John Ford may draw down "his melancholy hat," for we remember the play chastely rechristened the *Brother and Sister;* and Dekkar may hush his grim morality, for the very name of his masterpiece is unmentionable to ears polite. Shakespeare himself is only to be heard on sufferance.

THE MODERN STAGE.

And if we come down the years, seeking for a dramatist after the Lord Chamberlain's own heart, we must pass by Dryden, smudging with his careless finger the already well-besmurged Amphitruo of Plautus, and uttering in his very prologues and epilogues speech calculated to affright convention —much, by the way, to the delight of the King and Lord Chamberlain for the time being. Congreve, Wycherly, Vanbrugh, Farquhar, are no more to be heard than that quondam Court favourite, Mrs. Behn. Not until we find ourselves amongst the Dresden china literature of the age of Queen Anne do we begin to scent the air of virtue; but the air grows still purer as we proceed, until we find ourselves inspecting the stainless tragedies of Mr. Rowe, and, still later, the virgin pages of Mr. Sheridan Knowles. Unfortunately for the prospects of art, we discover that virtue and mediocrity, so far as the drama is concerned, have been synonymous, and that almost the only plays which (to quote Mr. Podsnap) "would not bring a blush to the cheek of a young person," are precisely the only plays to which lovers of literature are least disposed to listen.

In point of fact, British playgoers are quite virtuous enough without being encouraged to still more foolish prejudice by any official, however accredited. The one great obstacle to anything like high dramatic art in England is a conspiracy on the part of authors, managers, and actors to emasculate and conventionalise all their productions by a constant tacit reference to Mr. Podsnap's "young person." Plays must be simple in structure and succinct in plot to suit the comprehension of the young person; they must not touch on forbidden relationship, nor unnatural crimes, nor glimpses of morbid psychology, for fear of shocking the young person; they must be modern, for the young person's historical knowledge is limited; and they must be written as far as possible in modern English, for the young person dislikes poetical turns of expression. Any one reasonably familiar with that vulgar *deus ex machinâ*, the British manager, knows with how sure a gauge he professes to measure the dislikes of the typical playgoer. But recent experience has shown that the young person is not the mere inanity managers imagine her; that, in other words, people who go to the play possess, with all their ignorance, a fair share of human enthusiasm, and that a few touches of that nature which makes all the world kin will reconcile them even to pretty stiff attacks on their prejudices. They had a prejudice against "sensational" death-scenes, which Mr. Irving conquered in a night. They had another ridiculous prejudice in favour of "happy endings," which Mr. W. S. Gilbert has successfully violated over and over again. They disliked the "poetical" drama, but Mr. Irving has taught them to tolerate it. They had an aversion to "Irish" pieces, but were instantaneously converted by the *Colleen Bawn*. In a word, they are adolescent, ready to accept any decent education the enlightened may offer them. Education they want; who is to undertake the task of supplying it to them?

The managers being indifferent, and the actors at the mercy of the managers, the entire task of dramatic education—*pace* the critics, of whom I shall speak hereafter—must be performed by the authors. True, these gentlemen are themselves greatly at the mercy of the managers; but they have power, and they occasionally use it. This being the case, it is worth while to consider at some length the style and pretensions of dramatic productions; and, indeed, to do this, while adding some final suggestions as to how the cause of dramatic art may be advanced, is the main purpose of the present article.

Place aux dames! First let us see what the so-called poetical Muse has done for us of late in England. It is now many long years since the *Lady of Lyons* first made the theatrical fortune of its author, and it still remains at the head of modern romantic dramas; not on account of its writing, which is vapid in the extreme, but by virtue of an entertaining subject and excellent construction. Worthless as literature, worthless even as a vehicle for good acting, it holds its place on the stage as a thoroughly commonplace and interesting play. "You are just the author for a *Lady of Lyons*," wrote a London manager recently to a living author; "write me such a piece and there is a small fortune for you—and yours truly;" but the person addressed, unfortunately, did *not* think himself just the author for a *Lady of Lyons*. Of the same date as Lord Lytton's dramas are those of Sheridan Knowles; of these only the *Hunchback* and the *Love Chase* retain any firm hold of the stage. Unlike Lord Lytton, who succeeded by virtue of a compact and well-welded plot, Knowles got his effects from consummate command of verbiage and a masterly power of creating stage situations, not as part of a well-conceived whole, but from scene to scene. His characters are simply marionettes, admirably dressed and excellently managed. Their speech is wondrous. Listening to its endless interjections and repetitions, to its extraordinary flatulence of phrase and epithet, as uttered on the stage, one becomes so bewildered as almost to fancy one is listening to words of power, not sounds of fury signifying nothing. Knowles is the Chadband of dramatists, the Moody of the defunct classical school. His vigour in saying and meaning nothing amounts to genius, his skill in devising and connecting dialogues without a purpose, and yet apparently full of purpose, is fairly astounding. The following passage from the *Hunchback*, is a fair sample of the author at his best:

> *Enter* JULIA *and* HELEN.
>
> *Helen.* I like not, Julia, this your country life.
> I'm weary on't.
> *Julia.*   Indeed? So am not I;
> I know no other; would no other know.
> *Helen.* You would no other know? Would you not know
> Another relative—another friend—
> Another house—another anything,
> Because the ones you have already please you?
> That's poor content. Would you not be more rich,
> More wise, more fair? The song that last you learned
> You fancy well; and therefore shall you learn
> No other song? Your virginal, 'tis true,
> Hath a sweet tone; but does it follow thence
> You shall not have another virginal?
> You may, love, and a sweeter one; and so
> A sweeter life may find, than this you lead!
> *Julia.* I seek it not. Helen, I'm constancy!
> *Helen.* So is a cat, a dog, a silly hen,
> An owl, a bat—where they are wont to lodge
> They still sojourn, nor care to shift their quarters.
> Thou'rt constancy? I'm glad I know thy name!
> The spider comes of the same family,
> That in his meshy fortress spends his life,
> Unless you pull it down and scare him from it.
> And so thou'rt constancy? Art proud of that?
> I'll warrant thee, I'll match thee with a snail,
> From year to year that never leaves his house!
> Such constancy, forsooth! a constant grub
> That houses ever in the self-same nut
> Where he was born, till hunger drives him out.
> And so in very deed thou'rt constancy!

Julia. Helen, you know the adage of the tree :—
I've ta'en the bend. This rural life of mine,
Enjoined me by an unknown father's will,
I've led from infancy. Debarr'd from hope
Of change, I ne'er have sighed for change. The town
To me was like the moon, for any thought
I e'er should visit it—nor was I school'd
To think it half so fair.
  Helen. Not half so fair!
The town's the sun, and thou hast dwelt in night
E'er since thy birth, not to have seen the town!
Their women there are queens, and kings their men,
Their houses palaces.
  Julia. And what of that?
Have your town palaces a hall like this?
Couches so fragrant? walls so high adorned?
Casements with such festoons, such prospects, Helen,
As these fair vistas have? Your kings and queens!
See me a May-day queen and talk of them!
  Helen. Extremes are ever neighbours. 'Tis a step
From one of the other.

Of course, the less said of such very blank verse the better, for the author did not pretend to be a poet. His moral sentiments are on a level with his dialogue, and the occasional glimpses of good honest talent which Knowles undoubtedly possessed, are always spoiled by some ridiculous false note. The following little speech has merits, from a stagey point of view, despite its resemblance to a speech of Jacques:

Waller. Well, Master Wildrake, speak you of the chase?
To hear you one doth feel the bounding steed;
You bring the hounds, and game, and all to view—
All scudding to the jovial huntsman's cheer!
And yet I pity the poor crowned deer,
And always fancy 'tis by fortune's spite,
That lordly head of his he bears so high—
Like Virtue, stately in calamity,
And hunted by the human, worldly hound—
Is made to fly before the pack, that straight
Burst into song at prospect of his death.
You say their cry is harmony, and yet

> The chorus scarce is music to my ear,
> When I bethink me what it sounds to his;
> Nor deem I sweet the note that rings the knell
> Of the once merry forester!

But no sooner has Master Waller struck the natural note, than another speaker, Master Neville, interposes a note of moral philosophy.

> *Nev.* The same things
> Do please or pain—*according to the thought
> We take of them!*

Gems of this precious kind abound in Sheridan Knowles. Despite all his faults, he understood stage language thoroughly, and he was so well read in the literature of our best period, that he would have been a truly admirable writer if he had possessed ideas in proportion to his command of language.

Though Dr. Westland Marston is still living, his plays may almost be said to belong to the last generation. He does not attempt to compete with younger writers, and the only recent productions of his pen have been some capital little comedies for Mr. Sothern. His first play, the *Patrician's Daughter*, was produced in 1842, five years after the production of the *Love Chase;* and since then he has written five or six high-class plays. He possesses a true poetical instinct, which saves him, to a great extent, from the absurdities of that school of which he is the contemporary. His dialogue is bright and clever, his situations highly picturesque. He is deficient, however, in constructing power and sense of theatrical situation, and his dramas, therefore, have only been moderately successful when acted. Their value as literature has yet to be determined, and lovers of the drama will see with pleasure the announcement that they are now procurable in a collected form.

The name of Mr. Wills is now familiar to the public in its connection with the successes of Mr. Irving, but it has long been known to critics as that of an exceedingly clever, though undoubtedly careless, writer of plays. In a sort of collaboration with Mr. Vezin, who translated the German originals or "bases," Mr. Wills has written the *Man o' Airlie*, and *Hinko*, the first a really beautiful study of a poet's life and fate, the second a romantic drama of a school made popular by Kotzebue. The striking scene in the first-named play, where the senile poet, who is supposed to be dead, appears among the gay company assembled to uncover *his own statue*, belongs entirely to Mr. Wills, and is alone enough to prove him a dramatist of a high order. Unfortunately, his language is never on a level with his conceptions; it is seldom as strong and nervous as a little more care might make it. In the drama of *Charles the First*, Mr. Wills appeared to advantage neither as a poet nor as a politician. The picture of Cromwell (outrageously represented, by the way, by a comic actor [named Belmore) is without an excuse or a parallel; while that of the royal martyr is like a very mild piece in crayon by Richmond. Thanks chiefly to the easy grace and truly natural manner of Mr. Irving, even such scenes as this were listened to with toleration :

Huntley. I long have hoped to be an humble instrument
Of aid and comfort to your Majesty.
To show you something more than blind devotion.
To this end I have compass'd the acquaintance
And conversation of one Master Cromwell,
A leader in the Commons, and yet liberal.
King. I know him by report : a shrewd, strong gentleman,
Whose shrewdness and whose strength, methinks, are venal.
Huntley. In that your Majesty may do him wrong.
But be that as it may, I do profess

I come not an officious go-between,
But as an indirect and easy medium.
    King. I cannot say thy visit is more welcome.
What then?
    Huntley. Shall I bear back to Master Cromwell
The spirit of your Majesty's reply?
    King. Saint George forbid! Henry, of lusty memory,
Thy reign was set in happier days than mine.
Sooth, when thine anger flashed, thy thunderous voice
Announced it roundly. Huntley, we must temporize—
Thou hast not come as an official here,
And so thy message back commits us not.
Stay! Prithee tell them—nay, let's see—let's see.
    Huntley. Under your favour—
    King. Nay, under yours—I do bethink me now;—
Thou shouldst have told me earlier in our talk.
Say that the King repents his hasty act;
So we avoid that first rash burst of blame,
Which sudden measures, howsoever wholesome,
Provoke in England.
Let the five members sit as heretofore
(Our charges shall be laid most formally)
And let them bide the verdict of their peers.
As for their late remonstrance—tell my Commons
It is before us, and shall be considered
Most anxiously, and, point by point, discussed.
Some we shall cede at once, in other some
We shall require their counsel and review, etc.

But Mr. Irving in armour (Act iii.), resembling nothing more than the "Knight of the Rueful Visage," clad in a tin meat-jack, would have appeared comical to any audience less disposed to applaud the royal prerogative at all hazards. On the occasion of my visit to the Lyceum, the audience appeared to shed tears plentifully; but the situation was certainly only saved by the nervous energy of the popular young actor. A piece of higher calibre, *Eugene Aram*, showed Mr. Wills at his very best. No other living playwright could have produced, out of elements so simple, a success so genuine and unmistakable. Since *Eugene Aram* Mr. Wills has written a tragedy on the subject of *Mary Queen of Scots;* but as it was played, unfortunately, by people ignorant of the merest rudiments of acting, and has not been published, it is not easy to decide on its merits. One thing, however, is certain, that Mr. Wills seems to have some special delusions about Puritanism and Puritan leaders, for if anything could surpass his wonderful picture of Cromwell, it would be his delicious caricature of John Knox. The beautiful Mr. Rousby as Knox was a phenomenon to make the ghost of George Buchanan rise from the grave, and to darken the declining years of Mr. Carlyle.

Worthy to rank with Mr. Wills as a poetical dramatist, is Mr. Tom Taylor,* who is at once the most successful writer of his class, with only one exception, and the *bête noir* of a large clique of critics. Mr. Taylor is less original, but more diverse—less happy, but more careful, than Mr. Wills; and his dialogue, though bald like most modern dialogue, is more apt and to the purpose. I am certainly not among those gentlemen who deny Mr. Taylor the merit of originality; on the contrary, I believe his talents are underrated, simply because a foolish and erroneous idea has been circulated as to his indebtedness to foreign sources. To my mind he has seldom or never exceeded the allowable privileges of a dramatist, and almost all his success is due to dramatic faculties and instincts entirely his own. He is the author of some of the very brightest pieces of the day, and if in his historical and poetical productions he has failed to maintain a high level of literary excellence, he has merely failed in common with almost all caterers for the modern stage. The *Fool's Revenge* is, on the whole, his best serious play, and worthy of the translator of the *Barsaz-Breiz*. It is, to a certain extent, similar in subject to the opera

* Since deceased.

of *Rigoletto* and the play of *Le Roi s'amuse*. In most of its merits, however, it is Mr. Taylor's own, while its defects are just what might have been expected from one who, with all his talents, shows a sneaking regard for Mr. Podsnap's young person; and thus we are treated to a moral *dénouement* setting forth the prerogatives of Providence and the naughtiness of revenge.

> Vengeance is not man's attribute but heaven's!
> I have usurped it!

cries Bertuccio, "hiding his face in his hands." The piece trespasses on the borders of forbidden ground, but the danger is delicately avoided. The character of the Jester (admirably embodied at Sadler's Wells by Mr. Phelps) is cleverly worked out, through a series of nervous situations. The writing is on the whole excellent; the dialogue, though without imagery, being strong, pointed, and incisive. If faults are to be found in a really meritorious work, one may observe that Mr. Taylor is too consciously theatrical. Take the following little scene, which pleased the audience greatly:

[BERTUCCIO *stands for a moment fondly contemplating* FIORDELISA. *His dress is sober and his manner composed. He steps quietly forward.*
Bert. My own!
Fiord. (*turning suddenly and flinging herself into his arms with a cry of joy*). My father!
Bert. (*embracing her tenderly*). Closer, closer yet!
Let me feel those soft arms about my neck,
This dear cheek on my heart! No—do not stir—
It does me so much good! I am so happy—
These minutes are worth years!
    Fiord.   My own dear father!
  Bert. Let me look at thee, darling—why, thou growest
More and more beautiful! *Thou'rt happy here?*
Hast all that thou desirest—thy lute—thy flowers?
She loves her poor old father? Blessings on thee,
I know thou dost—but tell me so.

Fiord. I love you—
I love you very much! I am so happy
When you are with me— *Why do you come so late,
And go so soon? Why not stay always here?*
    Bert. Why not? Why not? Oh, if I could! To live
Where there's no mocking, and no being mocked;
No laughter, but what's innocent; no mirth
That leaves an after-bitterness like gall.
    Fiord. Now, you are sad! There's that black ugly cloud
Upon your brow—you promised, the last time,
It never *should* come when we were together.
You know when you're sad *I'm* sad too.
    Bert.   My bird!
I'm selfish even with thee—let dark thoughts come,
That thy sweet voice may chase them, as they say
The blessed church-bells drive the demons off.
    Fiord. If I but knew the reason of your sadness,
Then I might comfort you; *but I know nothing,
Not even your name.*
    Bert.   I have no name for thee
But "Father."
    *Fiord. In the convent at Cesèna
Where I was reared, they used to call me orphan.*
I thought I had no father, till you came,
And then they needed not to say I had one;
My own heart told me that.

Now it is, perhaps, superfluous to point out the gushing unnaturalness of this meeting between a father and daughter on a commonplace occasion. It might pass very well if the two had been separated for years, but they meet frequently, and hysterics are absurd. It is necessary, however, to recapitulate the nature of their relationship, for the edification of the audience, and so in the italicised lines, with a far too obvious side-glance at the spectators, the dialogue is studded with explanations. Faults of this sort disfigure too much of Mr. Taylor's work, and show too plainly that he approaches his subject more as a playwright than as a dramatist. There is a want of fusion in some of his conceptions, and a theatrical tawdriness in some of his designs. With all this, he has done the stage good service, and is certainly one of the leading theatrical authors of the day.

With the names already cited, the list of pseudo-poetical writers may cease. True, Mr. Albery has written a play in blank verse, in which the critics discovered original beauties, but his real talents lie in quite another direction. A word of praise, however, may ¦be given *en passant* to Mr. Hermann Merivale, who has made a very fair acting play out of *Le Lion Amoureux* of Ponsard, carefully avoiding the stilted style of that leader of the classic revival. Mr. Merivale has also written the *White Pilgrim,* a sort of poem for the stage, which failed as much by vile acting as by want of dramatic fibre. His productions have been few, but they encourage one to hope that he may take a leading place among contemporary dramatists.

Turning from the poetical drama, which is after all not poetical essentially, but rather a form of writing in which blank verse is used because great dramatists used it once on a time, we come to a writer who is perhaps more original than any we have named, and who also at times uses a sort of *monstr-inform-ingens-horrendous* style of writing, which is supposed to be blank verse. Critics have even gone to the length of calling his plays poetical, and of actually selecting poetic gems from their pages; but it would surprise me greatly to hear that he ever wrote a poetical line in his life. Mr. W. S. Gilbert, for it is he of whom I am speaking, is the greatest living writer of burlesques—not mere senseless inanities, composed of vulgar slang and breakdowns—but really first-rate comic productions, with an occasional touch of serious import. He began his literary career with the " Bab Ballads," maniac rhymes of perfect and convulsing originality, and he afterwards contributed to the vulgar burlesque literature of the day such absurdities as *Dulcamara; or, the Little Duck and the Great Quack*. His first genuine burlesque was the *Princess*, founded on Mr. Tennyson's pretty poem of that name; quaint in design, and clever in treatment. But in *Pygmalion and Galatea*, called a mythological comedy, and produced with conspicuous success at the Haymarket Theatre, he shows his talents at their very best. The myth of Pygmalion is a poetical one, and has been treated previously by our own Marston; but it remained for Mr. Gilbert to turn it into a first-class burlesque of the serious school. In his version, the statue, when brought to life, becomes a burden and a misery to its creator, and its perfect innocence and artlessness are made the cause of many diverting situations. The treatment is a vulgarising one, but has its merits; for while all the subtle loveliness of the primary idea is brutally destroyed, a good deal of strong satiric matter is gained. These are Galatea's reflections on first emerging from the stone:

Galatea. Then is this life?
Pygmalion.   It is.
Gal.   And not long since
I was a cold, dull stone. I recollect
That by some means I knew that I was stone,
That was the first dull gleam of conscience;
I became conscious of a chilly self,
A cold immovable identity,
I knew that I was stone, and knew no more;
Then, by an imperceptible advance,
Came the dim evidence of outer things,
Seen—darkly and imperfectly—yet seen—
The walls surrounded me, and I, alone,
That pedestal—that curtain—then a voice
That called on Galatea! At that word,
Which seemed to shake my marble to the core,
That which was dim before, came evident.

> Sounds, that had hummed around me, indistinct,
> Vague, meaningless—seemed to resolve themselves
> Into a language I could understand;
> I felt my frame pervaded with a glow
> That seemed to thaw my marble into flesh;
> Its cold hard substance throbbed with active life,
> My limbs grew supple, and I moved—I lived!
> Lived in the ecstasy of new-born life;
> Lived in the love of him that fashioned me;
> Lived in a thousand tangled thoughts of hope,
> Love, gratitude, thoughts that resolved themselves
> Into one word, that word Pygmalion! (*kneels to him*).
>   *Pyg.* I have no words to tell thee of my joy,
> O woman—perfect in thy loveliness.
>   *Gal.* What is that word? Am I a woman?
>   *Pyg.*   Yes.

Here is a dim gleam of what might have been a fine passage, but fine passages are not in Mr. Gilbert's line. Galatea immediately demands, "Am I a woman?" When Pygmalion replies, "Yes," she returns, "Art *thou* a woman?" and the house begins to titter. The ball now begins rolling. Galatea asks, "What is a man?" and being answered that man is a being framed to protect woman, work and toil for her, fight and die for her, observes quietly, "I'm glad I am a woman." "So am I!" Pygmalion responds; and the house titters again. So fascinated is the author by these subtle touches, that he repeats them, and when Galatea, observing her beauty in a mirror, exclaims, "So I'm a woman!" Pygmalion, to the intense delight of the audience, exclaims, "No doubt of *that!*" She continues:

>   *Gal.* O happy maid, to be so passing fair!
> And happier still Pygmalion, who can gaze
> At will upon so beautiful a face.
>   *Pyg.* Hush! Galatea—in thine innocence (*taking glass
>   from her*)
> Thou sayest things that others would reprove.
>   *Gal.* Indeed, Pygmalion; then it is wrong
> To think that one is exquisitely fair?

Pyg. Well, Galatea, it's a sentiment
That every woman shares with thee ;
They think it—but they keep it to themselves.
Gal. And is thy wife as beautiful as I ?
Pyg. No, Galatea, for in forming thee
I took her features—lovely in themselves—
And in the marble made them lovelier still.
Gal. (disappointed). Oh! then I'm not original?

The last expression is hardly tolerable in its psychology, even in a burlesque, where the whole subject is grotesque and unnatural. Though the other remarks of the statue may pass, it is difficult to believe her pouting over her own want of "originality." But I am fault-finding where I meant to praise. Taken as a whole, and seen as represented on the stage, this play has really a pleasant effect. It contains just enough imagination to redeem the dialogue from mere farce. Mrs. Kendal, who played Galatea, imparted to the character a delicate and dreamy beauty, noticeable even in her slow "swimming" movements about the stage, which lifted it into the high region of an Aristophanic creation ; she seemed indeed one of the great Athenian's own παρθένοι ὀμβροφόροι, descending into the region of modern comedy, and the ears almost listened for the music of strophe and antistrophe. And now, if Mr. Gilbert will forgive me for having found so many faults, I shall try to make amends by saying that in more than this particular he resembles Aristophanes. No living dramatist has his originality, and no living writer has his quiddity ; and if, with all his satiric gifts, he were capable of passion—that is, genuine satiric passion, he might do in a measure for our generation what Aristophanes did for his. The *Happy Land*, a burlesque of a burlesque, his own *Wicked World*, was perfect. Mr.

Gilbert has also perpetrated a delicious absurdity called *Trial by Jury*. Nothing could be better. It would have delighted Thackeray.

Reverting for a moment to *Pygmalion and Galatea*, which I suspect Mr. Gilbert regards as his masterpiece, I must regret that its general treatment was not either levelled to the broadness of the coarser passages, or raised to the level of the finer *nuances* of the situations. As it is, the effect is irritating. True, Aristophanes himself uses both absurdity and poetry, but he never *blends* them in this way; and his delicious lyrical effects are reserved for the chorus. Mr. Gilbert's play contains one truly imaginative passage, that where Galatea chronicles her first experience of sleep and dreams. It is as follows :

> *Gal.* I sat alone and wept—and wept
> A long, long time for my Pygmalion.
> Then by degrees—by tedious degrees,
> The light—the glorious light!—the God-sent light,
> I saw it sink—sink—sink—behind the world;
> Then I grew cold—cold—as I used to be,
> Before my loved Pygmalion gave me life.
> Then came the fearful thought that, by degrees,
> I was returning into stone again;
> How bitterly I wept, and prayed aloud
> That I might not be so! "Spare me, ye gods!
> Spare me," I cried, "for my Pygmalion,
> A little longer for Pygmalion!
> Oh, take me not so early from my love;
> Oh, let me see him once, but once again!"
> But no—they heard me not, for they are good,
> And had they heard, must needs have pitied me;
> They had not seen *thee*, and they did not know
> The happiness that I must leave behind.
> I fell upon thy couch (*to Myrine*), my eyelids closed,
> My senses faded from me one by one;
> I knew no more until I found myself,
> After a strange dark interval of time,
> Once more upon my hated pedestal,
> A statue—motionless—insensible;

And then I saw the glorious gods come down!
Down to this room! the air was filled with them,
They came and looked upon Pygmalion,
And looking on him, kissed him one by one,
And said, in tones that spoke to me of life,
"We cannot take her from such happiness!
Live, Galatea, for his love!" And then
The glorious light that I had lost came back—
There was Myrine's room, there was her couch,
There was the sun in heaven; and the birds
Sang once more in the great green waving trees,
As I had heard them sing—I lived once more,
To look on him I love!
Myr. 'Twas but a dream! (*coming down*)
Once every day this death occurs to us,
Till thou and I and all who dwell on earth,
Shall sleep to wake no more!
Gal. (*horrified, takes Myrine's hand*). To wake no more!

But a little after uttering this, Galatea is commenting vulgarly on the podginess of Chrysos (Mr. Buckstone), and exclaiming, " Mother! what is that? I never had one. Have people usually mothers?" to which Mr. Buckstone—I mean Chrysos—replies, with the leer and chuckle familiar at the Haymarket, "Well—that is the rule!" I do not say that Mr. Gilbert could by treating his theme in the highest manner have achieved as thorough a success, but I do lament to see an author of his talent, which commands the warmest admiration, descending to so vulgarising a treatment. The scenes with Chrysos were simply nasty, less, perhaps, through any intention of the author, than through the satyric unction of the male comedian. I have already expressed my opinion of the censorship of the Lord Chamberlain. Although censorship begins at home, the gentleman who interdicted the *Demi-monde* had nothing to say to certain portions of the *Wicked World*, or to that portion of *Pygmalion and Galatea* where Mrs. Kendal, in commenting on the shape of Chrysos, was to all intents and purposes compelled to pass her hand up and down Mr. Buckstone's abdomen, which resembled that of an African aboriginal blown out with "bang." I am not going to insist on the indelicacy of these matters. Perhaps, as the audience was not shocked, they contained nothing shocking. But I do insist that there is nothing in the *Demi-monde* or similar masterpieces to shock the delicacy half as much, and that the detection of indelicacies, if they exist, is the business and prerogative of the audience, and no business of any solitary person in authority. It is not for a moment to be argued that the modern French drama is clean. Such scenes as the supper scene in *Le Réveillon* are certainly indecent; and well might the *Pall Mall Gazette* complain that those who virtuously insist on adding an inch to the skirts of our ballet-dancers are comparatively lenient to foreign artistes. The Press and the Public, however, not the Court, are the proper authorities to settle such matters. Their power is at once indisputable and overwhelming. If a few super-sensitive souls complain that neither Press nor Public is severe enough, let them show their indignation by staying at home. So far as I see, it is not openly indecent pieces which most offend our Lord Paramount, but psychological dramas dealing chiefly with the violation of the marriage tie. Despite our breach of promise cases, and our Divorce Court, we are so virtuous here in England that we shiver at the very notion of a matrimonial breach of contract. To my mind, however, nothing but good could result even here from a free performance of French "social" pieces. We are not so good as we seem, and Mordaunt trials are merely the occasional eruptions of a volcano which is ever blazing under the surface.

Dumas *fils*, with all his faults, has purified his audiences. His ideal is not high, but to the French *bourgeoisie* it has been elevating, and it could certainly do us no harm. Moreover, there can be no question that the representation of a work of high artistic merit, full of accurate character-painting and delicate psychology, though its subject may be unpleasant and its treatment anatomic, is more in the interests of public morality than the representation of an apotheosis of vulgar virtue. The British Matron, whose ethics are those of the farmyard, and who deliberately sells her own young to the highest bidder, ruffles her feathers and squeaks her horror whenever naughty subjects are spoken of; but a more careful study of social complications, though shocking at first, might do her good. Marriage by her is held inviolable, and so true marriage should be; but the bond she means is a mercantile bargain, sacred to her as the contents of her pocket. Inspired by her, we in England value a purse more than a life, and deem an open violation of what is often a brutal fraud, the one unpardonable sin.

But I am forgetting my dramatists. The mention of the name of our leading burlesque writer naturally leads me to consider those others who call themselves burlesque writers also. But as an artist Mr. Gilbert is almost solitary. His are true comic creations, not mere monstrosities. Mr. F. C. Burnand is exquisitely funny at times; but his stage work is never done *au sérieux*—that is, with attempt to produce anything really admirable. His animal spirits are great, and his sense of incongruity perfect; he is an adept in stage tricks; and his pages are perfectly incomprehensible to one not adept in Cockney slang.

Here are Bacchus and Zephyr "returning from an evening party":

> *Bacc.* A very merry evening! for, as *you* know,
> There's no one gives a party like Queen Juno;
> They spoilt the coffee, tho', with too much chicory.
> *Zeph.* I say!—each dance, you flirted with Terpsichore!
> (*Digs him in the ribs—sly dog business.*)

Conceive the agony of an intelligent foreigner battling with the awful idiom of this stage direction. Mr. Burnand's Olympus is redolent of Cockaigne. Venus sings sweet ditties to the tune of "Billy Taylor," and the oracle at Delphi joins in chorus with "tiddy fol," etc. Zephyr talks of "taking a bus" while walking down "The Strand." Cupid talks about "Burlington Arcade" and Kew Gardens. The effect is sometimes funny, more often dreary. The author of "Happy Thoughts" should be capable of better work. His characteristic recklessness, however, has made his case hopeless. Even less amusing than Mr. Burnand's are Mr. Byron's. To the same rank belongs all the meretricious foolery of the day. Instead of Aristophanes, we have Joe Miller and the Ethiopian Serenaders done into dramatic scenes. The decline and fall of extravaganza has been rapid in the hands of its latest exponents. When Mr. Planché searched Fairyland for subjects, children of all ages could go to Covent Garden for delicate fun and picturesque romance. The spirit of "Once upon a time there were two kings," is almost idyllic, and the "Yellow Dwarf" is a genuine fairy tale for the stage. Even the succeeding school of Brough and Talfourd had great and distinguishing merits. Who that saw Robson in Brough's *Masaniello* can forget the tragic agony of the little conspirator, as pale and tremulous, the clammy perspiration on his brow, and his jaw dropping, he tottered in, crying,

"They've done it now—they've laid a tax on winkles!"

Not less striking was the pathetic reproachfulness of the same actor in *Fair Rosamund* when, as Queen Eleanor, he addressed the unfaithful king with one word, his own unaspirated Christian name, "'Enry!" This, with all its absurdity, was real burlesque. Something of a similar spirit breathes in a ridiculous production of Mr. Reece, wherein Romulus and Remus, two very naughty children, played by Messrs. James and Thorne, quarrelled while building up Rome with a "box of bricks!" The only surviving representative of fine extravaganza is Mr. Blanchard, whose yearly pantomime at Drury Lane is always what it professes to be—a dramatised fairy tale, full of light pictures, and without a shadow of vulgarity.

Passing from the dramatists who write in blank verse, and from the burlesque writers, who write in verse and worse, I come to those gentlemen who may be described as general dramatists, to whom nothing theatrical comes amiss, but who are perhaps most at home in plundering helpless novelists and adapting from the French. Towering before me rises a stately figure, with a head recalling the Chandos bust of Shakespeare, beautiful in its benignant baldness, with a twinkling eye and self-satisfied smile on the lips. I recognise him at once—it is our latter Shakespeare and our greater; a swan from the Shannon, uttering his wondrous notes in a delicious brogue, and breathing softly his own dulcet name of chaste "Dion." He has written one hundred and fifty dramas, some dozen of which have surpassed all modern productions in their successes. He might have been the editor of the *Times* and the President of the United States, but he preferred to devise amusements for a delighted generation: to turn *L'Homme Blasé* into a comedy for Charles Mathews; to take and mutilate the *Louis XI.* of Casimir Delavigne; to translate Dumas' *Corsican Brothers;* to dramatise the *Collegians* of Gerald Griffin. The first appearance of Mr. Boucicault was as a poet! When quite a young man he contributed to *Bentley's Miscellany* a poem called "Darkness," which, for some inscrutable reason, the publishers have reprinted in the "Bentley Ballads." Anything more dismal and uninstructed than this piece I have never encountered. It reads like a poem from Mr. Dobell's "Balder" turned into morality by Mr. Tupper, and then done into blank verse by one of Mr. Blimber's "young gentlemen." The author's first play was a comedy, *London Assurance,* which remains, with all its faults, his masterpiece. All the characters had done duty before in comedy. The languid old man about town with a rakish son, whom he believes to be an innocent; the rattling Londoner, who is ready to become bosom-friend with anybody; the rattling lady who hunts; the boobyish husband who follows at that lady's heels; the meddlesome lawyer; the confidential valet—all are familiar figures, farcical in outline, sketchy in drawing. The dialogue, brisk and telling, reads like Sheridan and water, faintly lemoned with Douglas Jerrold, and sugared by Sheridan Knowles. It is quick and jerky, to a great extent monosyllabic; when it rises to anything resembling emotion, it is simply insufferable. This is the rubbish a plain old baronet, whose other dialogue is simple in the extreme, is made to talk, in his enthusiasm over hunting :—" What state can match the chase in full cry, each vying with his fellow which shall be most happy? A thousand deaths fly by unheeded in that one hour's life of ecstasy. Time is outrun, and nature seems to grudge our bliss in making the day too short." The heroine talks gushingly, in the "Darkness" mood, of the "first tear that glitters in the eye of morning," and of "the shrilly choir of the woodland minstrels, to which the modest brook trickles applause." The lover, save the mark! informs his mistress that "the beams of that bright face falling on my soul, have, from its chaos, warmed into life the flowerets of affection, whose maiden odours now float towards the sun, pouring forth in their pure tongue a mite of adoration, midst the voices of a universe." It is clear that, when the stage secured Boucicault literature lost a Close. The success of *London Assurance* was secured by such artists as Farren, Harley, Keeley, and Mrs. Nisbett. Twenty years elapsed, during which the author continued to write indefatigably without any conspicuous triumph, but in 1859-60 the success of the *Colleen Bawn*, which ran for some two hundred and fifty nights, took London by storm. This drama, which is really a stage version of one of the most picturesque Irish novels ever written, brought its adapter a fortune. Its merits were great, but they belong to Gerald Griffin. Great successes rapidly followed; the *Streets of London, Flying Scud, After Dark*, and *Arrah-na-Pogue*, made the name of Boucicault a household word. Shakespeare was forgotten, but his mantle had fallen upon glorious shoulders. Now came the theatrical apotheosis of the railway train, the racecourse, and the town-pump. Now did the modern Orlando, disguised as the driver of a Hansom cab, prowl about the scene representing the Adelphi arches. Now did a fat female jockey sit in the weighing scales, to the delight of thousands; while a mighty stage mob of carpenters and scene-shifters applauded the racing of cardboard horses, running in the distance for the Derby. The triumph of realism had arrived, and the Shakespeare of the New Cut and Seven Dials had come.

As a constructor of stage plays, Mr. Boucicault is unequalled, and here, if anywhere, lies his special claim to distinction. If any one will take the trouble to compare the *Colleen Bawn* with the *Collegians*, he will see how the dramatist, while preserving everything, down to the tiniest detail, fuses all into a clever and more telling form. His dialogue is occasionally very happy, but comes from all sorts of sources. Turning from the mere form of his plays to the internal *morale*, the student perceives at a glance that, like most illiterate productions, they are thoroughly heartless. He has been styled the inventor of the Upholstery school of Comedy—upholstery doing in his comedies what pumps and steam-engines do in his dramas, and his ethics are, as might be expected, those of the bill-broker and the furniture-dealer. Indeed, his plays, like cheap furniture, seem made to *sell*. Though neatly put together, they are composed of cheap material and a great deal of veneer; and when he does introduce a fine, sterling, solid article, it is sure, on inspection, to prove second-hand. Such a gem as the character of Myles-na-Coppaleen is too fine to be his own; he has polished it up, however, to the highest pitch of stage brightness.

The mention of the Upholstery school leads me by a natural transition to that Cabinet school which is its natural successor, and which is generally known by the title of Robertsonian. Nothing could be more touching than the living career of the late Mr. Tom Robertson; he endured hardships and vicissitudes enough to crush any spirit, and only at the last moment awoke from his dream of poverty to find himself famous and rich. His talents were undoubtedly fine, his perception of his vocation delicate in the extreme; his defects belong less to his workmanship, than to his system. Born as it were on the stage, he early perceived the folly and absurdity of many stage traditions. He felt that acting as a rule was artificial and unnatural, that actors were too stagy and too stiff, and that this was partly a consequence of unnatural and stagy dramatic conceptions. Setting carefully to work, he produced, after several failures, his first and most popular comedy, *Caste*, the spirit of which is the simplest naturalism, the situations such as happen every day, the dialogue such commonplace as is spoken by commonplace people in real life. The effect was electrical, and Mr. Robertson was at once recognised as the Trollope of the stage. Without being original, the characters were life-like, and they did the ordinary business of life—such as laying table-cloths, carrying tea-kettles, and cutting bread-and-butter—in the easiest style imaginable. It is wonderful how modern audiences love on the stage the common facts of every-day life—how they thrill with joy at the sound of the postman's knock, or the muffin bell, and how they rejoice when they see an actor, dressed like a real gentleman, open a real umbrella or smoke a real cigar.* Mr. Robertson discovered this taste, and

---

* In a West-End comedy produced at this period, a leading scene represented a certain Park at dusk, when the chairs for visitors are gathered together and put away by a boy in buttons. The scene was recognised at once with delight, but the great

humoured it to the full. His comedies are minute cabinet pictures of society, admirably constructed for stage purposes, with a masterly perception of the tableau. As reading they are, of course, insufferable: that is no fault of the dramatist. Acted by the artistes of the Prince of Wales' Theatre, they were simply perfection. It has been argued against them, with some show of reason, that as they deal with the most commonplace persons and incidents, they are hardly worth the trouble and expense of seeing, since the real persons and incidents are unfortunately too common to every one's perception. "We don't go to the theatre," cry the severe critics of the drama, "to see lackadaisical schoolgirls flirting with imbecile Guardsmen, to contemplate crockery and inhale the steam of real tripe at a real supper, to listen to the vapid conversation of vapid people such as we encounter daily; we go to hear great thoughts expressed in grand language, to have our souls exalted by noble situations, to mark the fiery conflict of passions, and the subtle lights and shades of human character." This is all very well, and means just that they prefer Shakespeare to Robertson. But if we examine closely into the truth, we shall discover that Robertson, in his own way, was a poet too. No mere vapid realist could command such thorough success. His incidents may be commonplace, his characters may wear modern dresses and talk modern slang, but the fact is, he composed pictures which were pleasant to see on account of their artistic qualities. Those who do not

point was the appearance of the *real boy*, who after his real work in the Park was done, repeated it on the stage nightly, for the delectation of the delighted audience, many of whom recognised him at once.

understand how this can be, should read Mr. Browning's "Fra Lippo Lippi":

> Have you noticed, now,
> Your scullion's hanging face? A bit of chalk,
> And trust me that you should tho'?

And though Polly Eccles and Sam Gerridge, and the rest, may not be worth much notice in real life, they had real colour and pleasantness as figures on the little stage near Tottenham Court Road. The best of Mr. Robertson's dramas surpass the best of Mr. Boucicault's, as the best of Mr. Blackmore's novels surpass the best of Mr. Trollope's—by virtue of their gleams of simple poetic feeling. A maiden parting from her lover, a wife separated from her husband, a schoolgirl waking from her first dream, a soldier reading letters from home at the seat of war—all these are simple figures enough, but they grow interesting in the light of a genuine emotion. I do not for a moment affirm that Mr. Robertson's is high art; it is art of a kind. Its faults are those of the life it depicts: occasional heartlessness, shallow attempts at verbal wit, monotony of character-painting, the persistent representation of vulgar moods and modes.

> We call it pretty—that is, pretty well!

But to deny that it evidences poetic skill is certainly unfair. There is obviously poetry in it—of situation, of picture, though not of character and dialogue. This can scarcely be said of any other modern school of comedy. On another score, too, we owe gratitude to Mr. Robertson. He rebelled against the mock-heroic and stagy nonsense which had so long flooded the theatre. He determined at all hazards that his people should always be natural, his situations never artificial. He taught his actors to abandon their gasping "oh's" and "ah's," their stage strides, their unnatural looks and gestures. He suggested that they should endeavour to speak as men and women in real life do, and as French actors and actresses generally try to do. With this purpose he simplified his characters, his scenes, and his dialogues. At first there was a difficulty. "Gentlemen" were wanted, and actors, as a rule, were not like "gentlemen." The Gordian knot was solved by securing the real article, and more than one distinguished amateur was tempted, by the growth of society-dramas, to adopt the stage as a profession.

So far the gain was clear. The Scylla of artificiality was avoided, but the Charybdis of commonplace lay in the way; and, alas! on that fatal rock, the so-called Robertsonian school has split and sunk. The founder of the school died, having done good service to Art, and never, I believe, overstrained his natural pretensions. His very genius, however, deluded the public. A cry arose for realism, and the cry, which was answered to the heart's content of the crier, has hardly yet died away. Instead of being kept for gauging actors and acting of the Cabinet kind, the Robertsonian test has been applied to greater actors and nobler acting; so that English performances have become more and more distinguished for a dull, dead uniformity of mediocrity. Many people have gone to the extreme of renouncing the poetic drama altogether, on the score that it is not in the least like real life; forgetting that poetic language bears the same relation to high art that marble does to flesh, and though different in its superficial resemblances, resembles in its latent suggestions. Strong passions have been decried, strong gestures censured, strong emotions disliked, as offensive to the sense of realism. Dramatists have been afraid to take an imaginative flight, or to utter a flowery sentiment, from fear of the realist. The stage has lost dimensions, actors have lost dignity. Upholsterers and milliners have taken possession of a thousand theatres; and even the art of the scene-painter, who used to produce grand effects by Turneresque delineations of the brush, has been exchanged for the microscopic skill of the Cabinet designer. The best proof of Mr. Robertson's genius is that all these effects, which he instituted, are useless without him, and that in the one touch of poetry which redeemed all his imperfections he has never found a successor.

In the style of verbal wit of which he was so fond, he has found many. Perhaps the most conspicuous offender is Mr. H. J. Byron,[*] who began his literary career as a burlesque writer, and who is now the most indefatigable caterer of "comedies" for the London stage. Mr. Byron has two qualifications for theatrical success—he understands stage business, and he is an irrepressible punster. In his pieces, a number of infinitely vulgar people—labelled respectively "noblemen," "gentlemen," "authors," "ladies," "shopkeepers," "actors," but all bearing an indescribable family likeness, assail each other with vulgar verbal quibbles from scene to scene, in utter defiance of probability, and with no attempt whatever at suitability or sequence. Characters these plays have none, save such as may be detected in "Boz's" prentice-sketches, or extinct Adelphi farces. They do for the stage what Albert Smith's novels did for the library, and they are relished, I suppose, by the

---

[*] Since deceased.

same class of people. Their best feature is their innocence of all intent; their worst is their vulgarity. They might be passed over in silence, if they did not constantly occupy the London stage, to the exclusion doubtless of productions of real merit. Mr. Albery's *Two Roses* is of other and finer quality—a really genuine little play, although belonging also to the new school.

As I write, the reaction against mere realism, which began, doubtless, with the success of Mr. Wills and Mr. Irving, has culminated in some striking theatrical phenomena. A great actor, Signor Salvini, has appeared in London in an Italian translation of *Othello*, and his success has been in proportion to the originality—or what many think the outrageousness—of his conception. Sad to say, he has not entirely pleased the critics, some of whom accuse him of extravagance. The entire dramatic profession, however, with striking unanimity, has risen to do the great foreigner honour, and to recognise in his person the rights of the long-forgotten tragic Muse. Now for the first time, after long labouring under the delusion that Othello was a dull, hoarse-spoken blackamoor, who in the mildest possible way smothers his wife with an embroidered pillow, we discover the incarnate Moor, Titanic, terrible, striking down all opposition, raging on the torrent of his own wrath, haling Desdemona to death by the hair, and finally cutting his own throat with the most terrible realism of detail. A few years ago, this performance would have been hissed. To-day, audiences familiar with the horrors of *The Bells* greet it as the finest acting in the world. To my mind, it is entirely in the interests of Art that so powerful and original a reading of Shakespeare's drama should have achieved this popularity; it encourages the hope that attempts at originality may soon be the rule, and not the exception, on the English stage. Anything weaker than the stereotyped conception of Othello can scarcely be imagined. Mr. Fechter essayed the part after he had created an unparalleled sensation by playing Hamlet in a flaxen wig; his mild, gentlemanly *jeune premier* with a black face did not succeed in attracting the masses. He listened in the most well-bred manner to the insinuations of Iago, his strongest passions being conveyed by an open mouth, elevated shoulders, and turned out palms; and when he came to the murder, he did it as gingerly with his pillow as a careful father covering up a baby. It is said that Mr. Irving is going to try the character, and that he does not like Salvini's conception. It is difficult to imagine Mr. Irving in any part demanding powerful physique or mighty passion. His appearance is cadaverous, and his voice is weak. His manners on the stage are dignified without grandeur. His pathos, when he attempts pathos, is chiefly conveyed by a huskiness of the voice and a galvanic quivering of the hands. His success in *Hamlet* should not mislead him, for Hamlet is a character in which no actor has ever failed, so admirably helped is it at every point by the magnificent structure of the situations.* Mr. Irving is an actor of original genius, greater perhaps by reason of its very limitations than a genius more fluent in adapting itself to character foreign to itself. He would succeed as Richard III.; he might succeed

---

* Since the above was printed, Salvini's *Hamlet* has startled London. The character so represented becomes what Hamlet might have been, had he been born in Tuscany, during the ducal reign of Francesco de Medici; it is full-blooded Italian, and resembles as little the Danish Prince of Shakespeare as the legendary *Amleth* of Oehlenschläger.

as Macbeth. I believe he would comparatively fail in Othello, in Coriolanus, or in other parts characterised by intellectual robustness or predominant passion.

Simultaneously with the success of Salvini's passionate idealism, occurred the failure of Mr. Coghlan's mild realism. When first the announcement appeared that the management of the Prince of Wales' Theatre were about to produce *The Merchant of Venice* with Mr. Coghlan in the chief character, playgoers expressed a very natural astonishment. The theatre had been the temple of the Robertsonian Muse, and although since the dramatist's death it had despairingly betaken itself to such ghastly pieces as Mr. Wilkie Collins' *Man and Wife*, it had redeemed its own credit by the production of a pretty little trifle by Mr. Gilbert — *Sweethearts*. Mr. Coghlan was known as the *jeune premier* of the Robertsonian drama, an excellent actor, with occasional exhibitions of strength and insight, but certainly not one from whom was expected any high poetic exhibition. The experiment in the interest of realism has been made, and the failure has been complete. Mr. Coghlan's quiet, gentlemanly Jew has been voted an impossibility, and worse, a bore. The famous scene between Shylock and Antonio dwindles down into a mild conversation between two courteous merchants:

> *Shy.* Signor Antonio, many a time and oft,
> In the Rialto you have rated me
> About my moneys and my usances :
> Still have I borne it with a patient shrug ;
> For sufferance is the badge of all our tribe.
> You call me "misbeliever, cut-throat dog,"
> And spit upon my Jewish gaberdine ;
> And all for use of that which is mine own.
> Well, then, it now appears you need my help :

> Go to, then : you come to me, and you say,
> "Shylock, we would have moneys :" you say so ;
> You, that did void your rheum upon my beard,
> And foot me as you spurn a stranger cur
> Over your threshold. Moneys is your suit :
> What should I say to you ? Should I not say,
> " Hath a dog money ? Is it possible
> A cur can lend three thousand ducats ? " Or
> Shall I bend low, and in a bondman's key,
> With bated breath, and with a whispering humbleness,
> Say this :
> "Fair sir, you spit on me on Wednesday last ;
> You spurn'd me such a day ; another time
> You called me dog ; and for these courtesies
> I'll lend you thus much moneys."
>   *Ant.*   I am as like to call thee so again,
> To spit on thee again, to spurn thee too.
> If thou wilt lend this money, lend it not
> As to thy friends ; for when did friendship take
> A breed for barren metal of his friend ?
> But lend it rather to thine enemy,
> Who, if he break, thou may'st with better face
> Exact the penalty.
>   *Shy.*   Why, look you, how you storm !

Mr. Coghlan's conception, that Shylock is generally made too open and snake-like a villain, a mouther and ranter whose every look and word would awaken suspicion, was doubtless right enough ; but something more was wanted than mere negation of old readings to complete the part. It was foolish in the extreme not to perceive that the Muse of Shakespeare and that of Robertson are hopelessly apart. True, even Shakespeare gains by a more natural style of gesture and delivery, such as Mr. Calvert has been endeavouring to cultivate in his admirable revivals at Manchester ; mouthing and bellowing are always offensive and unsuitable, but one might as well play the Prometheus of Æschylus in gaiters instead of in the *cothurnus*, and modern wigs instead of the mask, as deliver the grand style of drama in the easy conversational style of modern comedy.

Of the resuscitation of that drama, I believe there is hope; if I did not, it would hardly have been worth while to take the above retrospect. Just now the theatre is shunned by the students, scorned more or less by *littérateurs*, despised entirely by philosophers. We are told on every side that the dramatic Muse is dead, and that she can never rise again.

> She is dead and gone, lady,
> She is dead and gone;
> At her head a grass green turf,
> At her heels a stone.

And over her stand Mr. Phelps and Mr. Hermann Vezin, in chimney-pot hats, while Mr. Chatterton intones her requiem. But the public know better. The dramatic Muse lives—will live as long as passions stir in men's hearts, as long as thousands delight in the mimic stage. It is simply absurd for poets and philosophers to glance contemptuously at the theatre —at an art hallowed by the grandest achievements of the human intellect, and glorified by godlike names; and it is equally insane to lay the blame on modern actors and the modern public, when the real fault lies with the intellectual barrenness of this generation. Let a great dramatist arise, and he will find great actors, and *perhaps* a great manager. I do not say there would be no difficulties in the way; but I do aver that the reward and honour of the highest probable dramatic success would be greater than that hitherto achieved by any writer of this generation. Just now, the world, wealthy as it is in feminine and fantastic writers, wants a great masculine dramatist above all things. Such an one would take the stage as it is, with all its deficiencies, and out of given materials evolve a noble series of productions. He would be harassed by misconceptions and absurdities; but so were Euripides and Racine. He would be often badly interpreted; but so were Sophocles and Molière. His grandest productions might be misunderstood; so were those of Æschylus himself. He might even have to "write in" inferior matter to tickle the groundlings; so did Shakespeare habitually. At no time in English history has the drama been recognised as the highest department of literature; it has always been more or less despised by serious professors; and this fact has deterred many, as it deterred Milton,* from casting their conceptions in the dramatic form. For this, English criticism is certainly to blame. Many of our poets, such as Coleridge and Byron, have deliberately written "plays for the closet," forgetting that the true home of a play is a theatre, the true destiny of a play to be acted—well or ill, as the case may be. This destiny has been filled by the highest masterpieces, from the *Prometheus* of Æschylus to the *Hamlet* of Shakespeare, from the *Ornithes* of Aristophanes to the *Tartuffe* of Molière. There are other dramas, like those masterpieces of Mr. Browning, compiled for representation, but not even the highest enthusiast in closet literature could represent any of these as of quite equal calibre.

"But," cry the wiseacres, "the public must be amused, and the highest products of the human intellect are not amusing." After this we shall be told that *Othello* does not draw the masses, and that *Le Malade Imaginaire* is not funny. "The finest productions of the Elizabethan period, for example, would fail to draw." The finest productions do draw,

---

* See some striking particulars under this head in Mr. Masson's admirable study of Milton's life.

whenever played; the inferior productions either fail, because they are ill-constructed and verbose, or are suppressed, because they are grossly indecent in subject and in language. There is an actor who parades the provinces, Mr. Barry Sullivan, a very clever performer of the old school, who succeeds so wonderfully, that a "Barry Sullivan house" represents the fullest triumph of the managerial exchequer; yet Mr. Sullivan's *répertoire* consists chiefly of Shakespeare; his leading parts are Hamlet, Richard, and Othello. The late Mr. Charles Kean, though by no means a first-class actor, made a fortune by Shakespeare. Many other obscurer stars do likewise. By his revival of a dull play, *Henry V.*, Mr. Calvert, of Manchester, achieved great successes, both in our provinces and in New York. Shakespeare, then, is amusing, after all. What the public find in Shakespeare, they would find in any writer of kindred endowments. They do not want dull plays written for students by students, by poets for poets; they want the living, breathing drama, whether in the shape of a play by the great master, or a trifle by Robertson; they want good construction, good situation, fair insight into character, lively dialogue. When a play, with these qualifications, fairly represented, fails, it will be time to talk of the indifference of the public. True, as I said at the outset, audiences are uneducated; it should be the task of dramatists to educate them—to guide their taste, which is on the whole excellent, into regular channels of legitimate enjoyment.

II.

A NOTE IN 1886.

SINCE the preceding notes were written, there has been little or no alteration in the condition and prospects of the modern stage. Two phenomena, however, have occurred, which are likely sooner or later to be noted as more or less historical : (1) The triumphant progress of Mr. Irving, followed somewhat timidly by Mr. Wilson Barrett and others, under the banner richly scrolled with the words " poetical " and " legitimate ; " and (2) the successful cynicism of Mr. W. S. Gilbert, exhibited in the production of pieces which are, in the most literal sense, anti-poetical. Of Mr. Irving and his *compeers* I need say little. They are fighting the good fight, and conquering fresh territory every day. Of Mr. Gilbert I am inclined to say a few words, since there is a large section of the play-going public ready to accept him as the typical playwright of the present period.

In the first place, let me observe that Mr. Gilbert, despite all his boasted cynicism, has been on more than one occasion a backslider.

In his bewilderment as to what is and is not literature, in his incapacity to perceive that a prettily-acted modern play, like *Arrah-na-Pogue*, is better than the best imitation or resuscitation of effete poetical models, he has shown curious misconceptions, among the most pathetic of which is his idea that a drama written in so-called " blank verse " is of necessity an attempt in the right direction. This misconception is curious in a dramatist who is radically unpoetic, and who has no more call to write blank verse than a nimble dancer has a call to use wooden legs. Thanks chiefly to such encouragement, Mr. Gilbert, who is well known as a grim wag and a most amusing writer of dramatic trifles, set to work the other day to write a play on the subject of Goethe's *Faust*, or, to quote his own words, "to remodel, for dramatic purposes, the whole story of Gretchen's downfall." I quite acquit Mr. Gilbert (to quote his own words again) "of intentional irreverence towards the grandest philosophical work of the century."

> Good in his blindness, he in goodness erred.

But his blunder was not in attempting to reach the poetical standard, but in falling almost wilfully below it. His *Gretchen* failed, not because it was literary, but because it was dull; not because it resembled Goethe's *Faust*, but because it possessed no portion of Goethe's magic. The first part of Goethe's *Faust* has been classed among the great literary successes of the world, not because (as Mr. Gilbert, speaking in the name of the provincial, or theatrical, mind would think) it is "the greatest philosophical work of the century," but because it is broadly and simply human, based on the commonest elements of human nature. It is beautiful because it is crystalline; it incarnates the sentiment of humanity, irradiated by the passionate poetical light. As a story it has an appeal to everybody, even to the theatre-goer, and if Mr. Gilbert, instead of tampering with it, had simply arranged its best scenes in their dramatic sequence, he would have certainly succeeded in arousing the public interest and securing the public applause.

Rash in his endeavour to justify himself, Mr. Gilbert appealed straight to the literary public by publishing his play. Some of his critics seem to have told him that it was too "poetical" to succeed on the modern stage, and failed in consequence of its superiority. This is an error. For once playgoers resented a provincial interpretation of a literary masterpiece; they did so, however, not because the piece was provincial, but because its provincialism was dreary. In Mr. Gilbert's play Faust is transformed into a very uninteresting monk, Mephistopheles into a talker of comic journal satire, and Margaret into a mincing young lady who lives and dies the mere echo of a monotone. On his first appearance Mephisto (as Mr. Gilbert calls him) says, with an eye to the gods:

> You see
> We devils have our consciences. In vice
> We can do nearly all that man can do,
> But not quite all. There are some forms of sin
> From which we shrink, and that is one of them.
> I have no stomach for such worldly work,
> But get a *man* to help you.

This, of course, is thoroughly provincial, thoroughly undevilish, but sure of a guffaw from the gallery. The character of Gretchen is pitched in the same key. Just as Mephisto poses as a dry dog, fond of his joke, does she pose as the incarnation of pretty virginity. She is, in fact, Miss Marion Terry, the very charming but particularly monotonous young lady who created the part, and to whom the published play is dedicated. Throughout the whole drama we never escape into the free air of passion and poetry; we are encumbered at every step by the mannerisms and platitudes of the boarding-school ideal. Goethe's Marguerite is supremely and essentially a woman. From the moment when she tries on the jewels before the glass to the hour when she dies raving mad in gaol, she is splendid and sublime by sheer force of typical womanhood. Her strength is that unconscious purity which comes of a soul thoroughly and simply human in all its passions, sorrows, and desires. This other Marguerite, or Gretchen, is a living doll, a thing of self-consciousness, simpers, and sawdust. When she dies in the atmosphere of poetry, with a stage sunrise reddening behind her, she says:

> Heaven wills that thou should'st live—that I should die—
> So let us yield ourselves to heaven's will.

The provincial mind is as fond of talking about "Heaven's will," as of that other "little article" (as Mr. Toole called it once in a comedy by Mr. Reade), "a father's curse."

I have made no quotations from Mr. Gilbert's play, because there are no passages to repay quotation. The best speech is one by Mephisto in the third act, where he calls down the curse of hell upon Faust's head; but even this is disfigured by conventional expressions—"false priest," "lying trade," "smug-faced brotherhood," "chicken-soul," and other jargon of the theatre. What is most extraordinary in the work, as the production of the dramatist by profession, is its utter negation of all dramatic effect; even when the situations are good, they are lost by want of technical skill. Mr. Gilbert shines as a writer of theatrical trifles, where dramatic insight is not wanted. He is a wag, and, to a certain extent, a comic poet, and I much like his adaptation to the stage of his own "Bab Ballads." But he has not even mastered the poetic vocabulary, and I trust *Gretchen* will be his last experiment in what writers call the "modern poetical drama."

It has remained for Mr. Irving, in his position of

champion extraordinary of the poetical drama, to exhibit before audiences bewildered by Mr. Gilbert, a play which adumbrates, with all its shortcomings, the true *Faust* of Goethe, which possesses the soul of poetry, though not its language ; which, when all is said and done, is worth a thousand such futilities as *Gretchen ;* and which, above all, supplies the one imaginative manager-actor of this generation with a *rôle* which absorbs the full resources of his undoubted artistic genius. It is little wonder, therefore, that the critics have taken heart of grace, and talked again hopefully, if mysteriously, of a possible "dramatic revival."

Periodically, say every five years, the great English-speaking public is startled by the eager voice of the quidnunc, announcing this prospect. Periodically, the voice dies away among other voices of the crowd, while the dear old moribund drama continues in its corpse-like coma, with spasmodic quickenings of death in life. When Robertson loomed above the horizon, the world prepared for something cosmic, only to discover that what it imagined to be a sun was a sort of gigantic tea-cup. When Boucicault rose radiant out of the sea of Irish woes, there was another portent, but what onlookers at first mistook for a potent magician's wand, turned out to be only —a shillelah. Meantime, the accomplished author of *Pinafore*, like a facetious Choragus of Choragi, has amused himself by poking fun at the Shape that once lived and moved and spoke the tongue of Shakespeare, by ridiculing its sock and buskin, by deriding its antique method, so persistently and so cleverly, with such a touch of Aristophanes-plus-Mr. Guppy and the "jolly bank-holiday-every-day young man"—that it has been a dangerous thing for any dramatist to view life seriously or sentimentally, or to attempt the grand manner so familiar to our fathers. Against the influence of sad wags like Mr. Gilbert, we have to set such phenomena as the beautiful "revivals" of Mr. Irving, which have reminded playgoers that after all there *is* a grand manner, and that it is a little better, when all is said and done, than the manner of the middle-class cynic.

But to do Mr. Gilbert justice (and no one is a warmer admirer of his saturnine humour than I am), his influence for good in this generation has, at least, equalled his influence for evil. He might be described, with some measure of truth, as the Mark Twain of the stage; for while the American humourist has succeeded in disintegrating so much of the shallow enthusiasm and false sentiment of ordinary life, the English one has done the same service in destroying what was false and meretricious in dramatic tradition. True, he has gone to the extreme length in disillusionising the public sentiment as to all the higher dramatic emotions; but that was inevitable, and the question will adjust itself by-and-by, since those emotions are practically indestructible. As the matter now stands, any attempt at pure poetry on the stage is very like skating on thin ice. There can be no doubt, nevertheless, that our grandfathers very often took platitude for poetry and heroic posturing for the acting of nature. A modern dramatist or actor must now reckon on a public prepared at all points to dispute and ridicule his method wherever it conflicts with common-sense. Love is not a passion à la mode, and there is a tendency to "guy" love scenes. Strong exhibitions of emotion are unpopular in real life and equally so in the theatre. At the same time the swift inspiration of genius can conquer the prejudice against the sentiment of love, or rather against its too maudlin expression, and justify the strongest and wildest of emotions under the right conditions.

Besides the revival of poetical drama, real or so-called, there has of late years been a revival of melodrama. Mr. Sims, Mr. Pettitt, and Mr. Jones have produced alone, or in collaboration, a number of bright and panoramic plays of human life. Mr. Sims possesses a true literary talent and a fine vein of workaday humour. Mr. Pettitt stands alone as a dramatic "constructor." Mr. Jones appears to have lofty aims and praiseworthy literary pretensions, while openly despising the craft in which he has sought for popularity. That the critics are eager to discover literary merit wherever they can is shown by their lavish praise of the following passage from the *Silver King*, put into the mouth of a rehabilitated drunkard and betting man :

O God, put back thy universe and give me yesterday!

Curiously enough, what is food for mirth to one generation becomes actual poetry to another, since the passage I have quoted is simply a paraphrase of the famous lines given by Martinus Scriblerus, in the "Art of Sinking in Poetry":

O God, annihilate both space and time,
And make two lovers happy!

If it were my wish or my business to find fault with Mr. Jones, I should say that he possesses one serious fault in a dramatist—that of sometimes mistaking "fine writing" for literature ; but of his earnestness there is no question.

Besides the gentlemen I have named, Mr. Sydney Grundy and Mr. Pinero are now diligent contributors to public entertainment. Mr. Grundy is a brilliant and an able dramatist, with an unique capacity for writing trenchant dialogue, and it may be confidently predicted that he will take a high place among contemporaries, if ever plays are judged on their merits as literature. Mr. Pinero seems to be a pupil of Mr. Gilbert's, without his master's cunning, but with much of his disagreeable cynicism. Another writer of note, Mr. Clement Scott, though better known as a critic, has done excellent work for the stage, both singly and in collaboration with Mr. B. C. Stephenson. *Diplomacy* was an admirable piece of rendition, and there was great ingenuity shown in *Peril*. I have not seen *Sister Mary*, but I hear it spoken of as a vigorous attempt at purely emotional drama.

While the drama remains moribund, the world is full of actors who may fairly be accounted virile. It is no exaggeration to say that the greatest of these actors are Americans. On this side of the water we have no artists, with the exception of Mr. Irving, worthy to rank by the side of Booth, of Jefferson, of Lester Wallack. Even to an Englishman familiar with the finest efforts of Charles Mathews, the acting of the younger Wallack comes with all the force of a revelation. I saw this princely comedian for the first time in *The Bachelor of Arts*. He had long been to me an illustrious name, one of the few American names known by familiar report on this side, but I had imagined him one of the "old school," in the Gilbertian and invidious sense. Of the old school he is certainly, in so far as his method puts all the efforts of the new school to shame; at once broad, subtle, swift, and penetrating, it is the method of the born actor, equipped with all the culture of his fascinating art. Nowadays, I fear, actors are made, not born, and made very badly. Young men flock upon the stage because it has become a lucrative profession. Formerly only those achieved histrionic reputation who possessed by nature a commanding, an interesting, or an amusing personality. Nature, even more than art, created, in their various lines of character, Mrs. Siddons, the Kembles, Macready, Kean, Harley, Robson, Charles Mathews, Buckstone, Keeley, Compton, Wigan, and Walter Lacy. Not but that the same kind of creation takes place occasionally even now. Nature, far more than art, has given us Ellen Terry.

The fact remains, however, that modern actors generally suggest the idea of professionals who have mistaken their profession. Let any one who doubts this go to Wallack's when the master is acting, and compare him with the ladies and gentlemen who surround him. There are clever people among them, but, with the exception of the tried veteran, John Gilbert, they strike the spectator as people who act to live, not live to act. In companies where there is no star of the first magnitude, the effect, of course, is different. At Daly's, for example, there is a combination so admirable in *ensemble*, so full of natural talent and acquired fitness, so excellently guided and directed, that it became last summer the talk of London. Nearly every member of the company has been chosen for his natural acting gifts, and from officers to rank and file, the whole regiment is fit for the field, and magnificently manœuvred.

In England nowadays, I regret to say, the tendency to what may be called, rather Irishly, professional amateurism, is much more marked than in America. It began with the Robertsonian successes, which in their excessive and somewhat insipid naturalism called into existence very little first-class talent, but opened the stage door to hundreds of average young men and women. Here and there, but almost by accident, an artist of distinction appeared to break the genteel monotony of the performances at the Prince of Wales' Theatre; there were brightness and natural gaiety in Marie Wilton, rich humour in George Honey, a pretty kind of talent for grasping small bits of character, in Mr. Hare. But when the Prince of Wales comedians exhausted Robertson and removed to the large stage of the Haymarket Theatre, it was plain that they were little more than amateurs after all. A cruder exhibition than the performance of *Masks and Faces* was certainly never seen on the amateur stage; and *The Rivals*, as we all know, was even worse. The public yearned for the old methods, and found them not very far off, at the Lyceum.

I am far from suggesting, as many do, that the loss of the fine old crusted performer of the past generation, the performer who played half-a-dozen parts a week with more or less incoherence, is a thing to be deplored, or that the inroad of good-looking walking gentlemen has been wholly without its advantages. Actors, nowadays, take pains to be natural, they conduct themselves like gentlemen on and off the stage, they dress well and appropriately, they seldom over-act or murder the Queen's English. But all this improvement, consequent on managerial recruiting among penniless dukes and impecunious earls, will not compensate for the genius, the natural adaptability, which used to be the actor's distinguishing qualification, or for the boldness and fearlessness of method, which made tragedy tolerable and comedy puissant. Turn again to Lester Wallack, and see him step upon the stage; then turn to any of our modern interpreters of comedy, and note the difference. The secret of the power and fascination is, that this man *is* the part he plays; that nature, in Lester Wallack, created the physical and intellectual type fit to wear the idiosyncracy of Charles Courtley, of Harry Jasper, of D'Artagnan, of Don Cæsar de Bazan. *Ars est celare artem;* the art is not manifest, because Nature herself is potent in establishing the verisimilitude. The finest of all acting, indeed, resolves into another Irishism—that, *au fond,* there is very little acting about it. Fechter in his young days *was* Armand Duval, Desclée was Camille, Lemaitre was Robert Macaire, Robson was Sampson Burr, Buckstone was Toby Twinkle, Compton was Touchstone, Helen Faucit was Cordelia, and so on all the world over. Natural fitness, plus the many resources and practices of the art, is what constitutes the true actor.

In England this fact is understood, perhaps, in only one direction. I have long wondered what quality it is in the English atmosphere, or in the English constitution, which breeds so many genuine "comedians." On the soil of America, so far as I have seen, they do not thrive; yet in England their name has been and is legion. Harley, Buckstone, Compton, Robson, Wright, Toole, Righton, Lionel Brough, George Honey, David James, Thomas Thorne, George Barrett, are names that will occur at once to many. The humour of each of these performers was, or is, something *sui generis*, but there is a family likeness in it all, indeed, a Cockney likeness. In other branches of the business England is not so excellent. It is doubtful, for example, if we possess a really first-class "juvenile" performer. Henry Neville—whose first appearance caused Planché to leap out of his seat and cry, "At last we have an actor!"—is still perhaps the best, despite his years, which he carries very lightly. Charles Coghlan has great talent, but is unequal and very weak in scenes of passion, where Neville is strong. Kyrle Bellew has shown abundant promise, but is somewhat too self-conscious and artificial; while Harry Conway, who began as the very weakest of walking gentlemen, has lately shown remarkable earnestness and latent strength. In personal attractiveness, William Terriss is the most endowed of them all.

The same lack of genius which is the fault of our juvenile actors, is to be found among our actresses. In scenes of power and passion, even Ellen Terry loses much of her charm. Mrs. Kendal is an inimitable *comédienne*, but quite without the pathetic fallacy in romantic and poetical characters, which she has sometimes attempted. Her Pauline, in the *Lady of Lyons*, is not a high-born beauty in distress, but a housemaid in a passion; her Claire, in the *Ironmaster*, is strenuously artificial in its pathetic solicitations. In pure comedy, however, Mrs. Kendal is supremely delightful. Much her superior in the higher graces of the art is Madame Modjeska, a somewhat artificial but exquisitely refined actress. Miss Ada Cavendish, though inferior in her method, has really inspired moments. The original freshness and sweet girlish grace of Miss Kate Rorke surpass all the attitudinising of more pretentious actresses. Mrs. Langtry is Venus from foot to forehead. Miss Mary Anderson is stridently juvenile, but splendidly beautiful. Passing away from leading ladies, we have *ingénues* by the score, and *soubrettes* by the dozen; one of the brightest of the latter being Miss Lottie Venne, an inimitable actress in her own peculiar line. Glancing downward through the ranks of the profession, we shall discover that the most noticeable artists are those who follow the good old method. There is Mr. Mead, whom I remember playing the whole range of the drama years ago at the Grecian; Mr. Howe, who graduated in the robustly vigorous Haymarket school; Mr. Willard and Mr. Speakman, both in Wilson Barrett's company; Mr. Hermann Vezin, perhaps the finest elocutionist living, and consummately excellent when suited; Mr. Charles Warner, full of electricity and splendid animal spirits; Mr. Fernandez, excellent in everything, but especially excellent in strong, rugged character studies; and Mr. Odell, who has a quiddity and oddity peculiarly his own. All the artists I have named are to be distinguished from the mob of gentlemen of the new school, who get upon the stage with ease, and act without intellectual conviction.

Why is it, then, that, with so many capable artists, and so warm an appreciation of their talents on the part of the public, we have so few virile plays? Because there are no great dramatic authors, say the critics. Because the managers are uninstructed, say the playwrights. Because the public is a great silly baby, to be pleased with a rattle, tickled with a straw, say the managers.

It may be quite true that we have no great dramatists, but it is also true that we have among us men capable of splendid dramatic work, if such work were in demand; not only within the circle of known writers for the stage, but outside of it, are such men to be found. But it is simply impossible to ensure the production of any drama which is not, to a certain extent, conventional after the known and approved fashions. The enormous outlay necessary in London to mount an important piece, the loss consequent on failure, the apathy of the public to new ideas of any kind, frighten the managers from making experiments. When *Claudian* was produced in London, everybody anticipated failure because it dealt with an ideal and far-off subject; and Mr. Barrett, himself, though a most enlightened manager and actor, had so holy a fear of the mere mention of "blank verse," that he caused the piece to be written in a sort of hybrid lingo, neither verse nor good prose, which utterly destroyed its value as literature. At a huge sacrifice of time and money, the play was forced along, till at last its novelty and beauty were recognised. Here, however, the circumstances were very exceptional; and moreover, *Claudian* furnished a star part for a manager of ample resources. Under any other conditions, the piece would have been withdrawn within a month. My own experience, which I may cite by way of illustration, is the experience of nearly every dramatic author living. Having an intimate and practical knowledge of stage requirements, acquired through early connection with the theatre, I find it possible to produce pieces which please the manager, and sometimes the public; but whenever I have proposed any drama lofty in method or unconventional in form, I have been met with the answer that such productions are inexpedient. Management is too precarious a business for experiments of any kind.

Then again, it is very difficult indeed to please both the critics and the public, and what pleases one will often repel the other. Nor are critics always unanimous. Two plays of mine, produced in London and afterwards repeated successfully in America, met with exactly opposite treatment from the newspapers here and on the other side. *Storm-beaten* (an adaptation of my own novel, "God and the Man") was received with no little praise by the leading critics of London; in New York it was roundly slaughtered in several quarters. On the other hand, *Lady Clare*, which some London critics treated coldly, and which gained its success in London in the face of lukewarm criticism, was praised liberally by the American Press, almost without an exception.

It is the custom in London, and often a sheer necessity, to force plays into success by large expenditures of money, and in the teeth of disastrous business. For many weeks *Pinafore*, the most successful of modern comic operas, played to quite inadequate receipts; so, I am informed, did the *Colleen Bawn*. *The Private Secretary*, when acted at the Prince's Theatre, involved the author in a loss of some thousands of pounds; but he held firmly on to it, and transferring it to the Globe, reaped a late but abundant harvest. Of course this can only be done where the play possesses great vitality in itself, or where the management is unusually sanguine and determined. It is seldom or never, I believe, done in America, where pieces stand or fall by a first night's reception, and by the perfunctory morning criticism. The exceptions are cases where the play is produced with an ultimate eye to the "road," rather than with any view of immediately making money.

I have touched upon the commercial side of the matter, because, in dramatic work, there is no golden mean between success and failure. A play is condemned absolutely, if it does not prove managerially profitable; no matter what its literary or technical merit, no matter how warm its reception, it is justified or condemned by the amount of money paid by audiences who wish to see it. Now, modern audiences are mixed assemblages of men, women, and even children. When a great drama flourished in England, playgoers were different, ready to respond to any kind of method, however daring, if it was justified by its cleverness; and if a prude sat listening under the rain or sunlight, her blushes were hidden by a mask. Later on, when we had a superb comedy, great in spite of its license, the conditions were the same; the subjects were selected without tremor, the treatment was slapdash, the speech vehement, reckless, and bold. It is too late in the day to reproduce these conditions, nor am I suggesting for a moment that their reproduction would be desirable. How far indiscriminate license may degrade and even emasculate art may be seen any night in Paris at the Palais Royal. But it is obvious at a glance that a dramatist writing for a mixed modern audience, with Mr. and Miss Podsnap in the stalls, must choose his subjects carefully and treat them very gingerly. Were he a very Sophocles, he would have to eschew the story of Œdipus; were he an Euripides, he would have to fight shy of the domestic life of Phædra. He must, in short, to be listened to at all, avoid all offence against moral and religious prejudices, follow the conventional ethics, humour the popular creeds, use language easily intelligible to immature persons. He must on no account attempt to edify; if he does, he is lost, and catalogued as a bore.

III.

THE DRAMA AND THE CENSOR.

THERE comes a time in the history of nearly every great literary movement when it is necessary for some member of the community to protest, in the name of himself and in the name of the class to which he belongs, against vexatious and quasi-providential interference from above. I think that time has come in the history of our modern stage, where some are pleased to perceive the dim dawnings of a dramatic revival; and I believe that I can count on the sympathy of readers of this book, if in citing certain experiences of my own I take leave to protest against an authority very much resembling persecution. I must premise, however, by saying that I have no private or personal feeling in the matter. For the present reader and licenser of plays, Mr. Pigott, I have the highest respect and consideration. Such as his spiriting is, he does it gently enough. But the position he holds, and the influence he brings to bear, are, in my opinion, so fatal to the interests of dramatic art, that it will soon be expedient to inquire into the true nature of his authority, its legality, and the prospects of its limitation, or best of all, its total suspension.

There was recently represented at the Adelphi Theatre, a drama from my pen, entitled *Storm-beaten,* and almost identical in subject with my novel, "God and the Man." This drama contained (I say it in all humility) a central idea as elevated, as pre-eminently religious, and I may add Christian, as is to be found, perhaps, in any other drama of modern times; an idea indeed embodying and adumbrating the very central conception of Christianity. How it was worked out, whatever might be its literary shortcomings, is another matter. My point is that the drama's purpose was the very highest and noblest possible from the spiritual point of view. That it touched the heart of the public, both here and in America, where it is still being represented, is now pretty well known. Now in this drama, as professedly ethical and avowedly religious, the name of " God " was used from time to time—never profanely, never being taken in vain ; that name had even been printed upon the playbill ; and in the last act, as the triumph of Christian love and brotherhood was proclaimed, the lovely Easter Hymn of our Church was sung by the village choir. I do not think any truly religious spectator, whatever his creed, could witness *Storm-beaten*, or listen to the holy music of its close, with any feeling of discomfort or sense of incongruity.

But the Lord Chamberlain, in the exercise of his traditional authority, thought otherwise. He objected to the mere mention of the name of "God" in a stage play, as unnecessarily impious ; he resented the printing of the name of God in a playbill as an additional outrage ; he denounced the singing of the Easter Hymn on the stage as a needless piece of profanity ; and, finally, he hinted to the management of the theatre that their license was in danger, if these things were not immediately reformed, as, I regret to say, they speedily were.

About that time there came to me a letter, written, not by any mere layman or outsider, but by an ordained minister of the Scottish Church, containing the following passage :

> What a wretched piece of official prudery that was of the Censor regarding your play ! It was good enough for a religious

magazine, but too good for a playbill. The Censor's objection implies that he is the controller of the Devil's work. *God must not be named in the documents with which he has to deal.*

This sarcasm, though bitter enough, certainly hit the mark. The drama, according to the Lord Chamberlain, must be eternally divorced from the Gospel according to any of the Apostles; the religion which animates our best literature is to have no influence upon our stage, which is to remain, what it has remained from Shakespeare's time, a mere excrescence, a thing for shallow hearts and idle heads, a spectacle for an hour's passing amusement—the Devil's pastime, and nothing more! The same Censor who is outraged at the word "God" in a playbill, would have swooned at the face of the "Holy Mother" on a wall; and Raphael would have been requested not to paint Madonnas. The same Censor who is outraged by the singing of a church hymn on the stage, would have been indignant at the musical description of God creating the world out of chaos, and Haydn would have been asked not to compose any more "Creations." Fortunately, however, painting is a free art, and sacred music has no Lord Chamberlain.

The question of mine is, I hold, one on which the whole fate of the English drama must depend. If the art of the dramatist is to be measured out to please the whim of a Court functionary, who condemns the clothing of religious symbols, but approves the nakedness of Gaiety burlesque; if the insane bigotry of the Church (with its rabid hatred of its hereditary rival, the stage) is to cripple the dramatist's work as it has done from time immemorial, the sooner we cease talking about a dramatic "revival" the better. Thanks to the Lord Chamberlain, the whole marvellous psychological drama of the French Empire has been interdicted to us, while there has been no real interdiction on the nudity of Châtelet spectacle or the ulcerous corruption of the Palais Royal. Thanks to the Lord Chamberlain, great themes of passion are forbidden to the dramatic poet and student of human nature, while the dramatic "Masher" behind the curtain has *carte blanche* to cater to the taste of the social "Masher" in the stalls. Thanks to the Lord Chamberlain, our drama is no drama, our art is no art, all the intent and purpose of stage performances being to amuse fools and chronicle small beer. But the drama, I trust, has a higher function than to please a modern Petronius and pass away an idle hour. It is the noblest of all arts, and should be the most free; and it embraces in its scope, not merely its kindred arts of poetry, painting, music, but from the days of Æschylus downwards it has held out the hand to Religion, its grave veiled sister. To paraphrase again the words of George Herbert:

> A play may find him who a sermon flies,
> And turn delight into a sacrifice!

Not that it is foredoomed to the heresy of mere instruction—that doom would be fatal to its claim as art; but there is no sphere of man's life, no phase of man's religion, with which it might not freely and candidly deal. True, there is a region of mystery, of spiritual sacredness, where it has never ventured since the days of the Greek, and there is no need that it should venture there again. The public is a wise judge, a judge that knows well with what sacred means the drama has a right to deal, and what others it ought to let alone; and I believe there is no public so sagacious as our English play-going one, in resenting inconsistency, mere edification, or idle profanity. But the dramatist should be able, like the poet, like the painter, like the musician, to go direct before his Rhadamanthus, to be condemned or approved, not in the ante-room, or in darkness, but in the broad daylight of the open court of public opinion.

I know well what arguments may be adduced by the friends and supporters of the Censor in support of the theory that a censorship of the drama is necessary; they are the same which have been used, from one dark age to another, to suppress free thought and free speech, and to limit literary activity. But the suppression of literature delayed, from century to century, the spread of natural knowledge, and the suppression of the drama (to compare small things with great) is likely to postpone indefinitely the resuscitation of our Elizabethan mummy, the dramatic Muse—which is not dead, but sleeping, after all. What man of genius would care to write poetry or fiction, if a gentleman in Court livery were placed at his shoulder, pointing out the kind of inspiration *he* thought expedient? What painter would care to produce pictures, what musician to compose music, if his work were to be regulated by the good taste of a special providence, salaried by the State? Such intervention would be the death of poetry, painting, and music, as it has been the death or syncope of the drama. But it is with the professors of dramatic art themselves that the remedy lies. The timidity of the old days, when the actor was an outcast, still clings to them; they are acquiring literary culture, but they still lack spiritual courage, so that we see every day the spectacle of artists cowering before the bottled thunder of Little Bethel, and feebly accepting the patronage which is an insult in lieu of the homage which is a right. Let the truth be uttered: that the Art which Æschylus made religious, which Shakespeare made humane, which Molière made reformatory, must and shall be *free*; that her true place is not at the feet of Religion, but at her side—sometimes even, during times of folly and superstition, in the empyrean above her head. Abolish the Lord Chamberlain, and we shall soon have virile plays. Free the tied tongue of the stage, and men of genius will soon teach it the divine speech of poetry and passion. But until this thing is done, until dramatists acquire the privileges and exercise the functions of manhood, the prospects of a dramatic revival, so fervently to be wished for, must be indefinitely postponed.

NOTE.—Since the production of *Storm-beaten* has come the Lyceum production of *Faust*, in which religious forms and expressions are freely and liberally used, and in which the Devil himself is a chief character. I have not heard that the Lord Chamberlain has remonstrated with Mr. Irving on the "blasphemous" nature of his production, or has requested him to cut out any of the christian hymns. So that there is one law for the Adelphi, and another for the Lyceum; a sanction for Goethe, and no sanction at all for the contemporary dramatist.—R. B.

FLOTSAM AND JETSAM.

I.

A NOTE ON ÉMILE ZOLA.

(1886.)

As one grows older, one wonders less at the proverbial philosophy of contemporary criticism. While the *Saturday Review* still exists, though toothless and moribund, a journalistic Dogberry proclaiming the watches of the literary night to a generation still unaware of sunrise and of Mr. Spencer, there will always be a class of readers which takes its opinions on faith and eagerly echoes the anathemas pronounced by senile watchmen against "one Deformed" and other disturbers of the public peace. We smile at Dogberry, though it is sad to reflect that never once, from the beginning of his official career, has he done a sane or a generous thing, has he recognised a new thought or a rising reputation, has he ceased to regard all men of genius as malefactors, and all mediocrities as men of genius. Among the great men of our time who are oftenest "run in" by the old-fashioned literary watch, perhaps the most phlegmatic of all is Émile Zola. Despite a chorus of uninstructed abuse he goes doggedly on his way, and even when hauled up before the magistrates he continues to assert his right of private judgment and his complete contempt for critical authority. I confess that I admire this stolid attitude, so different to that of most revolutionaries. I confess that I like to see this sublime contempt for Dogberry and Verges. Poor Thackeray was irritated when told by the watch that he was "no gentleman." Dickens was actually angry when informed on the same authority that his "Tale of Two Cities" was idle rubbish. *Nous avons changé tout cela.* We are merely amused when we hear the old cry, "This is your charge: you shall comprehend all vagrom men; you are to bid any man stand, in the Prince's name." It is only when men who should be wiser join in the persecution that one's amusement turns into indignation. For my own part I am amazed as well as indignant when Mr. R. L. Stevenson, who ought to know better, accuses the author of "Une Page d'Amour" of being possessed by "erotic madness!" Then I smile again, seeing the good Mr. Howells from Boston, gentle apostle of man-millinery, interpose for the defence, and generously affirm that Zola, though a sad offender against good taste, is a severe moralist, and, at the same time, the cleverest Frenchman alive!

The fact is, Zola is to literature what Schopenhauer is to philosophy—the preacher of a creed of utter despair. No living writer has a stronger and purer sense of the beauty of moral goodness; no living man finds so little goodness in the world to awaken his faith or enlarge his hope. But if Zola is "erotic," then a demonstrator of morbid anatomy is a sensualist, and a human physiologist is a person of unclean proclivities. True enough, he is conscious, even morbidly

conscious, of the great part which the god Priapus plays in modern life, more especially in those phases of life which are Parisian. Everywhere he diagnoses disease:
> Disease and Anguish walking hand in hand
> The downward slope to death!

Naturally, too, he is a little unhealthy, for the stench of the dissecting-room does not conduce to vigour. But of all men that wield a pen, he is perhaps the least "erotic." A little "mad" he may be, for, after all, some of us hold pessimism to be scarcely short of madness. His hatred of sensuality, his loathing of vice in all its forms, amounts to a passion. He finds, with Schopenhauer, that human nature is corrupt to the very core, but he always remembers, with Schopenhauer, that self-sacrifice and spiritual love, where they exist, are infinitely beautiful and noble. To him, the apples of the Hesperides are merest Dead Sea fruit. To him the god Eros is a corpse, smelling of corruption. To him, nevertheless, purity is a fact—the one grain of salt sprinkled on a putrefying world. As I write, the face of little Jeanne, gazing out of "Une Page d'Amour," rebukes the lie which brands its creator as infamous and unclean; but even over this divine child bends the Nemesis of Sin, cruel, piteous, and hideous—the same Nemesis that leant over the disease-disfigured countenance of Nana the courtesan, and over the figure of the old woman, paralysed in her chair, whose son married Thérèse Raquin. "Erotic," quotha! Spirits of mutual admiration, genial souls of the Savile Club, is this your indictment? Come, Messires Dogberry and Verges, arrest this rogue "Deformed," and haul him up for judgment; then, when Zola is sentenced to his fourteen days, go and seize Pasteur in his laboratory, suppress Huxley, stifle the physiologist and the philosopher as offenders against public decency, and put Herbert Spencer into the stocks!

Grim moralist and stern physiologist as he is, and as such supremely justified, Zola is nevertheless all wrong. To say that, however, is neither to impute his motive nor to deny his genius. Like all Frenchmen, he is possessed by one overmastering ethical notion, which causes him to sermonise *ad nauseam*. Even the French Empire, with all its faults, was something more than a subject for morbid anatomy. A man may die of syphilitic caries, yet be a living soul. In reading Zola, sane as he is, one has to hold one's nose; whereas life, real life, smells wholesome, and it is a very phenomenal city whose existence can only be determined by its lupanars and its sewers. Large as is the part which sensualism plays in life, and which it must play as long as the beast's brain subsists within the man's, it is merely a minor part after all. To Schopenhauer, the singing of the little birds was only one among many signs of their agony; to Zola, the music even of human love is a discord, ending in despair. Yet only a pessimist believes that the birds are utterly miserable, and that human creatures are completely vile or unhappy. So that, when all is said and done, the charge against Zola amounts to this—that he is a pessimist, and that pessimism is superficially impertinent and fundamentally wrong. As it *is*.

The subject of Zola's intellectual weakness is too long to discuss in a mere note, but it may be easily grasped by the reader who will refer to Zola's own notes on Proudhon. Proudhon is the philosopher who solves great social and literary problems by the power of generalisation. Zola is the artist who cannot generalise. "Une œuvre d'art est un coin de la création vu à travers un tempérament," says the artist; attempting a minor definition which in no way invalidates the philosopher's larger generalisation that temperaments and works of art are the products not merely of individuals, but of the collective temperament of nations and of humanity. ·Naturally, Zola misconceives Proudhon altogether. Great men, he thinks, are men who permit themselves to possess genius without "consulting humanity," who say what they have in their "entrails" (*sic*), and not what lies in the entrails of their "imbecile contemporaries." But perhaps no man that ever lived was ever so representative of his contemporaries, "imbecile" or otherwise, as Émile Zola. He is a Frenchman of the Empire, seeing the world *à travers* the temperaments of all his fellow Frenchmen—not seeing it clearly, not seeing it whole, not seeing anything in it but infinite corruption and infinite despair. "En un mot, je suis diamétralement opposé à Proudhon : il veut que l'art soit le produit de la nation ; j'exige qu'il soit le produit de l'individu ! " But that Proudhon is right, Zola himself offers the strongest literary demonstration.

Despite all this, Zola is an earnest man and a strong writer, and I am glad to be able to say even these few words in his justification.

II.

CHARLES READE.

A SOUVENIR.

It was in the summer of 1876 that I first made the acquaintance of Charles Reade, at a little dinner given by Mr. John Coleman, then manager of the Queen's Theatre. The occasion was one especially interesting to me, as the great novelist (for great and in some respects unparalleled he will be found to be, when the time for his due appraisement comes) had expressed a desire to meet my sister-in-law, who, though still a very young girl in her teens, had risen into sudden distinction by the publication of the "Queen of Connaught"—a work attributed in several quarters to Mr. Reade himself. Pleasant beyond measure was that night's meeting; pleasanter still the friendly intimacy which followed it, and lasted for years; for of all the many distinguished men that I have met, Charles Reade, when you knew him thoroughly, was one of the gentlest, sincerest, and most sympathetic. With the intellectual strength and bodily height of an Anak, he possessed the quiddity and animal spirits of Tom Thumb. He was learned, but wore his wisdom lightly, as became a true English gentleman of the old school. His manners had the stateliness of the last generation, such manners as I had known in the scholar Peacock, himself a prince of tale-tellers; and, to women especially, he had the grace and gallantry of the good old band of literary knights. Yet with all his courtly dignity he was as frank-hearted as a boy, and utterly without pretence. What struck me at once in him was his supreme veracity. Above all shams and pretences, he talked only of what he knew; and his knowledge, though limited in range, was large and memorable. At the period of our first acquaintance he was living at Albert Gate, with the bright and genial Mrs. Seymour as his devoted friend and housekeeper; and there, surrounded by his books of wonderful memoranda, he was ever happy to hold simple wassail with the few friends he loved. Gastronomically, his tastes were juvenile, and his table was generally heaped with sweets and fruits. A magnificent whist and chess player, he would condescend to spend whole evenings at the primitive game of "squales." In these and all other respects, he was the least bookish, the least literary person that ever used a pen; indeed, if the truth must be told, his love for merely literary people was small, and he was consequently above all literary affectations. His keen insight went straight into a man's real acquirements and real experience, apart from verbal or artistic clothing, and he was ever illustrating in practice the potent injunction of Goethe—

> Greift nur hinein in's volle Menschenleben !
> Ein jeder lebt's, nicht vielen ist's bekannt,
> Und wo ihr's packt, da ist's interessant !

His sympathy was for the living world, not for the world of mere ideas; and as his sympathy so was his religion—not a troubled, problem-haunted, querulous questioning of truths unrealised and unrealisable, but a simple, unpretending, humble, and faithful acquiescence in those divine laws which are written in the pages of Nature and on the human heart.

He read few books, and abominated fine writing. I well remember his impatience when, taking up a novel of Ouida, and being pestered with a certain abominable iteration about "an Ariadne," he sent the book flying across the room before he had reached the end of the first chapter. For the literature of pure imagination he cared little or nothing, perhaps not quite enough. Among the letters of his in my possession is one in which, referring to certain conversations we had had on the subject of poetry, he utters the following dicta, following them up with the charming playfulness which was his most pleasant characteristic :

"Even Tennyson, to my mind," he says, "is only a prince of poetasters * (!). I think with the ancients, in whose view the Poetæ Majores were versifiers, who could tell a great story in great verse and adorn it with great speeches and fine descriptions; and the Poetæ Minores were versifiers who could do all the rest just as well, but could not tell a great story. In short, I look on poetry as fiction with the music of words. But, divorced from fiction, I do not much value the verbal faculty, nor the verbal music. And I believe this is the popular instinct, too, and that a musical story-teller would achieve an incredible popularity. *Réfléchissez-y!* Would have gone in for this myself long ago, but can only write doggerel. Example :

"*Vive la poésie!*"
> "You and Miss Jay
> Hope to see my play :
> I hope so too.
> Because—the day
> You see my play,
> I shall see *you!*
>
> "Yours ever very truly,
>
> "READE."

---

* This remark must be taken *cum grano salis*, and only in reference to the argument which follows. Reade was a warm admirer of the poet Laureate.—R. B.

Here I may appropriately refer to his habit of signing only with his surname those letters which he reserved for intimate friends. In all his personal relations he was completely frank, charming, and gay-hearted. On the back of a photograph before me, taken at Margate, whither he had gone for the benefit of his health, he wrote as follows :

"DEAR MISS JAY,
 "I enclose the benevolent Imbecile you say you require. It serves you right for not coming down to see me !
"C. R."
"All previous attempts were solidified vinegar. This is the reaction, no doubt !"

This was written not long before he encountered the great trouble of his later life, when the good and gracious friend who had made his home delightful to all who knew him was suddenly and cruelly taken away. "Seymour," as he used to call her very often, possessed much of his own fine frankness of character, and knew and loved him to the last with beautiful friendship and devotion. From the blow of her loss he never quite rallied. His grief was pitiful to see, in so strong a man ; but from that moment forward he turned his thoughts heavenward, accepting with noble simplicity and humility the full promise of the Christian faith. Fortunately, I think, for him, his intellect had never been speculative in the religious direction; he possessed the wisdom which to so many nowadays is foolishness, and was able, as an old man, to become as a little child.

Any personal recollections of Charles Reade would be incomplete without some reference to his connection with the stage. From first to last he followed, with eager pertinacity, the will-o'-the-wisp of theatrical fame, descending into the arena to fight with wild beasts—among men who, neither in manhood nor in genius, had any right to be called his equals. Only in his latter days did he reap much pecuniary reward from the theatre, while to the very last he received scant respect from the ephemeral criticism of the day. But his love for the stage amounted to a passion, and more than once have I heard him say that he would rather earn five hundred pounds a year by writing plays than five thousand by writing novels. Unfortunately, he came upon a period when the dramatic art is without honour, and when the only standard of its success is commercial, and in his eagerness to meet halfway an uninstructed public, he had to call in the aid of the low comedian and the master carpenter. But if any reader would perceive how good work in this kind differs from bad, let him compare the literary workmanship of a play like *Never Too Late to Mend* or *The Wandering Heir* with any printed specimen of what is called in America the "nailed-up" drama, or set side by side with that by Charles Reade any other translation or adaptation of the French piece known as *The Courier of Lyons*. Even in his worst plays Charles Reade was a master of style.

Far away from and above his achievements in the acting drama stand the works by which my dear and lamented friend first made his reputation. The time is not yet ripe for a fit judgment on these works; but I am quite certain that if a poll of living *novelists* were taken it would be found that a large majority of them recognise Charles Reade, as Walter Besant some time ago nobly and fearlessly recognised him, as their Master. Yet I read in a newspaper the other day that Trollope considered Reade "*almost* a genius," and I am informed by the

Observer that "to speak of the author of 'Never Too Late to Mend' and 'Hard Cash' as a man of genius would be an exaggeration." "O sæclum insipiens et inficetum!" Trollope, whose art was the art of Count Smorltork *plus* the bathos of vestrydom, Trollope, who could write a book about the West Indies without putting into it one poetical thought or line, passes judgment on a literary giant and pronounces him a genius—"almost"! The Sunday newspaper, which would doubtless canonise the author of "John Inglesant," measures this Colossus, and finds him of "a tall man's height—no more"! Some of us, on the other hand, who are not to be daunted by bogus reputations, or to be awed by the idiocy of approven literary godhead, hold to our first faith that one man alone in our generation mastered the great craft of Homeric story-telling, and that this same man has created for us a type of womanhood which will live like flesh and blood when the *heroines* of Thackeray, Dickens, and George Eliot are relegated to the old curiosity shop of sawdust dolls. For my own part, I would rather have written "The Cloister and the Hearth" than half-a-dozen "Romolas," and I would rather have been Charles Reade, great, neglected, and misunderstood in his generation, than the pretentious and pedagogic Talent which earned the tinsel crown of contemporary homage, to be speedily dethroned, and, in the good time that is coming for Genius, justly forgotten.

III.

GEORGE ELIOT'S LIFE.

THE new life of George Eliot, by her last husband, Mr. Cross, has been justly praised by some English journals as a model of book-making, consisting, as it does, almost entirely of the lady's own letters, slightly and somewhat loosely linked together; but it is, none the less, about as dreary and lugubrious a work as men have met with during the last decade. Without any bold unveiling of the Sibyl, we are made to feel, not for the first time of late, that this biographical habilitation or rehabilitation of dead men and women, is, at best, an unfortunate business; for, though George Eliot is invoked to tell her own story, and tells it fairly well, it all amounts to nothing after all. We get few hints of honest human thought, not to speak of flesh and blood; we find that the Sibyl is still posing, and will not let us catch one glimpse of her real face. This statement may seem extraordinary to readers who are content to accept as self-revelation a good deal of feminine gossip, much talk about receipts and sales, some remarks on ganglionic cells, and a few quasi-editorial opinions on the advantages of beneficence. But Posterity, if it should interest itself very much on the subject—which I take leave to doubt—will want something more; something such as comes to us, with almost Biblical solemnity, in the terribly pathetic story of poor Carlyle.

When I met George Eliot first, over twenty years ago, she was living, with her husband, George Henry Lewes, at the Priory, St. John's Wood, London, and was then a tall, slight, not ungraceful woman, in the prime of life. As every one knows, she had a great reputation, which she had already begun to discount, however, by the production of " poetry." Every art and device of the experienced *littérateur* had been used by Lewes, a thorough man of the world, to make that reputation mysterious and sibylline; so that an unanimous press and a confiding public were leagued together in the faith that George Eliot spoke with authority, and not as the scribes. Seldom do works of art satisfy both the instructed and the uninstructed classes; yet " Adam Bede " and " Silas Marner " did so, and the author received the daily assurance of completed fame. A few, like myself, failed to recognise, in some of the author's works, the puissant touch which conveys literary immortality, while discovering in them, amidst so much that was admirable and exquisitely expressed, a distressing taint of intellectual conventionality, foreign to the nature of truly creative genius. What I saw of George Eliot personally confirmed me in my impression that the sibylline business, both publicly and privately, had been overdone. Naturally passionate, aggressive, sceptical yet impulsive, she had sat so long upon the tripod that her genius had become frozen at the fountain, and her character was veneered over with the self-pride of insight ; so that, with all her apprehensiveness, she lacked sympathy, and with all her moral enthusiasm, she was spiritually cold. The life she led was not one favourable to freedom of character. She saw few people, and those few were Sibyl-worshippers; her sex debarred her from the knowledge of at least two-thirds of humanity; her literary prosperity was untroubled by misconceptions or harsh criticisms; so it is little wonder that life at last became for her an ingenious physiological puzzle, to be pieced together with the assistance of M. Comte and Mr. Harrison. The result, I believe, is recorded in literary productions which, with all their brilliancy and subtlety, with all their friendliness of outlook, with all their well-weighed catholicity, became at last, in the worst sense, mechanical, and exchanged for lineaments of flesh and blood the deathly stare and ghastly ineffectiveness of a "waxwork"* exhibition.

A characteristic passage in these letters is the one where George Eliot describes her interest in Wallace's "Malayan Archipelago," and her particular delight in the record of the birth and babyhood of the young orang-outang. Here her sympathy with popular science warmly asserted itself, and, indeed, she was always most thoroughly at home in welcoming any suggestion which threw discredit on the superhuman pretensions of human nature. Very early in her career she had laid the spectre of "Anthropomorphism," and discovered that Comte's *Grand Être* was a more reasonable person than the *Pater Noster* of popular superstition. Forthwith it seems to have occurred to her that human types, possessing all the peculiarities of living beings, might be created for the world by a sort of intellectual evolution. But alas! the world has discovered by this time that these types, so scientifically fashioned, were homunculi and simulacra, not human creatures. No such process could have given us Tom and Maggie Tulliver, or Mrs. Poyser, or even Hetty Sorrel; but it gave us Romola and Daniel Deronda, and Dorothea Brooke, and the skittish marionette, Fedalma. It is

---

* This epithet of "waxwork" was very happily applied by Mr. Swinburne to "Daniel Deronda."

a pity, therefore, that George Eliot ever learned the vocabulary of science, or heard anything, even at second hand, about ganglionic cells. The radical defect of her mind, or rather of her education, is to be seen in her poetry. Striking novels may be constructed, as we have seen, with much cleverness and little inspiration; but great poems are all inspiration, from the first flush of thought to the last consecrating touch of form. Not even a contemporary critic would be rash enough to affirm that George Eliot's poems are much superior to poetic exercises. In only one of them, the series of sonnets called "Brother and Sister," is there either the rhyming instinct or the pathetic fallacy. In all she wrote, the editorial leaven is predominant. One instance out of many, serves to illustrate her radical want of imagination. Take, then, the opening lines of the "Legend of Jubal":

> When Cain was driven from Jehovah's land
> He wandered eastward, seeking some far strand
> Ruled by kind gods who asked no offerings
> Save pure field-fruits, as *aromatic things*,
> To feed the subtler sense of frames divine
> That lived on fragrance for their food or wine :
> Wild, joyous gods, who winked at faults and folly,
> And could be pitiful and melancholy.
> *He never had a doubt that such gods were.*
> *He looked within and saw them mirrored there.*
> Some think he came at last to Tartary,
> And some to Ind, etc.

Passing over the clumsiness of touch in the fourth line, there is not much fault to be found with the verses until we reach the fifth couplet, when the whole imagery of the poem falls asunder to show the writer's commonplace intellectuality. A poet, having just called up the vision of "wild, joyous gods," could never have paused to explain that Jubal had no doubt of their existence, because he saw them mirrored in his inner consciousness. Such a suggestion, at such a moment, is of the inmost nature of unbelief, of the very essence of prose. And what we discover here we discover everywhere in the Sibyl's later writings; keen intelligence and culture are predominant, and literary faith is wanting. Quite different is the impression gained on a fresh perusal of "Adam Bede," or the first volume of "Mill on the Floss," or, best of all, the "Scenes of Clerical Life." Here the emotion is almost poetical, and the insight quite delightful. The beautiful note, first struck in "Amos Barton," died away into a discord with the beginning of "Romola." A narrow but exquisite experience had been exhausted, and the period of manufacture had begun. George Eliot's books were full to the last of wise and clever things, her style to the end was that of honest workmanship, as of one who reverenced her art; but the Heaven that lay around her literary infancy seemed further and further off as her knowledge widened. Her writings reflected, not the lover of humanity, but the superior person. Pure literature is a democracy, however, where no superior persons are tolerated. Hence it is that the most noteworthy woman of this generation, a woman of unexampled cleverness and veracity, has left works which, I believe, will be speedily forgotten, while "Jane Eyre," and "Casa Guidi Windows," and the "Cry of the Children," will be remembered.

Indeed, when all is said and done, George Eliot was, not literally and technically, but essentially, a Positivist; and Positivism is not a creed out of which great imaginative literature is ever likely to spring. Such a Pantheon as Comte suggested, consisting of the wise men of the world, and presiding over a cosmos where the rapture of inspiration is exchanged for the miseries of evolution, is a poor exchange for the interregnum of the old gods of fable. It may produce half-hearted singers, but no poets; prodigious talents, but no geniuses of what Goethe called "daimonic" power. I am far from deprecating the influence of Science on works of art; indeed, I believe that out of the union of Science and Religion will issue, sooner or later, the supremest literature this world has ever known. But George Eliot was too much occupied with crude contemporary discoveries to grasp the full issues of human life and death. She studied, not on an observatory, but in a laboratory ; from conception and creation she turned to dissection and vivisection. Her influence was enormous for the time being, precisely because she appealed to an enormous public exercised in the same way, just waking up to the awful discovery that the moon was, not Diana, but green cheese, or magnesium. Of course we have no concern with a writer's creed, save in so far as it determines the quality of workmanship. In George Eliot's case, it changed what had originally been natural, fresh, and charming, into something tiresome, platitudinarian, rectangular. She began as an enthusiast, and ended as a bigot. The full extent of this change may be ascertained by contrasting her early letters, written before success came to her, with the later epistles, written when she was firmly fixed upon the Sibyl's tripod. Even when she was taster in ordinary to the propagandist publisher, Mr. John Chapman, she had not begun to take the literature of revolt too seriously ; indeed, she knew well that it meant "high jinks" generally, and had doubtful credentials ; but when it changed its machinery, and became the literature of a scientific priesthood, she was mastered by its novel pretensions, and went right over to it, as a ripe convert and eager auxiliary. From that time forth, her genius degenerated. As I have said, the life she led with George Lewes was not favourable to breadth of sympathy, or knowledge of the living world. They were a retired couple, generally in low health; and their visitors consisted chiefly of men of the new school—*e.g.*, Bastian, Harrison, etc. George Eliot's female acquaintances might have been counted upon the fingers of one hand. I have been at a gathering in the Priory where there were twenty or thirty gentlemen, and only one lady, the hostess herself. Now, George Eliot stood much in need of feminine companionship; she had a woman's heart under all her learning, and was capable of interesting herself even in feminine frivolities; and so there was something pathetic in her loneliness. Women, of course, tried to thrust themselves upon her, persons of the strong-minded sort, I imagine; but she rejected all such impertinent overtures. On one occasion, when she had been pestered by the solicitations of some more than usually pertinacious stranger, I heard her exclaim against the folly of troubling one's self to meet "persons with whom one has no sympathy in common." "Don't you agree with me?" she asked, looking at me with her grave, thoughtful eyes. I answered her in the negative, giving it as my humble impression that all human beings, however morally and intellectually different, had *something* in common with each other, and that, in any case, it was specially beneficial for literary people to encounter persons with no interest in literature, from whom they might at least discover how small a part mere literature played, after all, on this wonderful and many-featured planet.

Few works of permanent literary value obtain recognition from the criticism that is contemporary, and if George Eliot had been different, she would never have achieved her great popularity. Luckily, in all matters of knowledge, sympathy, and religion, she was well abreast of her time. She was content with the scientific solution of the problem of existence, and one of the best bits of verse she ever wrote was her prayer to join the "choir invisible," who, in the Comtean conception, make music to the great march of Humanity. Her first writings gave promise of a great writer, but, viewed coldly and dispassionately *now*, they do not justify the claim of her admirers that even her best work will be a permanent possession. Yet she was a great woman, though a genius *manqué*, a striking and commanding contemporary figure, if not a spirit whose labours may defy oblivion. She will be long remembered and always deeply respected; but her fatal mistake was that of writing as if the last words of wisdom had been spoken. Modern science is neither a hideous farce, as some theologians imagine, nor a thing to be taken, as George Eliot took it, too seriously. It is merely an interesting chapter in the complex philosophy of Human Life.

IV.

EPICTETUS.*

THE translation of Epictetus, executed by a gentleman who commanded a troop of black soldiers during the great American campaign, is doubtless popular in America, where the fiery breath of war and the wild winds of political change have rapidly dissipated the mists and fogs of transcendentalism, and converted a nation of speculators into a nation of men. The doctrine of fortitude, first growled by Zeno and his disciples at the pigs in the sty of Epicurus, and later still shaken like a lion's mane in the faces of pale emperors with unlimited control over human life—a creed somewhat narrow and practical, allied to the kind of speculation which forms bulwarks against contradiction and christens them moral principles, and expressed in a dialectic terminology as sharp as the whizzing of a cannon-ball—a rule of conduct which makes a fetish of individual "prosperity" (εὔροια) and sticks it full of pins—will answer the requirements of the typical Yankee, and even satisfy some of the cravings of the Concord school of philosophers. The negro, too, inhaling his new liberty, may glance with pleasure over pages which prove that there was nothing in a state of slavery inconsistent with high philosophic culture; and that all one has to do in order to secure the εὔροια (or "pumpkin," according to Carlyle) is to fold the hands on the bosom, look calm, and smile at the Infinite. For the

---

* "The Works of Epictetus." A Translation from the Greek, based on that of Elizabeth Carter. By Thomas Wentworth Higginson. Boston: Little, Brown, & Co.

rest, the "Discourses" of Epictetus are pleasant and easy reading for those who like the dialectic method, and they contain a good deal that is wise and eternal. I do not go the extreme length, with Mr. Higginson, of asserting that I am acquainted with no book so replete with high conceptions of the Deity and noble aims for man, or in which the laws of retribution are more grandly stated, with less of merely childish bribery or threatening. So far as I can perceive, Epictetus's devotion to the noblest aim of man, that of religious inquiry, is in the inverse ratio to his assumption of the possibility of personal virtue. And what on earth does Mr. Higginson mean by the "laws of retribution"? And what philosophic connection have such laws with "bribery" or "threatening"? It would have been better to let Epictetus speak for himself than saddle him with such sort of praise—especially as he is made, in this version, to speak very well indeed. The version, it is true, is not altogether faultless, and is perhaps, on the whole, inferior to that of Miss Carter in fidelity and force. The rendering of "office" for ἀρχαὶ is better than Miss Carter's "command," and there are many similar instances of *minute* care ; but "what is right and what is wrong," for τί μοι ἔξεστι καὶ τί μοι οὐκ ἔξεστιν, though correct in the strict signification of the English words as explained by Horne Tooke, does not convey to ordinary readers the sense of "what is and what is not permitted to me." Again, "phenomena" is improperly given as the equivalent for φαντασίαι, which looks all the more unpardonable when we find ὅτι φαντασία εἶ, καί οὐ πάντως τὸ φαινόμενον, correctly translated into, "you are but a semblance, and by no means the real thing." Yet, to do Mr. Higginson justice, in more than one instance, where he is not quite so literal, he is somewhat wiser. "Ἄπελθε πρὸς Σωκράτη, καὶ ἴδε αὐτὸν συγκατακείμενον Ἀλκιβιάδῃ, καὶ διαπαίζοντα αὐτοῦ τὴν ὥραν. Here Miss Carter had the boldness to translate literally, while Mr. Higginson converts the horrible Ἀλκιβιάδη into the harmless "his beloved," and thus saves his readers from the merest shiver of a repugnance which is felt too frequently in reading the heathen philosophers.

And Epictetus, in spite of all Mr. Higginson may say to the contrary, was as very a heathen as ever set up school in Rome—a fine, rough, self-sufficient type of heathen, practical and vaguely sceptical, even in those creeping moments when the breath felt stale, and the clouds of fantasy fashioned themselves into uncouth forms of Deity. It is in no religious mood that he exclaims, in a sentence which, perhaps, is the keystone of his whole philosophy, "Two rules we should have always ready—that there is nothing good or evil save in the Will [ἔξω τῆς προαιρέσεως]; and that we are not to lead events, but to follow them." He appears indeed to have held, with the earlier Stoics, that there is one unoriginated, unchangeable, and supreme God, but only such a God as bore the same relation to the world as the human soul is supposed to bear to the body, and whose power was limited to the laws of materials out of which things were originally fashioned. He utterly repudiated the doctrine of Chance, and described events as just sufficiently controlled by Law, or Fate, to allow of the freedom of human action. The souls of men he averred, paradoxically, to be parts of the essence of Deity, or the soul of the world—effusions, in a word, as Spinoza held them to be, but perishable with the body. The reward of goodness is goodness, of evil, evil; the bribe of heaven, or the threat of hell, as

Mr. Higginson would express it, is outside the circle of his philosophy; there is no Hades, no Acheron, no Pyriphlegethon. The business of life concluded, man is resolved into the four elements from which he emanated incarnate, and has no further personal existence. The prospects of felicity do not extend beyond dissolution, but man may be glorious and happy as a god in this world, enjoying perfect tranquillity of mind in many ways—stretched on the rack, beaten with the lash, or cut piecemeal to glut the pale, bloodthirsty hunger of an emperor. The philosopher, "when beaten, must love those who beat him"—a capital maxim, which Legree might have inscribed on the flogging-post for the edification of Uncle Tom. While holding life endurable under any circumstances, the philosopher was, nevertheless, not severe on suicide. True, Mr. Higginson states that there is one special argument against suicide, but that argument does not state that self-slaughter is wrong, but that it is extremely contradictory and unphilosophic in a man who counts the body as nothing. Suffering, the Stoic said, is no real evil, forgetting how Zeno, the father of the sect, hanged himself when his finger ached.

Much of all this becomes intelligible when we reflect that Epictetus speaks invariably in a fictitious character, that of the ideal man, perfectly wise and good. The "Discourses" are elaborate protests against human error, and confidential assertions of what *ought* to be. In more than one place the philosopher candidly confesses his own imperfections. "Believe me," he exclaims humbly, "I have not quite yet the powers of a good man," adding that such powers are of sure growth, but slow. Read in this way, and by the light of history, the fantastic fortitude prescribed in the "Discourses" seems noble and dignified in the extreme.

Had Epictetus invariably held forth in his simpler fashion, without attempting to launch out into the more airy region of abstract metaphysics, he would be more valuable as a teacher. Regarded as the description of a practical ideal, many of his sayings are, as we have suggested, true and eternal—admirable standards of perfection in human conduct. He seldom or never talks enthusiastically; there is little or no fire in his composition. He has no high theological insight, no white-heat thirst for spiritual food. The nearest approach we find in the remains preserved by Arrian to real grandeur of religious expression is perhaps the following, Συνεχέστερον νόει τὸν Θεόν, ἢ ἀνάπνει; but this is in all probability a spurious fragment. It is not in such a mood that he conceived his golden ideas of human conduct. His true mood was a household mood; he was ill at ease with a great conception, but at home with a sick mourner in an empty house. Cant, humbug, and pretence of all sorts were odious to him. He had a plain man's hate for tinsel. Had he been placed under more modern lights, he might have become a Calvinist; for he had a low, very low, idea of his fellows, and clear knowledge how far the average man stood below his ideal man; but he would never have swung a censer. He had much of the preacher in him, little of the philosopher, and was quite hard enough in many of his moods to accept a doctrine of downright damnation. It was clear to him that God, or Zeus, or the Spirit of the World, presided over a great deal of evil—that the pure of heart were few, and that the tyranny of circumstances was very terrible—and that the only compromise possible with Zeus was to set up invulnerable laws of private fortitude. On the whole, he conceived the world was not worth living in, but stubborn will might make it endurable—to a philosopher. Socrates was his great historical model, though he declined to agree with Socrates on many subjects, notably the subject of a future state. He was the toughest bit of slave-flesh that ever power had to deal with. Strength and force could not bind him, though they bound Prometheus; for Epictetus was a commonplace philosopher, no fire-filcher. What others did in theory he did in practice. We read of no other such Stoic in real life. Though many of the anecdotes preserved concerning him are doubtless spurious, there is enough in the bare skeleton of his life to show that he was made of iron stuff, and enough in the records of his disciples to convince us that his influence upon those with whom he came into contact was very extraordinary.

If we picture a deformed negro dwelling somewhere in South America while slavery still existed, abused, contemned, beaten, yet managing in despite of circumstances to persuade cultivated free people to hearken humbly to his discourses on fate, free-will, and private virtue, we form some idea of the position of Epictetus. We first hear of him as the slave of Epaphroditus, Nero's freed-man and Master of Requests—the same who assisted Nero to kill himself, and was slaughtered by Domitian for having done so. If report be true, the courtier was by no means a gentle master. We have it on the authority of Origen that when Epaphroditus put his leg to the torture, Epictetus, already a Stoic, smiled, saying, "You will certainly break my leg," which accordingly happened, on which the slave continued, still smiling, "Didn't I tell you, you would break it?" However,

Simplicius in his commentary expressly states that the lameness of Epictetus was owing to rheumatism. How or when he became free is unknown, but it is evident that by the time when the philosophers were hounded from Rome by Domitian, he had already gained considerable influence as a thinker. On the issue of the decree which turned thin-clad wisdom adrift, Epictetus retired to Nicopolis, and there founded a school, carrying with him in all probability his whole property and stock-in-trade, a bed, a pipkin, and an earthen lamp. Poor almost to starvation-point, a cripple, uncouth and sharp of speech, he assured the numerous persons of distinction who flocked to hear him talk that he was perfectly happy; expounded and illustrated, in fact, his whole principle of human fortitude; and taught that Arrian, soldier and senator, to whom we are indebted for the preservation of the "Discourses" and the "Manual." Practical and dogmatic, he, nevertheless, made his school a fashionable lounging-place for the questioning spirits of the unequally balanced Empire. He did all his teaching by word of mouth; he was no composer; but briskly wielding the club of dialectics, he hammered hard truths into many an unwilling conscience. Instead of flattering, he anatomised his hearers—mocked at those who came for mere idle pleasure—picked out their weaknesses with a grim humour which is sometimes lost in the diffuse and repetitive records of Arrian—and earned, by the sheer force of his practical example, unlimited influence as a portico philosopher. Now, for the first time, men beheld a true Stoic—one whose fortitude no Cæsar could bend, and who held unflinchingly by the strength of an invincible will. He taught much by illustration and anecdote, but his daily life was the best illustration and anecdote of all. He was, if we may use the word, a reformer. In the very centre of an unhealthy social life, he stood like adamant, erect, smiling, stainless, and indeed, if we mark closely one or two passages in his writings, not altogether ungentle. Perhaps, indeed, he used the terminology of the Stoic school as that best suited for purposes of practical reform, and would not have gone so far in following the merely abstract principles of that school, had he not feared to appear contradictory. What men just then wanted, for purposes of reform, was not a philosophic treatise, but a *life;* and Epictetus, with that view, gave up his life to them. Under the strong light of our whiter civilisation, such a figure as his may appear rough and rude; but picture the society of the Empire, think of the thousand enormities practised in the name of philosophy, contrast the life of Epictetus with the vagaries and inconsistencies of men like Seneca, and that human figure, uttering its doctrine of fixed principles and a particular Providence connected with the freedom of the will, seems noble and dignified beyond all the fantasies of metaphysicians and all the hair-splitting homunculi of the schools.

To the value of the records of Arrian many fine thinkers have borne testimony. Marcus Antoninus ranks Epictetus with Socrates, Aulus Gellius calls him the greatest of the Stoics, Origen avers that his writings have done more good than Plato's; and in more recent times, the very different tempers of Pascal and Bishop Butler have found equal delight in him. For my own part, while disagreeing with many of his ideas, I admit that his position as a reformer rendered them necessary, and I believe that the study of his precepts will be beneficial even now. Few philosophers are easier reading. The rough egoism, the absolute want of sympathy with the movements of the mass of mankind, the impracticable elevation of individual will, is at all events quite as wholesome as Carlyle's extravagancies of hero-worship and Goethe's science of culture. It is not by minds like that of Epictetus that the world progresses, but it is by such minds that it is purified at stationary periods; and just now England is in a stationary state, and America is pausing after action, and ready to digest new ideas or old ones that are eternal. Much good may the ghost of the old Stoic do us all!

V.

THE GOSPEL ACCORDING TO THE PRINTER'S DEVIL.

THE *Pall Mall Gazette,* in an article called "The Knife in Journalism," quoted recently from a book called "Oceana" some uncomplimentary passages concerning Mr. Frederick Harrison and Mr. Robert Buchanan; for though Mr. J. A. Froude, the author of the book, puts dashes in place of proper names, there can be no doubt as to the identity of the individuals so attacked. The *Pall Mall Gazette* supplies the blanks, and goes on to say that Mr. Froude's description of the plot of the "worst novel he ever read" applies literally to the "New Abelard"—a palpable mistake in so correct a newspaper, seeing that the book referred to is a story, by the same author, called "Foxglove Manor."

Now, to be bracketed for condemnation along with so earnest and high-minded a writer as Mr. Harrison is so great a compliment, that I could be well content to let Mr. Froude go stumping the Pacific Islands without one word of protest, if the question raised were a merely personal one. Mr. Froude at the Antipodes is so much more harmless a figure than Mr. Froude at Chelsea, that he might rail there to his heart's content, without darkening my sunshine. But the fault he finds with me being that I call him the "slipshod Nemesis," or mischief-making and meddling literary lady, who destroyed the reputation of the late Mr. Carlyle, I wish to repeat, here as elsewhere, my opinion that Nemesis in this instance did a service to society, and that, for once in his literary career, Mr. Froude was, unconsciously, veracious. Mr. Froude, wishing to know "what manner of man did not admire Carlyle," studied "Foxglove Manor," was shocked at its plot and scandalised at its morality. I, wishing to know what manner of man it is that did admire Carlyle, and think him the first of human beings, long ago studied Mr. Froude, and was not at all astonished to discover in him the "halting Fury" (as he himself expresses it) who was to avenge human nature on the worshipper of brute will and brute force. Ever since I could read and think, Carlyle's teachings, or preaching, or railings, however one chooses to term them, have been my abomination. Twenty years ago I said, as I say now, that the style was worthy of the man, and that both were worthy the admiration of a foolish and uninstructed generation as yet unaware of Mr. Spencer. This, of course, is one of many indications of what the *Pall Mall Gazette* calls my "fatal bad taste."

At the same time, I would not have the public think me blind to the infinite pity of Carlyle's biography; for even Mr. Froude's bungling could not destroy that. Noble and beautiful is the lesson that such a history teaches us; far more noble and beautiful, to my mind, than all the clamorous trash about *laborare est orare*, than all the sham of what I have christened the Gospel according to the Printer's Devil. What I gather there is what every man should learn—that literary fame and hard literary work are nothing, if the famous man and the worker, while preaching self-reliance and self-abnegation, forgets those who love him and makes of his own house a hell. The love or the hate of humanity begins at home, and we are lost or redeemed by the prayers of those near ones whom we, through love or hate, have made happy or unhappy. That the true insight of self-sanctifying affection came to Carlyle at last, we all know *now*. It came to him when he was a feeble old man, looking for a vanished face in the fire. It never came to him when he was coarsely fulminating against the suffering masses of mankind, drinking tea with Lady Ashburton, and talking platitudes about Work in the name of a God in whom he had never even the glimmer of a living faith.

Doubtless, Work is a good thing; but Carlyle liked his work, was by instinct and habit a literary worker, and found the whole business, in his ungracious way, pleasant. It would be sheer cant for a busy linendraper or an active bricklayer to make the welkin ring with praises of the dignity of linendraping and the nobility of laying bricks; it is even more insufferable cant for the literary man to sound pæans about the self-sacrifice of making books. Carlyle liked his work, got both fame and money for it, and was covetous of both. Posterity has now to appraise, apart from all tall talk and atrabilarious grumbling, what the work was worth. I believe that posterity will decide with me—that it was not worth one solitary hour of domestic misconception, that, cast in the balance, it would all be outweighted by one of Jane Welsh's secret tears. Carlyle's books, indeed, possess all the worst qualities of the lower transcendentalism. The Gospel according to the Printer's Devil was wrought in scorn and bitterness instead of love, and so its literary Messiah took the lineaments of Goethe, and its Apocalypse has been spoken at the gates of Paris by Bismarck. For my own part, I would as soon frame my religion on the scheme of Carlyle's choosing as I would base my ideal of biography on the masterpiece of Mr. Froude.

Bogus reputations tumble down like houses of sand. Simple truth and faithful love are things that abide for ever. I respect Mr. Froude for his fidelity to the king his bungling has dethroned, and when he himself has lost his master's scolding trick, I will cheerfully join with him in reverencing the ashes of Thomas Carlyle.

VI.

"L'EXILÉE" IN ENGLISH.*

IN poetry as well as in personal ornament, filagree is sometimes very charming. The mere ghost of an idea, set to tremulous music, appears more seductive than a substantial reality of the imagination ; while a

---

* "L'Exilée." By François Coppée. Done into English verse by J. O. L. London : Kegan Paul.

bit of sentiment, slight in itself but capable of being indefinitely beaten out, derives from its very slenderness a pathos which few can resist. A noticeable member of the filagree school of poets is M. François Coppée. Perhaps few writers, even of verse, ever started with so small a capital. Beyond the gift of verbal melody, which he certainly possesses in an unusual degree, and a certain pensive sweetness of mood, he possesses none of the stock-in-trade which forms the natural prerogative of poets: little or no shaping imagination, no great insight, no special love of nature, no passion, and no power. Despite all this, he uses his one advantage so admirably, he fashions his filagree so prettily, that it would be hard to deny him the name of poet. In what is perhaps his most original and coherent work, "Le Luthier de Crémone," a poem written for the theatre and acted with no little success, he fascinates attention by pure charm and simplicity of manner; while in "Le Passant," another contribution to the stage, in which Mdlle. Agar created a most witching impression, and Sarah Bernhardt played with a certain weird power, he produces, with materials even more slender, the same spiritualising effect. He is, nevertheless, more like the shadow of a singer than a real bard full of the knowledge and tendencies of his time; and his faint little melodies in the minor key win us like Æolian murmurs from Shadow-land.

In "L'Exilée," perhaps his most popular poem, or series of poems, M. Coppée passes from one dim mood to another with the ease of a melancholy spirit. Each poem is a little sigh, very human, yet curiously insubstantial. The difficulty of translating such pieces seemed to me insuperable, but the present translator, with a singular felicity and lightness of touch, turns French into English filagree most delightfully. Only a lady, I should fancy, could have done the work with such dexterity — in a man's coarse hand the little book would have been crushed like the nestful of delicate eggs mentioned in "Espoir timide":

> Chère enfant, qu'avant tout vos volontés soient faites !
> Mais, comme on trouve un nid rempli d'œufs de fauvettes,
> Vous avez ramassé mon cœur sur le chemin.
>
> Si de l'anéantir vous aviez le caprice,
> Vous n'auriez qu'à fermer brusquement votre main,
> —Mais vous ne voudrez pas, j'en suis sûr, qu'il périsse !

Here and there, of course, the necessity of faithfulness to the original causes awkward turns and involutions, but this was inevitable. Only those who have attempted similar work—who have tried to tackle Heine, for example—know the difficulty of producing such a translation as the following:

NATURE'S PITY.

In grief the senses grow more fine ;
   Alas ! my darling's gone from me !—
And in all Nature, I divine
   There lurks a secret sympathy.

The noisy nests, I half believe,
   Their bickerings for me restrain,
The flowers for my trouble grieve,
   The stars feel pity for my pain.

The linnet almost seems ashamed
   To sing aloud his joyous song ;
The lily knows her fragrance blamed,
   The stars confess they do me wrong.

Within their sweetness I discern
   Only my sweet, too long away !
And for her breath, eyes, voice, I yearn,
   Like lily, star, and linnet's lay.

This is felicitous, without being positively faultless.

The original is a mere tender breathing, hardly a lyric, lacking altogether the heart-crushing strength of the wail in " Ye Banks and Braes." When Burns takes Nature into his sympathy he does so like a strong man yielding to overmastering tenderness; his utterance is a deep-chested groan more than a sigh from the mouth. Even Tannahill is more robust than M. Coppée. In poems like the one I have quoted Coppée shows the influence of Heine more than that of any other poet, except, perhaps, Lamartine. The following piece is very much in Heine's manner, simple and symbolic :

THE THREE BIRDS.

" Fly over corn-fields," I said to the dove,
  " And beyond the meadow-land sweet with hay,
Pluck me the flower to win her love ! "
  Said the dove—" 'Tis too far away ! "

And I said to the eagle—" Mount with speed
  On soaring pinion—steal from the sky
The heavenly fire that perchance I need ! "
  Said the eagle—" It is too high ! "

Then I said to the vulture—" This heart devour,
  Borne down by its love and its sorrow's weight,
Spare only what has escaped the power ! "
  Said the vulture—" 'Tis too late ! "

" L'Exilée " consists of exactly twenty little poems of this kind, all more or less sentimental, and having for their subject the

Fair child with sweet eyes, O Norway's pale rose,

mentioned in the dedication. It is in fact merely the chronicle of the attachment of the poet for a young lady " seventeen years " his junior. Her charms are thus explicitly described :

Oft musing, with hand on my eyes, I behold
*Her lithe form and small head, with the pallid gold
Of her hair cut short on her forehead white.*

Poet and lady meet on the banks of Lake Leman, and after a formal introduction become acquainted. The progress of the gentleman's feelings is minutely described in the lyrics, which follow each other in thoughtfully devised sequence. In the piece called "Pre-existence" the poet fancies that they have met before in some serene world.

> And when in thine eyes I mirrored my own,
> I knew we had lived in the ages long gone;
> And haunted since then by a nameless yearning,
> To the heavens my dream is ever returning,
> Our birthland there to discover I try;
> And soon as night mounts up the eastern sky
> My glances seek in the glittering dome
> The stars that may, whilom, have been our home!

Of all this love nothing serious comes, and the lady passes gently away from the horizon of her admirer, reflecting, perhaps, that it would require even more sentiment than he possesses to get over the disparity of "seventeen years." "Then pity me not, though even I die!" the poet cries in conclusion. One does not feel much inclined to pity him. His grief is too insubstantial to last, and one feels that he will get over it. As for the poems, they are, as I have said, the veriest filagree or gossamer; yet as here translated, they are very attractive. The hand that can do such dainty work so well ought not to be idle in the future, and I hope that it will give us more translations. To have succeeded at all with so faint a singer as Coppée is a triumph of literary manipulation; but I should like the translator next time to leave this thin ghost of a poet alone and to touch something more robust.

VII.

THE CHURCH AND THE STAGE.

APROPOS of a poetical drama from my pen, on the subject of Lady Jane Grey, I was once accused of fostering religious dissension, by representing the Roman Catholic Church in an unfavourable light. Even a friendly foreign journal, *l'Indépendance Belge*, in criticising the *Nine Days' Queen*, observed: "Le rôle de l'évêque de Winchester est sacrifié à l'indignation publique, qui, après avoir applaudi l'acteur, accable de ses sifflets et de ses grognements le personnage antipathique." I am quite willing to admit that the nightly excitement, the applause lavished on the sentiments of Lady Jane Grey, the hisses and groans showered upon her persecutors, did seem to warrant the hypothesis of religious bias; but this hypothesis is only superficial after all, and the same sympathy and antipathy would follow the victim and the persecutor under any circumstances, quite apart from polemical predisposition. That Lady Jane belongs to the "royal army of martyrs," I am aware; I am aware, too, that Protestantism has indirectly canonised her, in the face of its rejection of all canonisation; but the great heart of the public yearns to her, not because she held certain dogmatic views, but simply because she was a beautiful and unfortunate human being, almost stainless in a stained and cruel time. Popular audiences care as much about Roman Catholicism and Protestantism as they do about Conservatism and Liberalism. They want interesting characters and dramatic situations; and, given these, they will sympathise as liberally with one side of the question as with the other. For my own part, as the author of this and other plays, I wish to record my complete indifference to religious bias. I have taken a few historical facts, which are indisputable, and tried to make a picturesque and pathetic play out of them; *voilà tout.* Personally, I feel as much antipathy to Lady Jane Grey's bigotry as to that of Mary Tudor. I know that both Catholics and Protestants have torn each other asunder from time immemorial, and that they would be doing so still if modern science and modern free thought—yes, and modern dramatic art!—had not arisen, to light the dark places of Acheronian controversy. Each side has its martyrs, and all martyrs, all victims of a tyrannical majority, appeal, by virtue of the pathetic fallacy overtaking them, to the tenderness and solicitude of human nature.

But putting aside this partly personal question, I wish to touch upon another point, of larger and deeper interest to society at large. I wish to ask, in the name of common sense, what reason there is that the Stage should spare the Church, seeing that the Church has been, and still remains, the implacable enemy of the Stage—nay, of Art and Poetry in general? I wish to demand on what ground the Drama is to hush up the monstrous crimes of Religion, when Religion parades so libellously the veriest follies of the Drama? I know that it is the opinion of many worthy people that dramatic art would be elevated if it could once conquer the prejudice of the so-called "religious" world; and we have therefore witnessed, in Church and Stage Guilds, at pious tea-drinkings, where the theatre has been discussed apologetically, a timid desire on the part of the theatrical profession to conciliate the hereditary foes of the theatre. Were

I the mouthpiece of dramatic Art, however, I should adopt a very different attitude. I should say to the Church: " Before you point out the mote in our eyes, remember the beam in your own. You tell us of the evil that the stage has done, of its tendency to corrupt society. Let us in return tell you what the stage has *not* done.. It has never usurped God's right over the consciences and the souls of men; it has never falsified documents, perverted facts, prostituted itself in the lust for power; though it has a long catalogue of martyrs, it has had no Inquisition and no official persecutor; the record of its bad deeds is not written in the blood of butchered women and children; it has never burned a Bruno or tortured a Galileo; it has never hunted down an Adrienne Lecouvreur during life, and refused her decent burial when dead; it has never, in a word, based its success or failure on the sorrow or the suffering of human nature." Then, if the Church retorted that these things were only of the past, I should explain that, if they are so, if religious intolerance is now reduced to a minimum, thanks are due, not to the Church, but to the Stage—to that art whose immortal teachers, from Shakespeare downwards, have exposed the false perversions and pretensions of other-worldliness. Tartuffe would still be a social possibility if the Stage had not sent society its deliverer, in Molière. For the rest, I am simple enough to believe that there is often more real religious teaching in the theatre than in the conventicle. I can find a grander spiritual lesson in such a presentation as Mr. Edwin Booth's King Lear than in the columns of the *Record* or the preachings of the Rev. Dr. Boanerges; when I want humour, or humorous pathos, I prefer Mr. Thomas Thorne to the Rev. Dr. Talmage; and altogether, as an unregenerate individual addicted to the excisable liquor of dramatic performances, I hold with pious Mr. Herbert:

> A verse may catch him who a sermon flies,
> And turn delight into a sacrifice!

Be that as it may, I for one shall certainly not avoid a good subject, but shall rather utilise it the more eagerly, because the presentation of certain historical facts is damaging to the Church. When the Æson of sacerdotalism is renewed by the elixir of liberalism, when he casts off its old lendings and recognises the divine brotherhood of all arts and all religions, then, and not till then, it will be time to say: "Let the dead bury its dead; no good purpose can be served *now* by recording the crimes and cruelties of the past."

VIII.

THE AMERICAN SOCRATES.

I AM very grateful to the *Pall Mall Gazette* for its kindly suggestion (Christmas, 1886) that Englishmen should send a little tribute to Walt Whitman, and it is satisfactory to know that there are some Englishmen with the courage, in the face of good and ill report, to express their sympathy with the great American. As usual, when Whitman's name is mentioned, it is strenuously denied that Whitman is either neglected or unfortunate. "We like the old fellow," said Mr. E. C. Stedman to me in New York, "and it is a great mistake to suppose he is unappreciated." This sort of pitying patronising praise may be heard everywhere. In the meantime, Whitman gets about as much honest sympathy from the literary class in America as Socrates did from the elders of the city. He is simply *outlawed*. I have no hesitation in saying that his little English band of admirers, headed by Mr. William Rossetti, have secured for him what little kindness he has received from his own countrymen. And who wonders? When Mr. Stedman can devote his talents to an ornithology of all the singing birds, putting the tomtit in the eagle's cage, and seriously discussing the chirps of the hedge-sparrow, when the ideals of American criticism are Mr. Lowell, Mr. Howells, and *Harper's Magazine*, when the reading public stupefies itself with the dull Eastern narcotic imported by Mr. Edward Fitzgerald, it is natural enough that Walt Whitman should be let severely alone. Fortunately, his worshippers out there are fit though few. I speedily discovered when in America the beneficent influence of his teachings on young men and maidens of the coming generation.

In March, 1885, I was in Philadelphia, bringing out a stupendous melodrama, and one day I found myself crossing the crowded ferry to Camden, on a visit to Walt Whitman. I soon found the house where he dwelt, for every one knew it, and every face brightened at the old man's name; it is a humble dwelling in a quiet street, very plainly furnished, but not uncomfortable. When I appeared at the door, which was opened to me by a middle-aged, motherly woman, I caught a glimpse along the lobby of a patriarchal figure seated in a back room, and I was informed that Whitman was at dinner, but would join me in the front parlour directly. He soon came in, supported on a stick, and looking rather feeble, his hair and beard long and white as snow, the skin of his face crimson with the influence of sun and wind. I need hardly say that I had a hearty welcome. I had a lady with me, and Whitman was very eager that she should partake of the feast on which he had been regaling—solid American pie, washed down with the strongest of strong tea. Inquiry elicited the fact that pie was the main pabulum of Whitman's life. He eats no meat, or hardly any, and beyond a little drop of whisky at bedtime, takes no stimulants. Year after year he dwells alone, waited on by the kindly woman who is at once his friend, his servant, and his nurse. He goes out daily, seeking generally the most crowded thoroughfares, his favourite amusement being to journey to and fro on the steam ferryboat, making friends with all and sundry. For Whitman's democracy is no mere literary sentiment, but a living instinct. He loves all forms of humanity. The movement of human life is divine music to him. He is quite happy thus, complains of nothing, girns at nothing, has a loving heart and an open hand for all the world. He has very few books, and these few are mostly gifts from the authors; one from Mr. J. A. Symonds had just come to him, with a respectful inscription on the fly-leaf. I found him alert and bright as any boy, greatly interested to hear about English authors, especially Tennyson, and very anxious to visit the old country before he died. He took us up to his bedroom on the upper floor, showed us the old arm-chair where he writes, and the old trunks where he keeps his books and papers. All about him was beautifully calm and "restful." I spoke of his detractors, and his blue eye brightened merrily, though he could not deny that some of them, and especially Emerson, had used him cavalierly. But what was all that to one who "heard the roar of the ages"? As might be expected, he cared little or nothing about modern reputations. Wagner, perhaps, was the only personality in Europe that greatly attracted him, as to a sort of equal. But I should convey a wrong impression if I suggested that he was without sympathy for the ideas of his contemporaries; on the contrary, every form of literary activity is interesting to him. He simply perceives as a philosopher the littleness of all literature in relation to life. Benignly gentle and universally tolerant, he sits apart, "holding no form of creed, but contemplating all."

About his poverty there can be no question. The pittance he gets from his books would not equal the wage of an ordinary labourer; the rest of his slender income is made up of loving gifts from people almost as poor as himself. Of course he is not "starving;" so long as pie and tea suffice for his nourishment, he can subsist! But his state is nevertheless, from our point of view, pitiful. His physical health is frail, his days cannot be long in the sunshine, and his necessities are pressing enough to make voluntary help acceptable. In a land of millionaires, in a land of which he will one day be known as the chief literary glory, he is almost utterly neglected. Let there be no question about this; all denial of it is disingenuous and dishonest. The literary class fights shy of him. The great reading public have been told that he is infamously immoral. There is nothing in his style to attract, everything to repel, the natures which batten on Longfellow's "Village Blacksmith" and the stories and engravings in the American magazines. Some years ago, when he was asked to contribute to a leading American review, there was an outcry, and the poor editor took fright. Countenance Whitman, hankering, gross, mystical, nude, whom even the good Emerson had abandoned? The thing was an outrage! The editor accepted the warning, and any future contribution was "declined with thanks." Whitman told me this, with the merriest of twinkles in his blue eye.

"I likes to be despised," said Uriah Heep. I don't know that Whitman likes to be outlawed, but he is fully alive to the prodigious humour of the thing. Sympathy, on the other hand, is sweet to him, as to every human being. He spoke with loving gratitude of the Rossettis and his other English friends.

When I shook hands with him there, at the door of his little house in Camden, I scarcely realised the great privilege that had been given to me—that of seeing face to face the wisest and noblest, the most truly great, of all modern literary men. I hope yet, if I am spared, to look upon him again, for well I know that the earth holds no such another nature. Nor do I write this with the wild hero-worship of a boy, but as the calm, deliberate judgment of a man who is far beyond all literary predilections or passions. In Walt Whitman I see more than a mere maker of poems, I see a personality worthy to rank even above that of Socrates, akin even, though lower and far distant, to that of Him who is considered, and rightly, the first of men. I know that if that Other were here, his reception in New England might be very much the same. I know, too, that in some day not so remote, humanity will wonder that men could dwell side by side with this colossus, and not realise his proportions. We have other poets, but we have no other divine poet. We have a beautiful singer in Tennyson, and some day it will be among Tennyson's highest honours that he was once named kindly and appreciatively by Whitman. When I think of that gray head, gently bowing before the contempt of the literary class in America, when I think that Boston crowns Emerson and turns aside from the spirit potent enough to create a hundred Emersons and leave strength sufficient for the making of the whole Bostonian cosmogony, from Lowell upwards, I for a moment lose patience with a mighty nation; but only for a moment: the voice of my gentle master sounds in my ear, and I am reminded that if he is great and good, it is because he represents the greatness and goodness of a free and noble people. He would not be Walt Whitman, if he did not love his contemporaries more, not less, for the ingratitude and misconception of the Scribes and Pharisees who have outlawed him. Praise, and fame, and money are of course indifferent to him. He has spoken his message, he has lived his life, and is content. But it is we that honour and love him who are not content, while the gospel of man-millinery is preached in every magazine and every newspaper, and every literary money-changer and poetaster has a stone to throw at the patient old prophet of modern Democracy.

FROM POPE TO TENNYSON.

IN the year 1733 that distinguished and prosperous poet, Mr. Alexander Pope, wonder of his age and envy of his contemporaries, published anonymously the first epistle of his "Essay on Man"; the second and third epistles followed in rapid succession; and, finally, twelve months afterwards, the fourth was published, with the poet's name. Pope had from the first been suspected of the authorship of this truly representative and "moral" poem, which was for ever afterwards to bear his superscription. The fame of the "Essay on Man," which, as everybody knows, was a sort of poetical adumbration (and perversion) of the views of Bolingbroke, was widespread and instantaneous. Translations appeared in all languages, and disquisitions, in which the poet's views were advocated or combated, were numerous in our own. Certainly no poem could be more typical of its period, or could represent better the elegant fatalism of that literary and philosophical group of which Pope was the mouthpiece and the ornament.

A century passed away. The reign of the distinguished Mr. Pope was forgotten, nay, almost mythical in its incredibility from the point of view of modern criticism.
Soles occidere, et redire possunt,

but a literary sun, once thoroughly set, seldom completely re-emerges. Mr. Pope was dust, and we were under the reign of Mr. Tennyson. Rather more than a hundred years after the publication of the "Essay on Man" appeared, also anonymously, "In Memoriam." The success of this fine poem, in which, as we all know, an elegant literary scepticism is lightly dashed with emotion and carefully spiced with science, was also instantaneous. The work was at once accepted as typical, and as representing the finest tendencies of the time. More than that, it became at once a text-book and a quotation-book. It was just philosophic enough to suit all poetic needs, and just poetic enough to please practical philosophers. Its power of supplying apt and memorable passages at least equalled that of the "Essay on Man." Our great-grandfathers, with quivering nostrils and faltering voices, could proclaim in measured cadence the wonders of that Deity,

> Who sees with equal eye, as God of all,
> A hero perish or a sparrow fall,
> Atoms or systems into ruin hurled,
> And now a bubble burst, and now a world;

and could add, not without solemnity,

> Know then thyself, presume not God to scan;
> The proper study of mankind is man.

We, no less fortunate, could speak gently of a God,

> That God, which ever lives and moves,
>   One God, one law, one element,
>   And one far-off divine event,
> To which the whole creation moves;

and could add, with a touch of tenderness unknown to our grandfathers, that

> Merit lives from man to man,
> And not from man, O Lord, to thee.

But in either case the fountain of quotation was a

poem representative, to use the slang expression, of "the best culture of the time," and of the time's most typical poet.

Doubtless in those days, as in these, there were dissentient voices, voices of a minority which rejected Mr. Pope's elegant fatalism as indignantly as it is possible to reject the refined scepticism of Mr. Tennyson. And in good truth the "Essay on Man" is not much more stimulating than a page of the renowned St. John himself. From the point of view of the period, nevertheless, it was simply sublime, and was accepted by its generation with a faith as implicit as that which the immortal "poor Indian," in its own pages, gave to his God. Its very defects hastened this happy consummation. Delightful beyond measure were its endless twists and turns of a tautological yet pliant metre; exquisite were its placid truisms, its fine platitudes, its fluent conservation of the popular sentiment. The age was one of moral essays, and this was a moral essay without an equal. Compared with the "Essay on Man," and judged by the standard of a later period, " In Memoriam" is, from every point of view, vastly superior; indeed, it is difficult to conceive a period when its finest passages will fail, as Pope's finest passages now fail, to awaken polite enthusiasm. As a piece of workmanship it is singularly beautiful—almost too beautiful, in a certain sense, to be quite satisfying as an intellectual stimulus. In the profundity of its philosophical insight, and the magnificence of its poetical images, moreover, it is as far above Mr. Pope at his best as Pope himself was above the herd he ridiculed in the "Dunciad." To say so much, indeed, is only to say that it is the peculiar outcome of a generation which was saturated in its youth with the sublime mysticism of Coleridge and Shelley, and which, a little later on, stood wondering at the "faery tales of Science." But with all this, and despite the charm of an incomparable lyric light, it is quite too fine a piece of work to answer our present speculative needs. Its grief is not moving grief, and its speculation is not kindling speculation.

The very structure of the poem, in its laboriously easy monotony, is against its permanence as a poetic force or a great literary stimulus. Readers at the present moment are not wanting who have forgotten its existence altogether, and who, in moments of anxiety and insight, would sooner turn for stimulus to a chapter of the Book of Job, or even a rugged page of the persecuted Walt Whitman.

The penalty of such perfection as is easily distinguishable in such widely differing poems as the "Essay on Man" and "In Memoriam," is the penalty which attends typical literary products of all kinds; for it need scarcely be added that it is not in acquiescent or explanatory moods, however representative of "the best culture of the time," that great poetical creations are developed. If Mr. Tennyson* were only the philosopher of "In Memoriam," there would be some danger of his being even summarily forgotten. Being what he is, one of the loveliest singers of this time and of all time, and an unique craftsman whose sign manual is sufficient to consecrate almost any piece of work, he need not fear the results of a criticism which must sooner or later leave him among the lyrical and perfecting, instead of among the philosophical and creative, singers. What the divine group, which preceded him, left ill-expressed, half-expressed, or only hinted, he has turned into miracles

---

* Now Lord Tennyson.

of musical speech. Ideas which the world passed by in the pages of Wordsworth and Shelley, it has hailed with idolatry in the Laureate's stately setting. Truths, which Science carelessly and clumsily revealed, have been turned by him into those jewels five words long,

> Which, on the stretched forefinger of all time,
> Sparkle for ever.

He differs, moreover, from Pope in this, that he is primarily and cardinally the poet of a poetical era, not, strictly speaking, the poetical oracle of the era of essays and essayists now again beginning.

Though all that I have said must be self-evident and even commonplace to most advanced students of modern poetry, it was still inevitable that many critics should accept Mr. Tennyson's more meditative utterances as a final gospel, and should pass by as irrelevant the utterances of such of his contemporaries as do not follow his school of literary perfection. In a little work which I have now before me,* it seems laid down as a canon that Mr. Tennyson's method of approaching the great questions of life and death is the only correct method of approach, and that the results of that method are finally and wholly satisfying. Mr. Selkirk, a man of undeniable cleverness and culture, has attempted in half-a-dozen striking essays to touch a subject which, as it seems to us, often eludes his method of treatment. His style is admirable, his manner finished in the extreme, but his summaries of the leading positions he wishes to establish are at times incorrect and not always convincing. Fortunately, or unfortunately, he does not

---

* "Ethics and Æsthetics of Modern Poetry." By J. B. Selkirk. London: Smith, Elder, & Co.

write with a clerical brief, but for all that writes with a religious bias. The general argument to be gathered from his book is that of Pope: "Whatever is, is right," with this corollary, that an attitude of emotional scepticism is highly admirable, provided it leaves the main problems *open* and does not infringe too much on the rights of the party in power.

This being the case, it may be easily understood that Mr. Selkirk is thoroughly satisfied with Mr. Tennyson's representation of current philosophical problems. His criticisms on Mr. Tennyson's method are quite admirable, while still, as I have suggested, unconvincing. He commends with strict justice the Laureate's "Socratean faculty of seeing both sides of a question with equal power, which has enabled him to become, in so important a sense, the interpreter of the transitional character of the philosophy, religion, and, to some extent, the politics of his time; his power to stand on the debateable ground on which these questions are discussed, giving strong poetical force to each of the opposing factions, and yet remain himself untouched and untainted by what he would himself call 'The falsehood of extremes.'" But, alas! it is this very "Socratean faculty," so much commended by Mr. Selkirk, which absolutely prevents Mr. Tennyson, in his philosophical flights, from achieving the very highest poetry. No sublime seer of the human race—call him what we will, Isaiah, Lucretius, Dante, Bunyan, Wordsworth, or Victor Hugo—has astonished his contemporaries by "seeing both sides of a question with equal power"—quite otherwise. The condition of inspiration in these and other great prophetic or prophesying poets has been the power of forgetting that there are two sides of a question at all! This is equivalent to saying that every great poet is, in a certain sense, a bigot, and that his inspiration is in proportion to his bigotry; and, making the necessary deductions, I believe this to be a true statement of the case.

Mr. Tennyson himself, who is certainly a great poet, if not of the highest order, is highest and best where his faculty is most fearlessly lyrical and least "Socratean."

Mr. Selkirk would doubtless dissent from my classification of Shelley and Hugo among the supreme seers. His treatment of Shelley is not altogether respectful. He tells about his "strangely persistent" denial of Christianity, "and indeed of God," but observes with surprise, nevertheless, that "in his inspired moments, he became the unconscious interpreter of the higher nature, and to a certain extent, became reverential and devout in spite of himself" (page 182). He adds (and here, for example, we have the clerical bias strongly marked): "It is not to be denied, however, that too many of our great poets, fevered by that kind of dithyrambic which so easily besets the *genus irritabile vatum*, have frequently made attempts to curse *what a higher power than theirs has seen fit to bless.*" It is a very common habit of critics far inferior to Mr. Selkirk to treat all forms of revolt as a sort of "dithyrambic madness," and to rebuke revolters for cursing what a providential dispensation has blessed—generally with the loaves and fishes. But if Mr. Selkirk means to suggest that Shelley in his "inspired moments," when "he became the unconscious interpreter of the higher nature," ever confounded that higher nature with Christianity or Deism, I beg to differ. Shelley was always "reverential and devout" in presence of those divine Mysteries which he declined to approach through the vestibules of any of the creeds; though certainly, in his inspired moments, he never achieved the "Socratean" distinction of seeing "both sides of a question at once." He was a revolter pure and simple, and in his sublimest moods he was pre-eminently a revolter. I really dislike this jesuitical plan of suggesting that such a man as Shelley was compelled at times, through providential inflation, to bear witness in favour of the enemy. It is not worthy of a writer so humane as Mr. Selkirk. Then, again, as to Victor Hugo; in a work devoted to the ethics and æsthetics of modern poetry, one would have expected some slight reference to one who is, without exception, the most didactic poet of the time, But Mr. Selkirk trots cheerfully along, as if quite unconscious of any living literary forces outside the Victorian circle. For all that I know, he has never even heard of one whom a few benighted individuals in England esteem the greatest living poetic teacher of all, Walt Whitman.

I have already said, and I now take the pains to reiterate, that there is a great deal of wisdom in Mr. Selkirk's book, but I must explain that it is at times rather old-fashioned wisdom. In spite of innumerable fine things, of many really superb passages, the whole effect is spoiled by the clerical (or conservative) bias, and by the complete absence of any leading or dominant idea. Mr. Selkirk is, in fact, like many others we might name, a microscopic critic; his minute observations are admirable, but his generalisations too often lack breadth and novelty. In order to sustain this statement with some slight proof, let me return for a moment to his treatment of Mr. Tennyson.

Mr. Tennyson is, of course, according to Mr.

Selkirk, the central sun of the Victorian system, the finish beyond which perfection cannot go. Words are insufficient to praise the masterly style in which the Laureate keeps the golden mean. He "beats his music out" to an accompaniment in which neither the sophistries of science nor the casuistries of a half-hearted orthodoxy find any place. "For such a task a brave and freedom-loving man was wanted, one that in his own phrase was ready to follow truth in scorn of consequence, and such an one the age has found in the author of 'In Memoriam.' The image of 'Freedom on her regal seat' has ever been one of the great sources of his inspiration, and since the days of Burns we had no more passionate worshipper of the great goddess, and no such divine Promethean scorn of anything in the shape of the quasi-spiritual fetter. Like the friend he consecrates in his immortal elegy, 'he will not leave his judgment blind,' and, speaking of himself, he tells us elsewhere how unendurable life would have been to him except in

> A land where, girt by friend or foe,
> A man may speak the thing he will!"

That such a poem as "In Memoriam" " should have presented difficulties to the orthodox mind is perhaps not to be wondered at, and cannot be helped. Without absolute freedom from the fetters and restrictions of authoritative human codes, poetry of the highest kind is impossible."

Now, surely, if words of praise were wanting for Mr. Tennyson, it was scarcely necessary to find them in so perverse and ridiculous a statement as the one I have just quoted. We may admire the Laureate's supreme philosophic calm, without crediting him with "passionate worship" of freedom, or with any sort of "divine Promethean scorn." I venture to say that there is not, in the whole compass of his writings, a single passage with a more rarefied ethical atmosphere than the one we breathe in the pages of the late Mr. Kingsley, or (greatly to descend the scale of comparison) those of Mr. Thomas Hughes. It is his characteristic, and it may possibly be his glory, that he is pre-eminently "an Englishman," guilty even, once or twice in his life, of actual Anglophobia; and I know of no single occasion on which his attitude of mind has been one solicitous of martyrdom. Only sheer bigots—and these happily are now in a minority—could find fault with so noble a piece of work as "In Memoriam." The British matron, with all her timid young clustering around her skirts, can find no offence anywhere in the pages of one who utters nothing base; for though he may tell her in sufficiently strong language that she is too fond of money, and that she buys and sells her offspring, he never on any occasion touches roughly on any of her institutions—say, for example, marriage, and the restitution of conjugal rights. Politically, I am so thoroughly at issue with Mr. Tennyson, that I find it difficult to discuss his political writings at all, and to preserve my reverence for a master's name and fame. Yet on more than one occasion, he has written in the purest spirit of "John Bull," has forgotten the divine prerogative of genius, and has sounded the charge for reckless war. That wonderfully fine poem, the "Ode on the Death of the Duke of Wellington," contains passages which I can scarcely read without a shiver, they are so manifestly beyond the mark even of a funeral eulogy; and, to conclude this sort of fault-finding, I am quite certain that it would have been better if the ballad on the death of Sir Richard Grenville—in itself one of the finest poems in the language—had never appeared, at the time it did, with the name of Mr. Tennyson.

These are positive recriminations, and my admiration of the subject is so great, that I almost shrink from making them. But really after all Mr. Selkirk is to blame, for Mr. Tennyson himself has never pretended to be a revolutionary or revolution-loving poet ; on the contrary, he has held throughout his grand career to the same fine middle-class ideal so much adored by the late Mr. Kingsley. " Throughout all our nineteenth-century British literature," wrote one whom England persecuted because he loved his country,* " there runs a tone of polite, though distant, recognition of Almighty God, as one of the Great Powers ; and though no resident is still maintained at His court, yet British civilisation gives him assurance of friendly relations; and 'our venerable Church' and 'beautiful liturgy' are relied upon as a sort of diplomatic Concordat or Pragmatic Sanction, whereby we, occupied as we are in grave commercial and political pursuits, carrying on our business, selling our altars, and utilising our heathen, bind ourselves *to let Him alone, if He lets us alone ;*—if He will keep looking *apart contemplating* the illustrious maremilkers and blameless Ethiopians, and never minding us, we will keep up a most respectable Church for Him, and make our lower orders venerate it and pay for it handsomely, and we will suffer no national infidelity, like the horrid French." This, of course, is only a sarcastic and almost brutal statement of the truth. As it

---

* John Mitchell.

stands, however, it is far nearer to the facts of the Tennysonian ethics than is the extraordinary thesis of Mr. Selkirk. My issue with Mr. Tennyson, if he for a moment assumed to be a great disturbing or creating force, would be that he was far too acquiescent and dispassionate a thinker. Being what he is and professes to be, the perfect singer of his time, he has a right to turn round upon us with: "Lyric poetry is perfect musical speech, and I simply decline the pressure of all disturbing influences. I am a musician, not a prophet; a great artist, not a great creator. I embody the best tendencies of my time, without aspiring to be beyond my time. It is no affair of mine to carp at Church and State, to reform society, to inspire revolutions. I am no iconoclast; my mission is to *sing*." This would be, and is, quite unanswerable. When the Laureate himself aspires to the position Mr. Selkirk claims for him, that of being the greatest ethical teacher of the time, it will be quite soon enough to discuss his claim to a position so close to moral and literary martyrdom.

A LAST LOOK ROUND.

I.

CIRCUMSPICE!

THE pursuit of literature has of late years become a lonely business. Beyond the narrow orbits of certain little merry-go-rounds of mutual admiration, few literary people are to be found who follow bright ideals in company, or exhibit much affection for one another. The great newspapers, with their monstrous machinery, swallow up our young men of talent by the dozen. If here and there a tricksy spirit escapes, it is to degenerate into a fashionable author or a fourth-rate politician. If by any chance a solitary writer attempts to be original and to think for himself, he reaps the privileges of literary martyrdom. Meantime, if we look quietly round in the world of life and literature, what do we see? The great waters of Democracy arising to swallow up and cover the last landmarks of individualism; a few isolated figures standing on ever-narrowing islets, and crying like Canute to the flood; bogus reputations going down into the angry living tide, volcanic notorieties springing up for a moment and disappearing, like certain earth-eruptions in the Mediterranean; the Ark of the Church, with a nasty hole in its sides, drifting hither and thither before the storm, with two archbishops, a Catholic and a Protestant, lashed to the rudder; minor prophets, in cockle-shells of Goethe's building, rowing leisurely out to the Ark's assistance, leaping jauntily on the deck, and offering to pilot the vessel into harbours of culture and light; and far away on the Mount Ararat of Science, the sun of some new creed dimly shining. Meantime, there is religious and social chaos, marked by a great confusion of tongues. Men no longer know what to believe or whom to believe. Literature is more like a blasted fig-tree than a healthy blooming English oak. Criticism flourishes on the grave of imagination. Encyclopædias, discursions, cheap manuals for the uninstructed, infantile manuals for lazy adults, take the place of living books. No sooner does one editor issue a series of ancient classics for English readers, than another editor cuts in with a series of manuals to our own classics, which are accessible to everybody in mother-English. The era of completed literary sinfulness is reached when people discuss seriously an article in the *Quarterly Review*, get up the "Pilgrim's Progress" out of a manual, and need cicerones to expound to them the beauties of our popular poets. Fiction flourishes like a noxious growth. Meantime, where are we, and whither are we drifting? After the School Board has come the Deluge. Let me take a last look round, and see the forces which are conditioning literature just at present.

At the very outset of my inquiry, two forces intrude themselves upon me. I will take them in their natural sequence.

II.
FIRST, HEAR THE CARDINAL!

"LIBERALISM in religion is the doctrine that there is no positive truth in religion, but that one creed is as good as another. It is inconsistent with the recognition of any religion as true. It teaches that all are to be tolerated, as all are matters of opinion. Revealed religion is not a truth, but a sentiment and a taste—not an objective fact, not miraculous; and it is the right of each individual to make it say just what strikes his fancy." These words, as many of my readers are aware, form part of the speech delivered by Dr. Newman at Rome, when he received the Pope's official message that he had been created a Cardinal. They are very sad words, as embodying the speaker's last farewell of free thought and free progress, and they have been received with a certain measure of respect, due to one of exceptional talents, and undoubted goodness of heart. But falser and more mischievous words were never spoken. True Liberalism in religion does not *deny* the positive truth of religion, but insists rather upon its relativity; so far from holding one creed as good as another, it insists that every man's creed is a law unto himself, to be broken at each man's spiritual peril; and because it reverences religion and its place in the human conscience, it preaches toleration in the widest sense to every creed under the sun. Here, as elsewhere, Dr. Newman shows a radical misconception of what Liberalism is and implies, for to him it is something abnormal and anarchical, instead of being totally simple and coherent. True, it is based on the assumption that in all matters of faith the individual conscience forms the last appeal; and hence, though it long ago pronounced its final opinion on the inspirations of the Vatican and the spirit of the Inquisition, it has enabled Dr. Newman to live his life in peace, and has provided for him at every stage of his career the cloistered shelter of popular esteem. Thanks to true Liberalism in religion, indeed, the author of the "Apologia" has prayed, worked, and spiritually thriven in a land which has formally renounced the thrall and, to some extent, the creed of Rome; every utterance of his has been circulated by the press, and commented upon in a kindly and a friendly spirit; his character has always been held venerable, and even his delusions have invariably been treated as sacred. And after all this, after years of solemn experience and mellowing wisdom, Dr. Newman, standing in the shadow of the Vatican, points his finger at his benefactors, and almost with his last breath abjures Liberty, and proclaims the gospel of intolerance, of torture, and of retrogression. The spectacle, to my mind, is a melancholy one. Not only does the old reason seem to have lost its cunning, but the gentle judgment appears to have become twisted and perverted. Such a definition of Liberalism as I have quoted is certainly unworthy of a divine trained among the free institutions of England. Accept that definition, popularise and legalise it, and we should speedily possess, instead of a free Church in a free State, not one Inquisition, but a dozen. Instead of "sentiment and taste," to which Dr. Newman has a characteristic objection, we should have "objective fact" —Catholic, Protestant, Positivist, and Materialistic. Dr. Manning would preside over one sort of Star Chamber, the Archbishop of Canterbury over another,

Mr. Frederick Harrison over a third, and Professor Huxley over a fourth. The end might, perhaps, justify the means ; but apostasy would then become a serious business, and quiet thinkers would no longer be left alone, even at Birmingham.

Of course what Dr. Newman means is simple enough. He has passed over into a Church which professes to hold the monopoly of objective and spiritual truth, and which has been historically distinguished for carrying the doctrine of protection even into the other world. He wishes to say, and in effect he says, as his Church has always said, that religion is to come from above, not from within, and that no man can be a Christian who denies the miraculous Virgin. The logical outcome of all this is inquisitorial. The creed of Rome is true, not merely relatively, but absolutely. Nay, the good Cardinal goes farther. " For thirty, forty, fifty years I have resisted to the best of my powers the spirit of Liberalism in religion." Yet for thirty, forty, fifty years Dr. Newman has been living under the beneficent protection of the Liberalism he has resisted. During all those years his protectress has never troubled him with questions concerning the material facts of his belief, but has left those facts to his own soul, which alone can apprehend them. He has seen everywhere around him the spectacle of a free people, eager to open all avenues of progress and of honour to all creeds, regardless of religious difference and tolerant to all opinion. How, and to what extent, has Dr. Newman resisted this Liberalism? Only, so far as I know, by expounding with strange clearness and beauty the meaning of his own faith, and by casting into the side of Rome all the weight of his private worth and intellectual ability. Such resistance, a Liberal would say, is holy and justifiable; that is to say, honest propagandism is justifiable. Our knowledge of Dr. Newman's life is limited to facts which he himself has made public. Well, there is nothing in these facts to warrant the assumption that he ever really resisted Liberalism; on the contrary, there is much to prove that he, more than most men, respected the sanctity of private judgment, enjoyed the moral atmosphere of Liberal institutions, and cherished the privilege of passing pensively from one state of edification to another under the safe protection of a free and Christian land.

My readers must perfectly understand that I pronounce no opinion on the creed which Dr. Newman holds and has held so long, or that faith which is built on miracles and has itself been most miraculously unsuccessful in its application to human needs. My business is not to discuss dogma on one side or another, but to protest against a definition of Liberalism in religion which would ultimately make all private judgment impossible, and render religion itself, in time, a mere affair of government from above. Dr. Newman's speech would be equally false and offensive if it came from the mouth of one professing any other form of creed. Suppose, for example, that Professor Haeckel, of Jena, were to say, in as many words, "Liberalism in science is the doctrine that there is no positive truth in science, but that one belief is as good as another. It is inconsistent with the recognition of any science as true." How Dr. Newman and all Churchmen would open their eyes at such a definition. Yet the cases are identical. Positive or absolute truth is one thing, its recognition by the human intellect is quite another. Unfortunately for Dr. Newman, the world is not so certain about the truth as it used to be; it has been driven to the conclusion that absolute truth is inconceivable, and that there a great many ways of looking at even one order of facts or miracles. So Liberalism says, " In God's name let all the creeds of God flourish, so long as they do not interfere with the due workings of the State; let Dr. Newman go to Rome if he pleases, and long may he wear his biretta; only he must let other men have their way too, and leave a little scope for taste and judgment, even in matters of opinion!" And Liberalism, true Liberalism, may add, with a sigh, " Since I *did* allow my good son, Newman, to go to Rome, and put no hindrance in his way, he might have remembered his first obligations to me and mine. He should not have abandoned me altogether, even to become a Cardinal."

III.

THE ATTITUDE OF SCIENCE.

I AM no blind admirer of the Professor who is just at present sending forth his saucy scientific prophecies from the University of Jena—indeed, there are many points, especially those affecting the psychological conditions of mankind, on which I am ready to join issue with him. In reading his two principal works, the "History of Creation" and the "History of Evolution," it is impossible to tell where certainty ends and wild poetical hypothesis begins, and equally useless to speculate to what heights of daring assumption the author may be led at any moment by his passion for logical symmetry and his fervour for the fancies of his creed. At the same time his power is great and his courage indisputable, while, concerning his mechanical conceptions of creation, this, at least, can be said—that they are a good deal nearer to the truth than the old dreams of theologians or the last romances of super-pious naturalists educated in the school of Cuvier. Fascinated, bewildered even, by the mighty hypothesis of Darwin, Professor Haeckel has pushed that hypothesis to its utmost limits. He has drawn up plans of natural progression which revolutionise all orthodox ideas; wherever links were wanting he has supplied them, with wonderful visions of the plastidule soul and the potentialities of carbon; and the result is a chart of Man's place in Nature which may be mistaken, which is certainly highly conjectural, but which, however false in detail, is in every way fascinating as a generalisation. As might have been expected, however, Haeckel's calm apotheosis of Darwinism has not been witnessed without protest, even from natural philosophers; and every one remembers with what warmth the orthodox party exulted, when Professor Virchow delivered his address on the "Freedom of Science in the Modern State," and held up to especial ridicule the evolutionary explanations of Haeckel. The name of Virchow, of course, carried extraordinary weight. "A Daniel, a Daniel, come to judgment!" cried the Churches and the journals; and the old Professor's words were flashed by the party of reaction all over the civilised world. The *reductio ad absurdum* came when the Prussian *Kreuz-Zeitung* bracketed Darwinism and Democracy together, and made the theory of descent responsible for the wicked attempts of Hödel and Nobiling!

The issue between the two Professors is very

simple, and may be briefly explained. Virchow condemns the precipitation of Haeckel, accuses him of assuming as certain what is not verifiable, and insists that public teaching should be limited to the statement and illustration of facts which are actually conquered and firmly established. Haeckel, on the other hand, censures the retrogression of Virchow, avers that all human knowledge is subjective, and shows—I think with considerable success—that the mission of science embraces illimitable conjecture. Even those "axioms," which are the basis of the teaching of mathematics, are incapable of absolute proof. Conjectural in every way is all we know of Matter, or Force; and even gravitation is hypothetical. The undulatory theory of Light, which we accept now as the indispensable basis of optics, rests on an unproved hypothesis, on the subjective assumption of an ethereal medium, whose existence no one is in a position to prove in any way. Again, the whole theoretical side of Chemistry is an airy structure of hypotheses, the common basis of chemical theories—viz., the atomic theory—being perfectly unprovable, since no chemist has ever seen an atom. In all this, perhaps, Professor Haeckel is perhaps a little ingenuous. He knows as well as any one that he is not fairly crossing swords with Virchow, but enveloping him in a cloud of verbal dust. The real matter at issue is not what every modern philosopher has already answered affirmatively to the public satisfaction, *i.e.*, whether hypothesis is admissible in science; but whether evolutionists, in using hypothesis wholesale and without due caution, and in mingling together material facts and subjective dreams, are not misleading both themselves and the public. Haeckel, for example, is a materialist pure and simple. Not content with leaving the evolution-hypothesis to illustrate itself and to point its own moral, he uses it as heavy artillery against the Cloud-Cuckoo-Town of popular Deism. He is eager at every step to show that Matter is everything, that Deity is impossible. He is never tired of ridiculing the religion which attributes, as he expresses it, "a dualistic existence to the psyche," his own certainty being that Matter and Spirit are identical; and he reminds his opponent that *he* too at one time expressed the same materialistic views. "He (Virchow) formerly supported with a clear conscience and with his utmost energy, in psychology as in the other collected departments of physiology (*sic*), that very mechanical standpoint which we to-day accept as the essential base of our monism, and which stands in irreconcilable antagonism to the dualism of the vitalistic doctrine. . . . He led me to the clear recognition of the fact that the nature of man, like every other organism, can only be rightly understood as an united whole, that this spiritual and corporeal being are inseparable, and that the phenomena of the soul-life depend, like all other vital phenomena, *on material motion only—on mechanical (or physico-chemical) modifications of cells.*"

The italics are mine, not Haeckel's. It seems to me that such language fully justifies Virchow's adjuration of "Restringamur." Haeckel not only exaggerates the monistic ideas formerly held by Virchow, but here, as elsewhere, he almost exaggerates his own conception of the theory. To assert that psychical or spiritual life is primarily or ultimately a material motion *only*, a mechanical modification of *cells*, is to use the language of wild hyperbole. It may or may not be true that such is the case; just as it may or may not be true that the moon is made of green cheese, but there is not the slightest evidence to justify the hypothesis. And the hypothesis itself is so charmingly easy and off-hand! What has puzzled philosophy since man began to think, what has eluded every kind of inquiry and research, all that wondrously complicated phenomenon which to this hour is the despair of physiology and the drunkenness of metaphysics, is only—mark the "only"—a mechanical modification of "cells." Why, this is no more than to say that to think is—to use the brain, and that the basis of life is physiological. Thought *may* be a mode of motion, as heat is, as electricity is supposed to be; but what then? Does that bring us an inch nearer to the central mystery, how cellular change, when such takes place, can possibly evolve psychic force? Haeckel's explanation, in fact, is no explanation whatever. It is a mere vision of a mysterious mechanism which no man has yet been able to explain. And when the Professor goes further and asserts that the mechanical nature of Matter and Spirit negates the idea of God, I cry again, with Virchow, "Restringamur!" How does the identity of Matter and Spirit affect the idea of God one way or another? Because we know how a monkey wags its tail, or how the mind of man receives its impressions and redelivers them, have we solved the riddle of the Universe? Quite the contrary, says Virchow; so do not let us be vainglorious. Here, certainly, Virchow is right.

But where Haeckel has his opponent on the hip is in his repudiation of the politico-theological assertion that the doctrine of descent leads to social anarchy, and supports the "Socialist theory." "What in the world," Haeckel naturally asks, "has the doctrine of descent to do with Socialism?" He proceeds to demonstrate, however, that Darwinism, at least, is the reverse of democratic, since it teaches the cheerful creed that "in human life, as in animal and plant life everywhere, and at all times, only a small and chosen minority can exist and flourish, while the enormous majority starve and perish miserably, and more or less prematurely." I cordially agree with him in his protest against Virchow's attempt to darken the discussion by awakening a political bias. I agree with him, moreover, whenever he takes his stand on the right of private judgment, and on the freedom of the truth. Yet this tract—with all its justice of polemics in certain particulars—forces upon us more than ever the fact that Virchow's protest was well-timed, and that pure scientists should clip their wings and lessen their fanciful flights, in which they try to rival theologians. Haeckel is a clever man haunted by one great truth, which casts a thousand delusive shadows. He seems utterly incompetent to give a philosophical opinion on the higher issues of the great religious controversy which his charts of facts and fancies illustrate so amusingly and so well; and he will leave the world where Aristotle found it, darkened by the shadow of its own doubt, and face to face with the everlasting Sphynx.

IV.

MINOR RESULTS AND INFLUENCES.

THESE are the two great forces which stand opposed to each other—authority and superstition, as personified in such men as Cardinal Newman; extreme scientific Radicalism, as personified in such men as

Professor Haeckel. The first still persists, to the great joy of many thousands of people, in affirming that two and two make five ; the second, elated with the discovery that two and two make four, encroaches so far as to deny the existence of any unknown quantity. Midway between the two forces, and full of a prescience and a sanity unique in this generation, stands Mr. Herbert Spencer, uttering supreme words of wisdom and of warning, but sadly disappointing those who crave for some creed of absolute certainty. While all other teachers of the age may easily be classed, while Mr. Mill, for example, may safely be relegated to the army of the intellectual revolt, while Messrs. Carlyle and Ruskin, despite all their divergencies, may as certainly be claimed by the leaders of the army of authority, Mr. Spencer alone confronts the problem of the universe, and while indefinitely enlarging the area of human knowledge, frankly postulates the Unknowable. His width of view, his catholicity of sympathy, his fearlessness in investigation, his faculty of crystalline exposition, appear to me almost superhuman. One sweep of his majestic vision has unveiled the whole mystery of human responsibility, one touch of his little finger has annihilated dozens of dilettante prophets—*e.g.* Mr. Matthew Arnold. Yet for all this he is solitary and scarcely happy, since, unlike the Cardinal, and unlike the Professor, he stops short at verification. His supreme proof is a supreme disappointment. His last word is, "Wait!" Fortunately, he closes no one gate of the universe, but leaves all wide open, while we stand awestricken at the dazzling vistas which open out beyond them all.

Below the sphere occupied by these greater forces quietly conditioning literature, work those innumerable minor influences to which we give, collectively, the name of criticism. Mr. Matthew Arnold, Mr. Mallock, Mr. John Morley, Mr. Huxley, Mr. Tyndall, Mr. Frederick Harrison, Miss Frances Cobbe, Mr. Picton, Mr. Greg, and many others, devote their powers, each in his or her own way, to the criticism of the "situation." From every great review, from every journal or newspaper, their voices are sounding. According to Mr. Arnold, here as elsewhere echoing Goethe, literature is merely a criticism of life. According to Mr. Mallock, literature is a criticism of religion, and the highest truth rests where it began, at the Empire Roman city. According to Mr. Morley, the criterion of progress is still to be found in the French encyclopædia. According to Messrs. Huxley and Tyndall, science now and for ever dispossesses imagination as well as religion. According to Mr. Harrison, there is no god but the *Grand Être*, and Comte is his prophet. And so on, through all the long catalogue of popular essayists. The whole matter, so far as it affects the literary calling, resolves itself into this. The imaginative creator must now, to use an American vulgarism, take a back seat, while criticism, with stern and pertinacious countenance, faces the religio-scientific sphynx. The world is tired of imagination; it solicits exposition, verification. All imaginative revolt is simple Philistinism. The Philistine novelist, the Philistine philosopher, the Philistine poet, and the Philistine journalist are told that their occupation is gone for ever.

The Philistine novelist is Victor Hugo. The antidote to his influence is the critical novelist-essayist loved by the critical journalist, Thackeray. Thackeray looked at life from the windows of the clubs, made silly Laura Pendennis the ideal of English womanhood, fought and wrought with criticism on his side till he based a splendid reputation on the theory of suckling fools and chronicling small beer. Thackeray was to literature what Major Pendennis was to society —a delightful *flâneur*, a charming exponent of the philosophy of *laissez faire*. Thackeray "trusted to Heaven (*e.g.*) that German art and religion would take no hold in our country, where there is a fund of roast beef that will expel any such *humbug* in the end." Thackeray protested, apropos of George Sand, against "women who step down to the people with stately step and voice of authority, and deliver their twopenny tablets, as if there were some Divine authority for the *wretched nonsense* written there." Thackeray, in his hatred of all imaginative revolt, belonged to the party of the Cardinal.

The Philistine poet is Walt Whitman. Against his influence, such as it is, may be set the influence of the critical poet loved by the critical journalist ; for example, Mr. Matthew Arnold.

There must be a certain charm in the didactic verse of this writer, for it has been liberally praised and widely read. I have, nevertheless, to record my impression that Mr. Arnold is not, in the strict sense of the word, a poet at all, and that, even where the form of his thought appears poetical, its primary inspiration is crudely intellectual. In saying so much I do not deny that this writer has written charming verses, and has attained poetical credentials ; all I mean to convey is that he is not an inspired writer, in the sense that certain of his contemporaries are inspired writers, as Mr. Swinburne for example is inspired, and that his verses lie on the wrong side of the border-line which separates true poetry from eloquent prose. As a prose writer, whether he is writing verse or not, he is invariably self-collected, sagacious, and sane, but he is at all times a prose writer, never a poet, either "born" or "made." For the besetting sin of his style I should say that his master, Goethe, was responsible. That sin is didacticism. Where he reaches the highest level of his attainment, as in the verses to Obermann, he is didactic in the best mood of our contemplative essayists; where he sinks to his lowest level, he is didactic in the manner of a leader writer in the *Daily News;* but in either case his object is not poetry but criticism. He offers to our eyes that strangest of all spectacles, an inquirer who keeps his temper, who never gets angry, but who is calmly and insinuatingly irritating in all his moods. After a careful study of his verses, I can quite understand how he came to utter the dictum that Shelley's prose would be remembered when all Shelley's verses were forgotten. A writer who finds nothing better in verse to say of Heine than that the world smiled, and "*that smile was Heine,*" was never born among the laurel-bushes of Parnassus.

The Philistine philosopher, for all practical purposes, is Thoreau. People who pass him by with indifference turn with rapture to Mr. Mallock or Mr. Percy Greg.

V.

THE NEW GIRONDE.

MEANTIME, in the dearth or the neglect of literary individualism, we have witnessed for a short season the apotheosis of the dilettante.

The writers and critics to whom I am about to allude may be called the Girondists of contemporary literature. Being called to power some few years ago, at a period of literary depression, they have had their opportunity—and lost it; because, like their namesakes, they have had nothing to offer mankind but a dainty scepticism, an enervating æstheticism, an elegant theory of *Art pour Art*, founded on a foolish indifference to the great facts of religion and life. Their overthrow was certain from the first. Totem-worshippers, they carved their own images on pieces of wood, and when the hour of trial came, they were found without a living faith. They are liberals, I know, but that is all; their liberalism is not vital. In the meantime, that other liberal party in literature, which may be compared to the Jacobins, have undergone no little persecution. Combining with their advanced religious views and scientific sympathies a vital belief in God, that is to say, in the supreme Moral Power which guides the universe, they have been branded as sentimental and transcendental; nor could they hope for any assistance from the exponents of popular creeds, seeing that like their great prototype, Rousseau, they reject all dogmatic solutions of the dark problem of life. But should they ever be called upon to govern, as is not impossible, it will perhaps be found that their faith is not dead but living, that they understand mankind, and that their programme includes a method by which Religion, Science, and Art may be reconciled.

It is a favourite assertion of the gifted leaders of the English Gironde that Art itself is all-sufficing and that literature, to be acceptable to the dilettante, must be destitute of any kind of edification. For the artist, no theory of life is necessary, no philosophy, no moral aspirations, no religion; his nature may exhaust itself in triumphs of mere reproduction, with the most satisfactory literary results; his world may be Bedford Park, his culture need not extend beyond the literature of poetic terms, his outlook on life may be, and indeed had better be, confined to the tea-roses in his own back garden. Unfortunately, just at the present moment, something more is wanted in literature than this kind of teaching. Poetry founded on elegant indifference to the great problems of life may be very well suited for schoolboys and their tutors, but it is of little or no value in times of great revolution, such as that through which we are now passing. My friends of the Gironde have reigned for a few days, and fallen under the derision of the very citizens who were at first eager for them to govern. Nor have they fallen merely through negative incapacity to grapple with the difficulties of the situation; they have committed positive sins against literature and against society. The predominant vices of the age are its lust for worldly success, its love of mere amusement, its indifference to moral sanctions, its mindless pietism on the one hand and its dapper scepticism on the other, its irreverence, its contempt for emotion; in one word, its materialism. All these vices have been approved, tacitly or openly, by the party to which we Jacobins of the new Republic are in opposition. Members of this party have long contended that this world is all-sufficing, that mere pleasure is the end of Art, that morality is a mere matter of opinion, that orthodox religion is imbecile and scientific religion irrelevant, that sentiment is preposterous, that the true basis of belief is, in the worst sense, materialistic. Life is an "empty day," and that is all. Well, our friends have been heard, have been honoured, have said their say, have reigned, have fallen. They still command several of the bastions of criticism, but every day their fire grows weaker and more straggling, and soon, I have no doubt, it will be silenced for ever. The strife between them and the party at present called Philistine is the everlasting strife between moral enthusiasm and artistic indifferentism, between spiritualism and materialism, between Art for Religion's sake and Art for its own sake, between idealism and realism—in a word, between Jacobinism and the Gironde.

VI.

THE OUTCOME IN SOCIETY.

WHILE religion is waning, while literature is failing, while the dilettante still survives in the shadow of the busy man of science, how is Society progressing? According to the evidence of many who speak with authority, very badly.

There is no smoke without fire; and although modern society may not be quite as bad as its own scribes represent it to be, although virtue may still be a moral factor even in fashionable circles, there can be no doubt that the progress for the last decade has been a progress downward. In politics, in social affairs, in literature, art, and the drama, as well as in the mere records of the Divorce Court and the milliners' shops, we read the same dark truth—that luxury has increased in proportion to the decline of domestic ideals, and that all standards, even the merely commercial one, have been lowered in answer to the popular demand for wild mental or moral stimulants. It is no task of mine to preach a sermon on this old theme, or to play Cassandra in the manner familiar to students of reviews. No words of mine can change the condition of things. Time and patience alone can effect any reformation, for the day is long past when any single utterance, however prophetic, could have much effect in guiding the popular mind. And yet it has been repeatedly forced upon me of late that, of all things wanted by the present generation, a Satirist is wanted most; one who would tell the world its sins and foibles, not with the sneaking snigger or familiar wink of a Society journalist, but with a voice loud and clear enough to reverberate from Land's End to John o' Groats. It would matter little where this voice was first heard. It might be in the pulpit, it might be on the stage. It might sound as the voice of one crying in the wilderness, or it might be heard, as more than once heretofore, from the very heart of the crowd. Since Dickens dropped the scourge, satire has been sadly at a discount, and we are in reality worse off for *censores morum* than were our prototypes, the prosperous *bourgeoisie* of the Second Empire.

So closely do our present social conditions resemble that of the *bourgeoisie* alluded to, that even a course of the comedy of the Empire would do us nothing but good; but, unfortunately, instead of a real we have a spurious *censor morum*, and the instruction from abroad is interdicted. The late Licenser of Plays, animated by a too blind enthusiasm of morality, thought he was doing a wise thing when he forbade the performance in this country of the masterpieces of Dumas Fils and Sardou; and the present Licenser, though a man of more liberal instincts, still sets an adamantine countenance against the innovation. True, dramas of this sort, though, doubtless, open to the criticism which has been lavished upon them, and which has caused them to be classed in France under "*l'École Brutale*," are, in the best sense, works of art. They are, moreover, fiery social satires—and true satire is never quite unwholesome. Under the foul rule of the French Empire society grew luxurious, reckless, libidinous, and rotten; extravagance in dress, in manners and customs, in conduct, became the fashion; it was the epoch in real life of the "Faux Bonhommes" and "Madame Bovary." As a bitter comment on this state of things came the so-called "comedy" of the Empire. Dumas Fils, a melancholy man, began by picturing the pathetic side of the life of courtesans, and continued by preparing for Parisian acceptance an entire system of theatrical ethics—or rather, as a critic of the period called it, "la logique appliquée au théâtre." And what, after all, was the sum total of his philosophy? "Se marier, quand on est jeune et sain, choisir, dans n'importe quelle classe, une bonne fille franche et saine, l'aimer de toute son âme et de toutes ses forces, en faire une compagne sûre et une mère féconde, travailler pour élever ses enfants et leur laisser en mourant l'exemple de sa vie : voilà la vérité—le reste n'est qu'une erreur, crime, ou folie." If, sooner or later, this good girl becomes like the "Femme de Claude," shoot her; if she forms a grand passion, like "Diane de Lys," and it is encouraged, after due warning, by its object, kill *him*. Horrible morality, doubtless, but grimly appropriate notwithstanding. The comedies of M. Dumas are a series of propositions on the theme of the married state, but their moral is unmistakable; it is the moral of all plays, from Scribe's *Trente Ans dans la Vie d'une Femme* downwards, viz., that to become adulterous is natural, but inexpedient. Sardou, another melancholy man, preaches the same lesson. The French comedy of the Empire, so far from being an incentive to vicious living, is subacid, platitudinous, rectangular—on the whole not very entertaining, but edifying as a social study. It was, at any rate, the nearest approach to Juvenal's terrible manner that the Empire could furnish; and though it was Dead Sea fruit enough, many who devoured it were healed perhaps of a portion of their disease.

I am not defending the comedy of the Empire, though I infinitely prefer it to the vile importations in which what, in the stage directions of Goethe's *Faust*, is called an "obscene gesture" supplies the place of all moral teaching or rational meaning. He who accepts *La Marjolaine* and rejects *La Femme de Claude* must be either a *roué* or an ignoramus. Be that as it may, there can be no doubt that we here in England would be the better if some one would hold the mirror up to our follies, even to our vices. It is useless to look for such a satirist in the direction of the stage; the whole drama is usurped by the spectre of that British matron who in the flesh never patronises the drama at all. Our novelists are pigmies, clinging to the cast-off coat-tails of departed giants, and their social satire, when they do attempt social satire, is at once timid and verbose. Our poets are *dilettanti*, with each other for a public, and Mr. Tennyson's mildest verses for a precedent. In all the lower departments of art and literature a sad, unsocial diffidence embarrasses the speech of genius, and instead of "human nature's daily food" we get mannerism, affectation, and the cynicism of complete indifference to practical social problems.

Meantime Society, mœnad-like, twines flowers in

her hair, and goes from bad to worse. The only individuals who tell her of her vices are those who flourish through them, and the cue of these is to lament over the ideals they first overthrow, and to pretend that goodness is useless, since there is no power but evil left. Well, even a comedy of the Empire would be better than this; better than a journalism which degrades the social standard with every quip and turn characteristic of blind snobbery; better than a literature which hushes up every vital question, covers up every social sore, reduces life and thought to the "prunes and prism" insisted on by Mr. Mudie; better than a stage which is either unclean and corybantic or pure and prurient to the verge of imbecility. The only straightforward and truth-telling force at present at work is modern Science, but it is not sufficiently aggressive in the social sphere to be of much avail. So the feast goes on, so the soothsayer is put aside, and the voice of the prophet is unheard. Some fine day, nevertheless, there will be a revelation—the handwriting will be seen on the wall in the colossal cypher of some supreme Satirist. How much of our present effulgent civilisation will last till then? How much will not perish without any aid from without, by virtue of its own inherent folly and dry rot? Meantime, even a temporary revelation would be thankfully accepted. Such satire as Churchill suddenly lavished upon the stage would be of service to Society just now. Even satire as wicked as that with which Byron deluged the "piggish domestic virtues" of the Georges would not be altogether amiss. Only, it must come in simple speech, not in such mystic dress as that worn by St. Thomas of Chelsea when he gave forth his memorable sartorial prophesies.

VII.

CONCLUSION.

WHAT, then, is the *status quo* of our literature just at present? Too much intellectual activity, and too little; too many teachers, and too few; too few creative books, and a plethora of "criticisms." Fortunately, great stars still shine in the literary heavens. The fame of Spencer, of Tennyson, of Browning, of Whitman, of Hugo, lends us assurance that the godlike mood is still possible, that the godlike speech may still be heard. But against such divine influences must be set those of men, of cicerones, of newspaper columns. Authorised critics abound. It is an authorised critic who tells us, as Mr. Arnold, that Shelley's prose is likely to be remembered when his verse is forgotten; it is an authorised critic who informs us, with Mr. Lowell, that Thoreau is a thoroughly unauthorised and almost offensive person. Mr. Arnold and Mr. Lowell are cultivated men, who speak with authority; their temper fascinates the spirit of mediocrity, and their culture is in perfect harmony with the culture of the period. Open any newspaper, and we shall find that these are the leaders of critical opinion who are honoured in their own country and whose dicta are accepted at second hand. I pass these cicerones politely by. Their message is not to me, their inspiration is not mine. I have refused to listen to their master and inspirer, Goethe, and I shall certainly not spend my time with any of his disciples.

What, then, some may ask, does the world want, since neither mere science, nor dilettantism, nor culture, nor bogus reputations, will serve its turn? It wants poetry, and not criticism; it wants earnest thought and life, and not a philosophy of the schoolroom; it wants fearless truth and imagination, applied to all the great phenomena of creation; it wants, in one word, a living creed, not a rehabilitation of creeds that are indeterminate. Much of Carlyle's early teaching was beautiful; we *believed* when he taught us that manly dignity and independence, that honest work, were better than worldly honours. Part of Goethe's teaching is wise, that there is a law which makes for righteousness, independently of all dogmas. Mill was sane in his generation, while Comte was even saner in his. But what all these men have missed is the great truth that literature is not a criticism of life, but only one of its phenomena; that manly dignity and belief in culture, and the belief in the utility of culture, are not personal possessions differentiating men from each other, but part of the universal privileges of humanity; that "goodness" and "badness" are terms of mere relation, applied to certain incidents of human action, or applied to living books, but possessing no absolute truth whatever; that Love and Love's sorrow alone are true, and, being so, are the indisputable possession of the noblest hero and the lowest criminal under the sun. A creed of this sort has been called optimism, or cosmopolitanism, and what not; it has been confronted of late years with the arid creed of pessimism, which has one merit, that of perfect logical symmetry. It has been described by the contemporary satirist as the creed which "proves wrong is as good as right, you know, and one man as good as another." Well, those who hold it are quite willing to accept all these definitions. Their faith is that God will be justified, even to the very lowest and least of His children. As poets, they believe in all the gods, from Jesus to Josh. They believe in Professor Haeckel and they believe in the Cardinal. As men of the world, they turn their ears of sympathy to everything human. As students of literature, they decline to accept any work as supremely creative or authoritative which does not take count of *all* the forces which condition the moral immortality of the human race.

Brought down to the lowest platform of modern expediency, what does this creed imply in letters? The rejection of all dilettantism, the apotheosis of the highest and *truthfullest* of human teachers, whether dead or contemporary, the recognition of every kind of noble effort, whether in the region of the lowest "cakes and ale" or the highest sphere of the ideal. Above all, it implies distrust of individual judgments or "criticisms," and faith in the all-embracing catholicity of the laws of life and literature.

Literature cannot be divorced from life, any more than poetry can be divorced from religion. The two are one. A man is great or wise, not because by humouring his reputation he succeeds in hocussing the world into an opinion of his greatness or wisdom, not because he is corroborated by the folly of his inferiors—as Napoleon was, as Goethe is; but because, like Lincoln, like Whitman, he is saner than his fellows in the purest sanity of goodness and love. A book is great, not on account of its cleverness, its brilliance, its literary pretences, but on account of that integral wisdom which discharges cleverness, and brilliance, and even pyrotechny, through the magical chemistry of *style;* the style which is neither superficially effective nor openly meretricious, but which unites perfect harmony of meaning with sanity of expression. Words are the merest counters, apart from what they are used to represent. Books are the merest waste of force, unless they tell us something new, or lend a new significance of beauty to something that is old. Judged in this way, not one book in a thousand has a right to live.

All this proves only that criticism is really a series of private judgments, more or less fallible, and that the value of a man's life and work can only be estimated after a very long period of probation. Meantime, all one can do is to record *impressions* as honestly as he can. I can advance no scientific reason for seeing a great genius in Robert Browning, or a fine painstaking talent in George Eliot, for thinking George Meredith almost alone in his power of expressing personal passion, and Walt Whitman supreme in his power of conveying moral stimulation. I can take a skeleton to pieces scientifically, but not a living soul. I might prove the absurdity of the writer who calls herself Ouida, but I could not prove the absurdity of any honest original thinker, however low in the intellectual scale. I am helpless before Mr. Swinburne or any authentic poet, while quite at my ease before Macaulay and Professor Aytoun.

Finally, it must not be understood that a reader has a right to judge a thinker by the nature of his *opinions*—in other words, by the points of his agreement or disagreement with one's own philosophy of life. This would be to say that I could not enjoy Thackeray, because I thought him *au fond* narrow-minded, or appreciate Sterne, because I knew him to be a sham sentimentalist. A writer may be very provincial yet very delightful; in that case, however, though his scope of view and his sympathies may be narrow, his spirit must be faithful and completely sane within its range. At the same time, the greatest writers are those who possess, in combination with technical gifts, the grandest and most all-embracing power of sympathetic vision. No writer can be truly great who believes, like Carlyle, that God Almighty intended the negro to be a servant, who avows, like Lamb, that he is miserable anywhere beyond a London street, or who upholds, like Zola, that the world is a sink of sensual corruption. For great writing is great wisdom, and great wisdom means great goodness, that is, love for and sympathy with all created things, animate and inanimate. Judged by this standard, great writers are very few, and when they appear, are, for a long time, dimly guessed.

THE END.

CHARLES DICKENS AND EVANS, CRYSTAL PALACE PRESS.

www.ingramcontent.com/pod-product-compliance
Lightning Source LLC
Chambersburg PA
CBHW030426300426
44112CB00009B/877